A Season To Remember

Finding the right balance without tipping the scales

Craig Briggs

By the same author

The Journey series

Journey To A Dream

Beyond Imagination

Endless Possibilities

Opportunities Ahead

Driving Ambition

The Discerning Traveller

A Season To Remember

Short story

Roast Pig and Romance

Copy editing/proofreading by Louise Lubke Cuss at wordblink.com
Cover design and Photography by Craig Briggs
Portrait photo by Melanie Briggs

ISBN-13:979-8580406367

In Memory

Amelia Puentes Yañez (Meli)
(1940 – 2020)

Richie Kennedy
(1980 – 2020)

CONTENTS

Introduction

If life deals you a bad hand, don't fold, take a chance; a good player will always come out on top.

I entered this world on the 12th of July 1962, in St. Luke's Hospital, Huddersfield. The second child, and only son, of Donald and Glenys Briggs. Donald, a humble lathe operator, worked for one of the town's largest employers, David Brown Tractors of Meltham.

The birth of their first child, Julie, had been a joy. The arrival of a son would make the family complete. Donald couldn't wait to groom his boy for sporting success. Notification of my arrival came via a phone call to his work, a call that dashed his parental hopes. Young Craig was not a 'normal' lad: he'd been born with congenital feet deformities. I cannot imagine a crueller message.

Unaware of my disability, I got on with life as any infant would. My first birthday brought a gift that would change my life forever. Not a cuddly toy from Mum and Dad, nor a silver-plated trinket from friends or relatives. My life-changing gift was a marvel of modern engineering, manufactured by J. E. Hanger and Co. of London for and on behalf of the National Health Service. Bespoke footwear gave me what the Vespa had given the youth of the fifties: freedom and independence. They weren't quite as stylish as an Italian built scooter but I didn't care. From now on, Master Briggs was on the move and no one would hold me back.

Over the next five years a series of surgical procedures changed the way I moved. Recollections are few but these infant experiences would influence the rest of my life. In the 1960s bedside visits were restricted to one person for one hour per day. The anguish of a young mother listening to the tortured screams of her infant son begging her to stay must have been horrific; it wasn't much fun for me either.

When the time came, Mum walked me to school like other proud mothers. For his part, Dad gave me his first and only piece of worldly advice. 'If anyone hits you, hit 'em back.'

With one exception, my mind proved sharper than my boxing prowess. Kids can be cruel, particularly to those who stand out, but only once did I break down in tears and ask, 'Why? Why me?' It's a question I sometimes ask myself today, but for very different reasons. Academia was not my thing. I found it difficult to concentrate on anything that didn't interest me.

I left secondary education with a mediocre haul of four 'O' levels and drifted aimlessly into an 'A' level course. It seemed preferable to starting work. If my 'O' level tally was disappointing, my 'A' level results were pitiful. I blamed a perforated appendix, two months before my finals, but if truth be known I'd had my fill of education.

In May 1980 I left college and entered the employment market. Margaret Thatcher was busy dismantling British industry and unemployment was running at a post-war high. I signed on to receive unemployment benefit and spent the summer lounging around the house watching the

Wimbledon Tennis Championship on telly. As the tournament drew to a close, parental pressure to find work intensified. In September, during one of my many visits to the Job Centre, a job card caught my eye: 'Wanted: trainee retail managers'. The idea of becoming a manager appealed, so I applied.

Five hundred and sixty applicants chased six positions. I pleaded my case at an interview and ended up being selected. After a two-week training course in the seaside town of Southport, I passed with honours, achieving the rank of assistant manager. When asked where I'd like to ply my newfound retail skills, I chose London, a city paved with gold.

In October 1980, I left Huddersfield a naïve child and returned three and a half years later a wiser and more mature young man. A brief period of letting my hair down followed, catching up on lost time and lost youth. During these wild and hedonistic months, I met the love of my life and future wife, Melanie.

My career in retail spanned six and a half years with five different companies. Each one expanded my experience and knowledge but to realise my dream I would have to go it alone. Not long after my twenty-sixth birthday, I handed in my notice. My future lay in leather jackets. Unfortunately, no one shared this vision and my aspirations fell at the first hurdle.

The prospect of returning to the retail trade pushed me into pursuing a different path. I reached a compromise and worked as a self-employed agent for one of the nation's largest insurance companies. The job title, Financial Consultant, exaggerated the role. In reality I was nothing more than a desperate insurance salesman. Life was hard and the insurance industry ruthless. Trying to sell a product that nobody wants, and which by its nature will never benefit the payee, is not easy. Unlike most recruits, I managed to survive and learnt some difficult but valuable lessons.

My 'Big Break' came when two of my clients asked me to invest in their fledgling printing business. The first year's accounts showed greater losses than actual sales. Against all professional advice I jumped at the chance, remortgaged the house and bought an equal stake.

By accident rather than design, I'd finally found my true vocation. The company was losing money hand over fist. The bank had taken a second charge on the partners' homes and my investment was swallowed up in a black hole of debt. Just when things couldn't get any worse, the bank called in the overdraft. While others worried, I applied myself to the problem. Through hard work and determination, we weathered the storm, but casualties were high.

After thirteen years of blood, sweat, and holding back the tears, I ended up owning a modestly successful little business. The time was right to begin my journey to a dream.

In May 2002 my wife Melanie and I decided to sell up and chase our dream. We packed all our worldly belongings, including our dog Jazz, into my ageing executive saloon, and headed off to Spain.

Not for us the tourist-packed Costas of the Mediterranean or the whitewashed villages of Andalucía. Our destination was Galicia: a little-known region in the northwest corner of Spain.

The contrast in lifestyles from England's industrial north to Spain's rural interior proved far more traumatic than either of us had imagined. Three and a half years at night school studying the Spanish language was little help. Galicia has its own language, galego. A proudly spoken tongue that has more in common with Portuguese than Spanish.

Dubious estate agents and questionable property descriptions turned our search for a new home into a lottery. Clear objectives became blurred and after several failed attempts to buy a property, we were forced to reassess our goals.

Eventually, we found our dream house, a tiny bungalow on the outskirts of the sleepy village of Canabal. Coping with Spain's laid-back approach while managing a building project tested our resolve. What could go wrong did and by Christmas we were ready to throw in the towel and head back to Blighty. But Yorkshiremen are made of sterner stuff.

A timely visit from my dad re-energised our ambitions. Twelve months and ten days after arriving in Galicia, we moved into our new home and completed the first part of our *Journey To A Dream.*

Choosing a name for our renovated property proved difficult; eventually we settled on El Sueño (The Dream). After the challenges of the first twelve months, we settled into a more relaxed lifestyle. Drinks at sunset, or Teatime Tasters, became an integral part of our daily lives and the warmth and generosity of our village neighbours made us feel at home.

With Melanie's help, I set about transforming our barren plot into a garden paradise. It wasn't all plain sailing and dealing with Spanish bureaucracy proved difficult. As time drifted by we started to enjoy a life *Beyond Imagination.*

For the first time in a long time, I had the freedom to take up some hobbies. Little did I know that writing and viniculture would become my pastimes of choice. With help from our neighbour, Meli, I took my first tentative steps on the road to winemaking. The success of my fledgling hobby was left in the hands of Mother Nature. Initial results were encouraging. My love of winemaking had begun.

As with viniculture, my efforts at writing took time to develop. Under the tutorage of Peter Hinchliffe, former editor in chief of Huddersfield's daily newspaper and founder of an online magazine, my writing slowly improved.

Hobbies are one thing but the financial requirements of day to day living were never far from our thoughts. After successfully buying, renovating, and selling a second property, we decided to look for another. Eventually, we found the ideal project, a romantic ruined farmhouse with *Endless Possibilities*.

Events have a way of keeping our lives in perspective, and this was particularly so when Melanie's dad was diagnosed with terminal cancer. A surprise fortieth birthday party turned into an emotional, but happy, final family reunion.

Later that year we offered to help our friends, Bob and Janet, convert their unloved house into a luxury holiday rental. Weeks before the first guests were due to arrive, the builder had a serious on-site accident. We had no alternative but to roll up our sleeves and finish the job. A season that could have turned into a disaster ended in success and satisfied customers. The question was, could we duplicate that success and build our own holiday rental property?

Finding the perfect place was challenging; buying it proved far more difficult. The lack of official paperwork led to lengthy delays. Thirteen months after agreeing the purchase, we finally took possession. That's when the problems really began. The wisdom of buying a house without water or electricity was put to the test. By the time we resolved those issues another twelve months had passed. The time had come to put the frustrations of the past behind us and concentrate on the *Opportunities Ahead*.

Throughout the wait we'd kept ourselves busy. There can't be many people who can add moonshine distillation to their curriculum vitae. Our second year in property management presented an unexpected opportunity, a house swap to the far side of the world. All we had to do was make the arrangements. After all, how difficult could it be to organise the trip of a lifetime?

We soon discovered that restoring a Spanish ruin requires a unique skill set. The two most important are a vivid imagination and a great sense of humour. Above all, be prepared to sacrifice your sanity: if you're not crazy when you start, you will be by the time it's finished.

Keeping the costs down came at a price. The work was hard and the hours long. Suppliers and subcontractors tested our patience but throughout it all we manged to maintain a healthy work-life balance.

During our house swap holiday to Australia I realised a *Driving Ambition.* The trip of a lifetime took us from rural Galicia to Wollongong in Australia via Shanghai in China. A forty-nine-day tour to six countries on three continents, flying 27,000 miles and driving over 13,000 kilometres. On our return the house restoration had moved on apace but there was plenty still to do before we could welcome paying guests to our holiday rental home.

By the end of May the main contractor had finished his work. The gardens and grounds would take a little longer to complete, but Melanie and I could finally make a start on designing the interior. Our mission was to provide quality accommodation for *The Discerning Traveller.*

Hard work and quality fittings helped transform our blank canvas into a cosy home. Choosing a name is never easy but after much consideration we settled on *Campo Verde.* A luxury farmhouse in the Galician countryside with a name that rolled off the tongue in any language. We'd put our hearts and souls into creating this romantic hideaway, and invested a large part of our savings. Only time would tell if we'd made the right decision.

1

What a Charmer

When Benjamin Disraeli coined the phrase, "Hope for the best but prepare for the worst", I doubt he had a Spanish holiday rental in mind. We'd worked tirelessly to ready the house for the start of the letting season, but doubts remained. Had we done enough? It's not the problems you envisage that catch you out, it's the ones you don't. Years of hard work and planning would soon be put to the test. Our financial future was hanging in the balance. Thumbs up, and we'd live to fight another day; thumbs down, and the consequences could be catastrophic.

We'd spent the last three years managing a rental property for our friends Bob and Janet. During that time, we'd perfected our Meet and Greet (the slogan we'd adopted for our official welcome). Now we were owners, and I for one was feeling a little nervous. We'd left home and driven the twenty-four kilometres to the sleepy village of Vilatán, location of *Campo Verde*, our holiday rental property. I'd pulled up outside and Melanie was about to jump out and open the gate.

'Are you ready?' I asked.

'As ready as I'll ever be.'

'Just remember, happy smiling faces and nothing is too much trouble.'

Melanie grinned at me like a Cheshire cat.

The guests presiding over our fate were Dr Gerald Cann and his wife Elizabeth, from Strathclyde. They'd arrived yesterday. We'd left a key in a secret location and a contact phone number just in case. The fact that they hadn't rung was a positive sign.

Melanie hopped out, pressed the doorbell mounted on the gatepost and opened the gate. I drove through and she closed it behind me. By the time I'd crept slowly to the end of the driveway, a woman, who I presumed was Mrs Cann, had opened the front door and stepped outside. The palms of my hands felt sweaty as I fumbled for the door handle. I glanced in the mirror; Melanie was almost alongside. I stepped out, beaming like the proverbial village idiot.

'Good morning, I'm Craig, and this is my wife Melanie,' I said, offering my hand.

Melanie stepped forwards, smiling in such a way it looked like she was trying to hold in a fart. I couldn't believe how nervous we were.

'I'm Elizabeth, please come in to your lovely home.'

A sweeping arm gestured us inside.

'It's your home for the next two weeks,' said Melanie.

Elizabeth smiled.

Without further ado we climbed the staircase to the first floor where Dr Gerald Cann was awaiting our arrival.

'I'm Gerald,' he said.

Their friendly nature melted our anxiety. They loved the house and thought we'd done a great job. Compliments rained down and their interest in us and our endeavours seemed genuine and comprehensive. Time flew by and before we knew it, an hour had passed.

'Anyway, we must let you good people get on with your holiday. If there's anything at all, don't hesitate to give us a call,' said Melanie.

'We'll be back at the same time on Saturday to change the linen and mow the lawns. Don't worry if you're going out, we can let ourselves in,' I added.

We shook hands one final time and left.

'That seemed to go well,' I said, as we drove through the village.

'They were a lovely couple.'

'Definitely not a Gerry though.'

My remark brought a smile to Melanie's face. When Gerald had made the reservation, we had wondered if he'd be a Gerald Cann or a jerrycan.

If their reaction was anything to go by, our decision to pitch the house at the upper end of the market had been justified. We drove home with a renewed sense of confidence. Today we could relax in the knowledge that our best efforts had been good enough.

Swapping the six-and-a-half-tog duvet for the four-tog confirmed the arrival of summer. Even the weather gods were playing their part in the success of our new venture.

'We've got another,' I announced, as I stepped outside.

Melanie was pegging out the washing and I'd been checking the inbox.

'Another what, darling?'

'Another booking.'

'That's good.'

We'd set ourselves a target of ten weeks and had passed that by mid-April. Since then, enquiries had dried up which led me to believe the booking season was over. This reservation threw cold water on that theory, much to my surprise and delight.

'How long is it for?' she asked.

'One week, from the 11th until the 18th of July.'

'It's your birthday that week.'

'It doesn't matter.'

'How many people is it for?'

'Just two.'

'Good.'

We preferred small parties; it meant less work for the same money.

We spent the rest of the day lounging in the sunshine and dipping in and out of the pool to keep cool. In the evening I fired up the barbecue and we dined alfresco.

'What's that?' said Melanie.

Something had startled her. She jumped to her feet and dashed towards the pool. I wasn't hanging about to find out and scampered after her.

'What's what?' I asked.

'Over there, something is moving,' said Melanie, pointing in the general direction of the kitchen door.

The dog couldn't wait to see what all the fuss was about and wandered over for a closer look. That's when I saw it.

'Jazz, come here,' I called.

The urgency in my voice did the trick and she retreated immediately. Hiding in the shadows was a small grass snake. It had slithered unnoticed into the garden and seemed intent on finding out what lay beyond the flyscreen guarding the kitchen doorway.

'What is it?' stammered Melanie.

'It's only a grass snake.'

'It's going in the house. Get rid of it.'

From holiday rep to snake charmer in less than twenty-four hours. Are there no limits to this boy's talents?

'Wait here,' I said.

'Where are you going? Don't leave me on my own.'

'I'm going to get the net.'

'What net?'

'The net for the swimming pool.'

'It's a snake, not a dead fly.'

'Do you have a better idea?'

That silenced her.

The pool net is attached to a three-metre-long pole. A reassuring length when faced with a slippery serpent. My plan was simple: scoop the snake into the net and throw it over the garden wall.

'Do be careful,' cautioned Melanie.

I knew from experience how fast these little critters can move. Any sign of resistance and I was out of there. Cautiously I approached my quarry.

'Come on then, fella.'

Speaking nicely to it was unlikely to assist its capture, but it helped relieve my tension. The creature hadn't moved a muscle since I'd first clapped eyes on it. I had the distinct impression it was weighing up its options: fight or flight? I was hoping for neither. Slowly, I edged the net towards it.

'Here we go.'

My heart was racing as I eased the net under its stomach.

In the blink of an eye, it flicked its body and made a beeline for the kitchen.

'Stop it!' screamed Melanie.

What did she think I was trying to do?

'Oh no you don't.'

My reactions were equal to the task. I darted forwards and crashed the net down between it, and the open doorway. It didn't stand a chance. With that route blocked, it had no other option but to bypass the door and head towards the corner of the house.

'Now I've got you.'

It was out in the open. I had to move quickly. I slid the net across the tiled terrace and was just about to catch our uninvited guest when it darted between the wall and the drainpipe and disappeared.

'Where's it gone?' asked Melanie, fear reverberating in her voice.

I couldn't believe it. Like a magician's illusion, Hissing Sid had transformed into Harry Houdini and done a vanishing act.

'It must be hiding behind the drainpipe,' I replied.

'Well, take a look.'

That was easy for her to say; she was standing on the other side of the terrace.

Nervously I edged forwards, straining my eyes in the darkness to see where it'd gone.

'I can't see a thing.'

'Get closer.'

I had visions of it coiled up behind the drainpipe waiting to launch itself at the first idiot stupid enough to get within range, and sink its fangs into their eyeballs.

'Where are you going now?' she asked, as I moved away.

'To get a torch.'

I thought it wise to close the kitchen door on my return, just in case it made a break for freedom. If it got inside the house, I'd never hear the last of it. I kept my distance and shone the torch into the cavity between the wall and the drainpipe.

'There you are,' I said, spotting our slithery friend.

Two glass-like eyes stared back at me.

'Come on, I'm not going to hurt you. We just want you to find somewhere else to spend the night.'

My sweet talking fell on deaf ears. It seemed I wouldn't be adding snake charmer to my CV, after all.

'We'll have to leave it,' I said.

'What?'

Melanie was horrified at the thought.

'What am I supposed to do?'

'I don't know. Can't you poke it out with a stick?'

'It's not doing anyone any harm.'

'What if it gets inside the house?'

'If it's clever enough to use the door handle, I suggest we sell it to the highest bidder.'

Melanie was not impressed with my attempt at humour. I checked my watch.

'We'll be going to bed in half an hour. If we leave it be, it'll be gone in the morning.'

'And if it isn't?'

'It will be.'

We spent the rest of the evening sitting on the half turn with one eye on the drainpipe.

'I've been thinking,' I said, as Melanie nudged open the bedroom door carrying our morning coffees.

'Oh yes.'

'Yes.'

'And what have you been thinking?'

'I've been thinking we ought to invite guests from *Campo Verde* to come here for a wine and tapas night.'

Melanie was used to my hare-brained schemes but this one had her stumped. Over the last three years we'd learnt a great deal about managing a holiday rental property. Our biggest disappointment was the lack of repeat customers. In all that time only one party had returned for a second stay. Anything we could do to encourage guests to return would mean one less client to find the following year. We knew from our own holiday experiences that once we'd found somewhere we liked, we would go back year after year. Why we'd failed to attract repeat customers was something of a mystery. One theory was that Galicia is a bucket list destination; once experienced, most people move on to the next place on their list.

In many ways, this corner of Spain isn't exactly user friendly towards international tourists. When it comes to communication, priority is given to the Galician language, *galego*. Its use was banned during Franco's dictatorship, but has enjoyed a resurgence since his death. Nowadays, most public information is written in *galego* first and *castellano* (Spanish) second. As for English, you can forget it. This makes the simplest tasks, such as ordering a meal, far more difficult. To make matters worse, many restaurants deliver their menu orally, at breakneck speed, and in a little-known language. For some travellers this is exactly what they're looking for, but the more specialised the marketplace, the fewer the opportunities.

In an effort to compensate for these shortcomings, we'd produced a list of the most common dishes along with an English translation, and left printed copies at the house. We'd written a series of restaurant reviews for over a dozen local restaurants, and created a book of self-drive tours complete with tourist information and driving instructions to help guests discover those off-the-beaten-track places mainstream guides often overlook. All this effort was to enable guests to make the most of their stay in Galicia. What we now needed to do was encourage them to return.

'Wine and tapas night?' repeated Melanie.

'That's right. We could invite guests to come here and share a glass of wine and a few traditional tapas. What do you think?'

'How many tapas?'

Melanie was more interested in the practicalities of hosting such an event than the overall principle.

'I don't know … two or three.'

'Well, is it two, or three?'

'Three would be better.'

Melanie's bottom lip dropped while she considered the proposal.

'Why exactly do you want to do this?' she asked.

'To encourage people to book again.'

'And why do you think hosting a wine and tapas night will do that?'

'I don't know it will, but what have we got to lose? Do you remember the Crockfords?' I asked.

'Remember, how could I forget them?'

Mr and Mrs Crockford were one of the first couples to stay at Bob and Janet's rental property. At their Meet and

Greet, we discovered that Mrs Crockford had a severe case of conjunctivitis and spent the next twenty-four hours ferrying them between the hospital in Monforte de Lemos, and the pharmacy in Ferreira de Pantón. They were very grateful for our help, and showed their appreciation by inviting us to share a glass of wine with them. While we were there, the conversation turned to a holiday they'd taken the previous year in France. The owners of that property had invited them to take refreshments in their chateau.

'Don't you remember how keen she was to tell us about it?'

'I do, but it didn't make them book again.'

'You don't know that.'

'They came here.'

She had a point.

'They might have had two holidays that year.'

'I don't suppose we'll ever know. Anyway, what makes you think people would like to come here; it's not exactly a French chateau?'

'Your delicious tortilla perhaps.'

'Tortilla! It would have to be a chuffing big tortilla to hide this house.'

'Tsk! There's nothing wrong with the house.'

'I know, just kidding. Actually, I think it's a good idea.'

'You do?'

'Yes. What else can we serve besides tortilla?'

'I thought Flaming Pig might be nice.'

'That's a great idea.'

Flaming Pig is our name for a dish called *chorizo al infierno* (flaming chorizo). Rounds of sliced chorizo are skewered and flambéed over a brown glazed earthenware bowl using the local firewater, *aguardiente*, as the accelerant. Diners are encouraged to turn the skewers over the bouncing blue flames. It's quite a spectacle.

'And your third tapa?' asked Melanie.

'I don't know, what do you think?'

'What about *pimientos de Padrón*?'

'Excellent.'

Pimientos de Padrón are a variety of small green peppers. They're served deep fried and sprinkled with rock salt. Not only are they delicious but they'd make an excellent vegetarian option.

Having created a menu, Melanie was far more enthusiastic about inviting strangers into our home. We hadn't a clue if it would result in more repeat customers, but if we didn't try, we'd never know and besides which, it sounded like fun.

'When shall we start?' asked Melanie.

'If the Canns are around when we do the mid-stay linen change, let's ask them if they'd like to join us.'

'OK, why not?'

'There's one other thing,' I said, sheepishly.

'Oh yes, what?'

'What do you think to the idea of giving each guest a gift?'

'A gift, what sort of gift?'

'More a souvenir than a gift.'

'Like a fridge magnet?'

'I was thinking of a pencil drawing rather than a fridge magnet.'

'A pencil drawing!'

'That's right.'

'And who's going to do this pencil drawing?'

'It's funny you should ask that. I've found an online program that converts a photo into a drawing.'

Unbeknown to Melanie my plans had been taking shape for some time. We finished our morning coffee and readied ourselves for the day ahead.

'Come and take a look at this program,' I said.

'Aren't you forgetting something?'

'What?'

'The snake.'

I'd forgotten all about our unwanted guest. I needn't

have worried; a thorough search of the garden revealed no trace of our night-time intruder.

'Not a sign of it,' I announced.

Melanie had been waiting in the kitchen with the door closed.

'Where have you looked?'

'Everywhere. It's gone. Come on, let me show you the drawing.'

We went through into the office and I booted up the laptop.

'Well, what do you think?'

I'd used a photo of *Campo Verde*, fiddled about with the contrast and run it through the program. After a bit of practice, I found the style I was looking for.

'That's amazing.'

'It's clever, isn't it?'

'How does it work?'

'I've no idea, but once it's framed it'll look really good.'

'How much will all this cost?'

'I don't know. Let's see if we can find a frame and then decide.'

'OK.' Melanie turned to leave before saying, 'Would you like another coffee?'

'Yes please.'

By the time she'd returned, I had something else to share with her.

'Guess what?' I asked.

'What?'

'Guess.'

'I don't know, Elvis has been spotted in a karaoke bar in Benidorm.'

'He might have been, but I was thinking more on the lines of another booking.'

'Another?'

'Yep.'

'That's great.'

'A certain Michel DeVille.'

'Oh la la. I take it he's not from the UK.'

'Belgium,' I replied.

Our new enterprise was nothing if not cosmopolitan.

That afternoon we drove into town to check out the cost of picture frames.

'This would be ideal,' I said.

I'd found a twenty by thirty centimetre pine picture frame.

'How much is it?' asked Melanie.

'Only €4.95.'

'Is that all?'

The pine was a little lighter than I would have preferred but beggars can't be choosers. The end result looked excellent and significantly more expensive than it cost.

On Saturday morning we drove to *Campo Verde* for the mid-stay linen change. Gerald and Elizabeth were at home. Elizabeth gave Melanie a hand with changing the bedding while I mowed the lawns. Before leaving we invited them to the inaugural Wine and Tapas night.

'We'd love to come,' they said.

We set the date for Thursday the 4th of June.

The Canns arrived at 7:30 pm and we retired to the back terrace to chat. During the conversation we discovered that Dr Cann was a doctor of geography, and a professor at Strathclyde University. Their claim to fame was that they once lived close to the home of Sir Frederick Anderson Goodwin, aka Fred the Shred. He gained notoriety as the head of the Royal Bank of Scotland who, at the time of the Global Financial Crisis, was held responsible for the bank's flawed investment strategy and subsequently had to go cap-in-hand to the government for fifteen billion pounds of public money. After the revelation, Sir Fred went into hiding taking his £342,500 annual pension with him. In 2012, the powers that be thought it fitting to strip him of his knighthood. I'd say he got away lightly.

The wine flowed and all three tapas were a resounding success. By the time they were ready to leave the clock had ticked around to 10:00 pm.

'We have a gift for you. A souvenir of your stay at *Campo Verde*,' I said, handing Elizabeth the framed drawing which I'd neatly wrapped.

'Thank you. Can I open it now?'

'Of course.'

Carefully, she pulled the tape off one end and slid out the frame.

'Oh, look Gerald, isn't it wonderful?'

'Yes, that's very nice, and thank you,' he said, directing his final comment towards Melanie and me.

'You're very welcome and we hope you return to see us soon.'

We shook hands one final time, wished them a bon voyage, and waved them off.

'That seemed to go well,' I said, as we stepped inside.

'Yes, and they loved the tapas.'

'That settles it then, from now on we'll invite all the guests.'

'It's got to be worth a go.'

Melanie's endorsement was a sure indication that, despite her reservations, she'd quite enjoyed entertaining the guests. For the time being, the Wine and Tapas night would become part and parcel of our customer service. Only time would tell if going that extra mile was a worthwhile investment.

2

Wet and Dry

No sooner had the Canns left *Campo Verde* than the weather changed. Dark clouds filled the sky and rain began to fall. Fortunately for us, the next guests weren't arriving for another week.

'Can you believe this weather?' I said, as we trundled through the narrow lanes of Vilatán.

Melanie said nothing. We'd driven to *Campo Verde* to collect the dirty laundry and make sure everything was OK. If truth be known, we were feeling a little nervous. The Canns were a lovely couple, but you never know what you'll find after guests have left. Melanie went straight to the Visitors book to see if they'd written a comment while I checked every room. We needn't have worried; they'd taken great care of the place.

'Come and read this,' said Melanie, calling me over.

Gerald and Elizabeth Cann – Strathclyde, Scotland

An outstanding holiday with good weather for visits to Lugo, Santiago de Compostela and four of the tours in the Self-Drive Guide, without which we might have missed many gems. The farmhouse – Campo Verde – is splendid and Craig and Melanie delightfully hospitable hosts. Our memories will be forever of the miles and miles and miles of hillsides covered in bright yellow Spanish broom – a marvel to behold.

Muchas Gracias! Hasta la vista!

'That's really nice,' I said, closing the book.

A comment like that made all the hard work worthwhile. We were in the business of surpassing people's expectations and could rightly be proud of our efforts. We'd set the bar very high; maintaining those standards would keep us on our toes.

'Right then, let's get the laundry.'

We gathered up the bedding, towels, tablecloth, and tea towels and hauled the laundry bag downstairs.

'Do you need a hand?' asked Melanie, as I lifted it into the back of the car.

One final push and in it went.

'Done.'

A key part of any business is organisation. Over the last three years we'd developed our own clearly defined roles. I was responsible for marketing, reservations, and property maintenance, Melanie looked after housekeeping, and we shared the workload on changeover day.

'If this weather doesn't improve soon, I'm going to have to use the tumble dryer,' said Melanie.

I could hear the frustration in her voice. She'd been trying to get the laundry dry for days but every time she pegged it out the heavens opened. The next guests would be arriving soon and she was desperate to get everything dried and ironed. To keep costs down, we'd decided to limit the use of the tumble dryer to airing the towels. Melanie had insisted on them being soft and fluffy. 'There's nothing worse than towels that feel like sandpaper,' she'd argued.

'Can't we use another set of linen?' I suggested.

'We can, but that doesn't get these dry, and if I wait much longer they'll go musty and I'll have to wash everything again.'

Who would have thought that a washer and a dryer could become a rock and a hard place?

'What's the forecast looking like?' I asked.

'I don't know.'

'Let's give it one more day.'

'We can if you want, but are you going to iron everything?'

When Melanie starts using four-letter words like iron, it's time to blow the budget and let her get on with it.

'On second thoughts, you're right. It can't harm to use it this once,' I replied.

Melanie rolled her eyes and pulled the sheets off the airer and into the clothes basket. Before the day was out, we had a freshly ironed set of linen ready for the new arrivals.

'What are the next guests called?' asked Melanie.

'Mr and Mrs Panton.'

'Panton?'

The irony wasn't lost on her. Ferreira de Pantón is the name of the village where *Casa de Elo* is located, the house we rented when we first moved to Galicia.

'Yes, I thought we might treat them to a bottle of Mencía.'

Mencía is a local grape variety. It produces a very distinctive red wine with a price tag to match.

'Why?'

Given my reluctance to use the tumble dryer, she had every right to ask. As part of our customer service we provide guests with a grocery starter pack to see them through the first day or so. It includes staples such as bread, eggs, cheese, ham, milk etc, and beverages, water, beer, and a bottle of cheap red wine. Swapping that for Mencía would almost certainly add to the cost.

'I'm sure I've seen one in the supermarket called Pantón.'

'You're joking.'

'No. I think it's got a purple label.'

'That's a great idea.'

'It'll depend on the price, of course.'

'Of course.'

We'd decided to prepare the house a day early. That way we could buy the starter pack en route instead of making two trips, leaving Saturday free for me to spray the grapevines.

On Friday morning we loaded the linen into the car and called into Monforte to buy the groceries.

'This is it,' I said, picking a bottle of Ribeira de Pantón off the shelf.

'How much is it?' asked Melanie.

I pointed at the price.

'That's not too bad.'

'Shall we get it?'

'Why not. It'll look great.'

When we arrived at *Campo Verde*, Melanie made a start inside the house and I mowed the lawns. By the time I'd finished, they looked fantastic. Not quite the turf at Wembley Stadium, but the grass was lush and green and the tramlines gave the whole exterior a lift. Three and a half hours after leaving home we arrived back, tired and hungry. Jazz had spent the morning dozing in the sunshine. As soon as she saw us, she hauled herself to her feet and waddled over to greet us. That afternoon we took a leaf out of her book and enjoyed a siesta in the sunshine.

We woke early the following day. Melanie went to switch on the kettle and take Jazz outside for her morning constitutional. I held my breath and flung open the window shutters. Perfect spraying weather: bright sunshine but most importantly, not a breath of wind.

'Are you going to spray the vines this morning?' asked Melanie on her return.

'Yes.'

Work on the grapevines started in March with the challenging job of pruning. Left unchecked, the vines would quickly grow out of control and produce poor quality fruit. There are two main parts to a grapevine: the trunk and the fruiting canes, some of which grow to over four metres long. In autumn the vines shed their leaves. This is where new buds begin to develop. Deciding which canes to trim and which to remove is a puzzle I have yet to master. Fortunately, grapevines are very forgiving. The deeper the cut, the more aggressive the following season's growth.

The canes I chose to keep were cut short, leaving just two buds for the coming season, all except one cane per vine which I left with six. It all sounds logical and straightforward; in reality, it's anything but. To make matters worse, the decisions I'd made in March would determine the success, or otherwise, of this year's harvest.

Husbandry is another important part of viniculture. To ensure a good crop, vines have to be protected from pests and diseases. Regular use of a fungicide is essential for maintaining the health of the plant. The first treatment of the season is a dusting of yellow sulphur powder. Many people swear by it, but I've yet to be convinced. A few weeks later, when the new shoots are between ten and fifteen centimetres long, the spraying can begin.

The product of choice is called *sulfatar*. It's a generic term for most types of copper sulphate-based fungicides. To listen to the locals, you'd think it was a wonder product capable of solving all cultivating problems and even enhancing the flavour of the wine. I'm not sure about that but it does protect the vines from some of Mother Nature's less desirable afflictions.

'Right then, I'm going to make a start,' I said.

'OK.'

'Keep Jazz inside until I've finished.'

When it comes to health and safety, one can never be too careful.

'Haven't you forgotten something?' asked Melanie.

'What?'

'The car.'

'Oh yes.'

If I didn't roll it down the driveway it would end up getting covered with bright blue spots of copper sulphate. I don't need to tell you how I found that out.

The sprayer uses a pressurised air system to apply the liquid fungicide. Mine is a manual machine that works by pumping a handle on the side of the holding tank and squeezing the trigger on the spray gun. The tank holds twelve litres which might not sound much but try wandering around your garden with twelve bags of sugar strapped to your back and you'll get an idea of how heavy it is.

I began by measuring the correct amount of *sulfatar* into the measure. The owner of the local agricultural shop had kindly indicated the correct amount by drawing a thick blue line around it with a permanent marker. That said, it's not exactly scientific. The thickness of the line and an unsteady hand can have quite an impact on the final quantity. I tipped the measure into the top of the sprayer and dissolved it in cold water. At this point I donned my safety equipment: gloves and a face mask. The spraying could now begin.

Through trial and error, I'd found the kitchen windowsill to be the perfect height for strapping the sprayer to my back. I balanced it on the sill, remembering to lower the pumping handle before backing into position and pulling the carry straps over my shoulders. Within seconds of lifting it off the sill my prescription spectacles had fogged up; heavy breathing and a face mask has that effect. To make matters worse, I'd accidentally knocked the pumping handle upwards and out of reach. Time after time I tried to grab it but to no avail. Talk about a dog chasing its tail.

'Melanie!' I called in frustration. 'Melanie!'

If she'd taken the dog for a walk, I'd have to unstrap the sprayer and start all over again.

'Mel …'

'There's no need to shout, I heard you the first time. What do you want?'

'Just pull this handle down for me, will you?'

'This one?'

'That's it. Thank you.'

Melanie went back inside. I could finally make a start.

Using a manual spraying machine is not as easy as it looks. It's a bit like taking a coordination test where you have to rub your tummy with one hand while patting your head with the other. In this case I had to pump the handle with one arm while operating the spray gun with the other. Within the hour, I'd finished. I washed out the sprayer and put it back in the shed until next time. From now until a month prior to harvest, I'd need to treat the vines every ten days, more often if it rained. By doing this, the grapevines should remain healthy throughout the season.

'Coffee?' called Melanie.

She was standing at the kitchen door.

'Yes please. Let's have it outside,' I replied.

I plonked myself into a garden chair and waited. Minutes later, Melanie stepped outside balancing two steaming mugs.

Ring, ring … Ring, ring!

'I'll get it,' she said, placing the mugs on the table and running inside.

My heart skipped a beat. A ringing phone takes on a whole new significance on arrival day. Was it the new guests at *Campo Verde* and if so, did they have a problem? I waited nervously with my fingers crossed.

Suddenly, Melanie burst through the beaded flyscreen and stepped out onto the terrace.

'One minute,' she said, holding her hand over the microphone.

I held my breath, expecting the worst.

'It's Janet,' she said.

Phew! My racing heart began to slow.

Janet is Bob's wife, the couple whose house we used to look after. We'd met them in Galicia seven years ago and hit it off straight away. They too had dreamed of living here but things didn't turn out as they'd hoped and they returned to the UK. Since retiring, earlier in the year, they'd spent more time here.

'She wants to know if we'd like to go out for the day on Tuesday.'

'Where to?'

'The castle at O Bolo and the sanctuary in As Ermidas, and then on to Viana do Bolo for lunch.'

'Why not? It sounds like fun.'

Melanie confirmed the arrangements. They'd pick us up at 10:30 am and we'd take it from there.

'I thought it might be the guests,' said Melanie.

'So did I,' I confessed.

Sunday morning meant Meet and Greet. We'd set the alarm but woke in plenty of time to enjoy a morning coffee before readying ourselves. The rain we'd had earlier in the week had gone and normal service had been resumed: bright sunshine and a cloudless blue sky.

'What did you say they were called?' asked Melanie.

'Panton. Robert Panton.'

'And his wife?'

'I don't know. He's dealt with the booking.'

I picked the car keys off the top of the wine rack and stepped outside. Melanie opened the gates and I reversed out into the lane.

'They can't complain at this weather,' I said, as we made our way to Vilatán.

I pulled up in the entrance and Melanie hopped out. She pressed the doorbell and opened the gate. It seemed ironic that Félix, our electrician, had spent days feeding the cable for the doorbell from the house down the length of the driveway only for us to be too far away to hear it ring. I drove in slowly, giving Melanie time to close the gate and catch me up. Unlike Mrs Cann, no one came outside to meet us.

'Do you think the bell rang?' I whispered.

'I don't know.'

'I'd better knock.'

Knock, knock, knock!

The heavy wooden door gave as good as it got. We waited in silence.

'Can you hear anything?' whispered Melanie.

'Not a sound.'

It was hardly surprising; the walls were a metre thick

and the door was solid chestnut. All we could do was wait, and wait, and wait.

'What do you think?' I asked.

'I don't know.'

This dilemma highlighted the flaw in our arrivals procedure. We hadn't had this problem at Bob and Janet's house. Their doorbell was clearly audible from outside. The disadvantage of leaving the keys in a secret location and allowing guests to let themselves in was that we didn't know what time they'd arrived. For all we knew, the Pantons might only just have gone to bed.

'Perhaps we should go around the back,' I suggested.

The house is built into the surrounding bedrock. The front has a two-storey façade while the back is single storey and the living accommodation is on the first floor. With this in mind, it seemed reasonable to assume they were more likely to hear me knocking at the back door than the front.

We tiptoed around the side of the house.

'I'm not sure this is such a good idea,' I whispered.

'Why?'

'It doesn't feel right.'

We looked more like burglars than property owners.

'I think you're right.'

We turned around and tiptoed back to the front door.

'What are you doing now?' asked Melanie.

My action was obvious.

'I'm going to knock again.'

'Are you sure?'

'What else can we do?'

Melanie shrugged her shoulders.

Knock, knock, knock!

Seconds later we heard the key turning in the lock. The door inched open and a slim woman in her mid-sixties greeted us.

'Hello, I'm Shirley. Do come in,' she said, gesturing us inside.

What a relief.

'I'm Craig and this is my wife Melanie.'

Mr Panton was waiting for us when we reached the top of the stairs and led us into the lounge.

'Would you like a drink?' asked Shirley. 'The kettle has just boiled.'

Melanie and I looked at each other. It would have been rude not to.

'A coffee would be lovely.'

The conversation focused on us and our move to Galicia. I was more interested in them. Robert was the former head of an international school on the Costa del Sol. It was a private, fee paying school and one of the best in the area. It was clear from his enthusiasm that he'd loved his job but times change and he seemed quite relieved to have retired when he did.

'The last few years weren't the same,' he admitted.

He blamed the changes on the collapse of the Soviet Union. In the aftermath, modern-day gangsters made huge sums of money, some of which found its way into exclusive resorts such as Marbella. Trying to explain to a Russian gangster why his darling little Boris couldn't enrol in such a prestigious educational institution despite Daddy's net worth didn't go down too well.

'Were you threatened?' I asked.

'On more than one occasion.'

'I'd like to ask a question,' interrupted Shirley.

We all turned to face her.

'Is it usually so warm at this time of year?'

'More often than not,' replied Melanie.

'Oh.'

She sounded disappointed.

'It's usually bad weather people complain about,' I joked.

'I'm sure. It's just that our friends suggested we pack our winter woollies. I'm afraid we might have the wrong attire.'

It never fails to amaze me how misinformed some people are about northern Spain and Galicia in particular. It's true that winters here are wet. That's why it's such a stunningly beautiful place. We also have our fair share of showers in spring and autumn, but summers couldn't be more perfect and often run from May through to October. During summer we enjoy glorious sunshine with temperatures warm enough to enjoy but not too hot as to be intolerable. Anyone who had suggested packing winter woollies in the middle of June had obviously never visited the area at this time of year.

Thankfully for us, the Pantons would return south with tales of beautiful scenery and excellent weather.

3

Tripping the Light

During the summer months our social calendar becomes quite congested as holiday homeowners return for their seasonal getaway.

'That was Carol on the phone,' said Melanie, as she stepped outside.

We met Carol and her partner Gerry the first summer we moved to Galicia. It's fair to say that Gerry was something of a pioneer when he bought his house back in 1989.

'Oh yes, what did Carol want?'

'She said it's the *feria* in Escairón this Friday.'

Ferias, or markets, are a regular feature of Galician life. Most towns and large villages host a bi-monthly event. Each location has its own fixed dates which enables nomadic traders to travel around the area peddling their wares. Accompanying these travelling traders are hospitality tents specialising in the region's two most popular gastronomic delights: boiled *pulpo* (octopus) and chargrilled *churrasco* (a selection of barbecued pork and beef, accompanied with a *criollo* or plump pork sausage).

'Is it really,' I replied.

I had a good idea what was coming next.

'She wondered if we'd like to meet them there and then go back to their house for lunch.'

'Lunch?'

'Yes. She's going to make a curry.'

'Excellent.'

'I thought you'd say that so I said yes. She asked me to see if Bob and Janet would like to join us. Oh, and I said I'd make some naan bread.'

'Good idea, and I'm sure they will.'

'That's what I told her.'

The chatter of songbirds nudged us into a new day. I rolled over and stared bleary-eyed at the digital display: 8:23 am. Ample time for a leisurely start before Bob and Janet picked us up for our trip to O Bolo and beyond. The weather couldn't have been better, bright and sunny without a cloud in the sky. Bob and Janet arrived as arranged and parked in the entrance. Melanie and I went to meet them.

'Aw look at her. She hates the sight of us,' said Janet, as she opened the gate.

Jazz trotted across to greet her.

'No, she doesn't, look.'

Jazz was rubbing up against Janet's leg, seeking some attention. Janet obliged and bent down to stroke her.

'She doesn't mind being on her own for the day. Do you lass?' I said.

Looking into her eyes, you could be forgiven for thinking her world was about to fall apart. I had no doubt that as soon as we'd gone, she'd be curled up asleep in the sunshine.

'I spoke to Carol yesterday,' said Melanie.

'How are they both?' asked Janet.

'They're fine. She asked if you'd like to join us at Escairón *feria* this Friday and then go back to theirs for lunch?'

Janet looked at Bob who nodded.

'That would be lovely.'

'That's what I told her.'

'Right then, let's get off,' said Bob.

From home we joined the *carretera nacional* N-120 heading east. It took us forty minutes to drive the fifty-nine kilometres to the town of A Rúa where we picked up the OU-533. After ten kilometres we caught sight of O Bolo Castle, perched atop a hill in the middle of the Galician countryside. The town's older properties are clustered around the hillside below the castle's impressive *torre* (castle keep).

We exited the main highway and continued along local roads. The *torre* skipped in and out of view as the route took us uphill and down dale through Galicia's undulating landscape. Eventually we entered the town. Access to the castle is not immediately obvious and first-time visitors can be forgiven for believing they have to park at the foot of the hill and walk the rest of the way. Fortunately, we'd been before and knew that holding our nerve up the steep and narrow approach road would have its rewards. At the top of the hill lies a small square surrounded by quaint cottages. At the far end is a 12th century Romanesque church and walled cemetery. Strategically planted trees provide leafy shade for those brave enough to make the climb. Bob parked under one and we made our way towards the *torre*.

The town of O Bolo has a long and turbulent history dating back to the 1st century. The origins of the original castle are unclear, but by the 12th century, title had passed to the Counts of Lemos. The original castle was destroyed during the 15th century Irmandiño revolts (peasants' uprising). What remains today was rebuilt from the ruins a century later under the patronage of Juan Francisco

Pimentel, the Count of Benavente. Over the next two centuries the castle and *torre* fell into disrepair, but in 1999, under the supervision of the town council, parts of the castle, including the *torre*, were restored. It now hosts a visitors' centre and interactive museum. Three euros each seemed a fair price to pay for admission.

'Are you on holiday?' asked the young curator.

'We are, but these two live here,' replied Bob, pointing at us.

'Where do you live?' she asked.

'In Canabal, close to Sober,' replied Melanie.

The young lady looked puzzled.

'Near Monforte de Lemos,' I added.

'Oh yes.'

'Can we climb the *torre* first?' asked Janet.

'Of course, and you're in luck. The kestrel chicks have just hatched.'

The young lady explained that every year a pair of kestrels nest in one of the loopholes (narrow windows that were used to launch arrows through) and this year there were five chicks.

Bob listened intently. If truth be known, I think he's a bit of a twitcher.

'You'll see them when you get up there,' she added.

'We'll be able to see them?' asked Bob.

'Yes. There's a peephole.'

The prospect of a peephole had Bob bolting for the steps.

Torres are like a Tardis but in reverse: they're much smaller on the inside than they are on the outside, which is hardly surprising given the walls are at least two metres thick. These medieval monoliths were built as a final redoubt. If this defensive structure was breached, death was inevitable.

The old stone steps had been replaced with a modern, safe staircase and handrail. Halfway up we reached the loophole housing the family of kestrels. I'd expected to find a high-tech observation window; I should have known better. A pane of glass had been wedged into the loophole and sealed with a rough bead of silicone. This had been hand-painted with a thick coat of black gloss and there was a tiny peephole scratched out of it. Bob was first to take a look. He pressed his face into the glass and stared through the hole.

'Wow, that's fantastic. One, two, three, four … and there, there's the fifth.'

All we could see was our dull reflection in the painted pane and the back of Bob's head.

'Can I have a look?' asked Janet.

Bob moved to one side and Janet assumed the position.

'I wonder if the parents will return. Oh, oh … one of the chicks has just stood up. Here, take a look,' she said, stepping aside to let Melanie see what all the fuss was about.

'Ah, they're so cute.'

The shortcomings of the viewing arrangements didn't go unnoticed.

'Oh, oh … another has just stood up. Do you want to take a look?' she asked.

Finally, it was my turn.

'Yes please.'

I stepped forwards and peered through the hole. My first impressions weren't exactly earth-shattering. The daylight streaming in from outside made it difficult to focus on the chicks. It was almost as if they were in silhouette. The most striking thing was the state of the nest: it was filthy. When my eyes had adjusted to the dazzling backlight, the chicks themselves seemed very clean. Watching them interact with each other was quite fascinating although I doubt I'll be morphing into a twitcher anytime soon.

'Are you coming?' called Melanie.

When I turned around Melanie was standing at the top of the next flight of steps and Bob and Janet had disappeared from sight.

'I'm coming,' I replied.

By the time I'd caught up with everyone we were standing on the roof, staring out between the merlons at a landscape of undulating hills, blanketed with a patchwork of natural woodland and grassy pastures. The *torre's* location was an obvious choice. Defenders had a clear line of sight for miles in all directions. No one would sneak up on this place unannounced.

'Right then, shall we see what the museum has to offer?' I suggested.

On the way down we stopped for one final look at the chicks.

'Hello, did you see the birds?' asked the curator.

'Yes, it was wonderful.'

Janet echoed our sentiments.

'Would you like to watch a promotional film? The narration is Spanish but the pictures are very beautiful,' she added.

How could we refuse? We followed her into the viewing room. Melanie and I understood most of the audio and the cinematography lived up to its billing.

'Did you enjoy that?' asked the curator, as we filed past her and into the final part of the museum.

'Very informative,' I replied.

The museum had a number of interesting artefacts but what caught my eye was a life-sized model of a horse standing in the middle of the room. The jet-black stallion was draped in a medieval-style red and yellow robe with matching reins and a tan leather bridle.

'Look at that,' I said.

A mounting block invited visitors to mount the horse.

'And look,' said Melanie, pointing at a wardrobe of knights' attire and an assortment of wooden weaponry.

'Come on, let's have a go,' I said, making a beeline for a suit of leather armour and matching helmet.

'I'll have this,' said Melanie, pulling on a coat of chainmail.

'Here you go.'

I'd handed her a helmet. Bob and Janet looked on as Melanie donned her fake headwear. The helmet resembled the business end of a large artillery shell and sat high on her head. If anything, it made her look more like an extra in a *Monty Python* sketch than a medieval knight.

'Go on then. You know how to ride,' I said, encouraging her to mount the statuesque steed.

Melanie straddled the beast and I whipped out the camera and snapped a few frames.

'Right then, your turn,' she said, sliding off the mare.

'One minute. I can't do battle without my tackle.'

Janet smiled as I picked up my weapons of choice, a wooden Excalibur and trusty shield.

'I can't see a chuffing thing with this hat on,' I said.

'It's a helmet,' said Bob.

'Well I still can't see anything.'

Carefully, I climbed the block and cocked my leg over the mount.

'Whoa boy.'

'Steady on Craig, it looks a bit frisky,' joked Bob.

I shifted my weight from right buttock to left and slid onto the nag.

'Hold that pose,' instructed Melanie, as she snapped away.

'OK, that's enough.'

Melanie and I disrobed and put away our toys. We thanked the young lady on our way out and headed back to the car.

'We'll definitely do that again,' I said, as we strolled through the square.

Despite being parked in the shade of a plane tree, the interior of the car was hot enough to roast a chicken. Bob switched on the air conditioning and the fan kicked into action. The next stop on our mini tour was the sanctuary at As Ermidas or to give it its official title, Santuario de Nuestra Señora de las Ermidas. En route we passed through the hamlet of Santa Cruz, home to a very unusual monument.

'Have you visited the cross?' I asked, as we approached the outskirts of the hamlet.

'What cross?'

'It's an unofficial viewing point marked by a concrete cross. It's just off the main road.'

'Let's call on the way back,' suggested Melanie.

The road from the OU-533 into As Ermidas is not for the faint-hearted. It's a steep and winding descent with spectacular views of the sanctuary. On first sight, it's difficult to imagine anyone visiting this mountainous wilderness, never mind building such an impressive structure. Only when you hear the story does it begin to make sense.

The sanctuary dates back to the 17th century and was built as a testament to the miraculous power of God Almighty, at least that's how the custodians of Catholicism frame it. However, the story begins much earlier than that in the 12th century when local herdsmen unearthed an ancient artefact. The herdsmen noticed that every time their cattle passed one particular patch of thorny and overgrown land, they became noisy and agitated. On closer inspection they discovered the entrance to a cave. Curiosity overcame fear and a group of them entered. Their audacity paid dividends. Hidden in the darkness was a carved sculpture of the Virgin Mary cradling Baby Jesus. In reverence to their good fortune the herdsmen built a small shrine to house their treasure.

Skip forwards five hundred years to 1624 and the arrival of Don Alfonso Mejía de Tovar, Bishop of Astorga. He was in the area doing a promotional tour when things started to go wrong. We'll never know if it was a bad batch of wine or some dodgy pork, but Alfie fell gravely ill. Physicians were summoned from as far afield as Monforte de Lemos. Their prognosis was certain death. On hearing the news, his faithful parishioners began praying for his recovery. As the poor bishop lay helpless on his deathbed, he saw an apparition of the Virgin Mary and hey presto! Alfie made a miraculous recovery. In appreciation of this divine intervention, Don Alfonso visited the herdsmen's shrine to give thanks to the Virgin, only to discover that the ancient artefact was a manifestation of his earlier apparition. To cement his legacy in the annals of history, Don Alfonso ordered the building of the sanctuary. The fact that four hundred years later I'm alluding to these events is a testament to his foresight.

Cynicism aside, there's no denying the splendour of this magnificent building. There are those who say it's the best example of baroque architecture in the whole of Galicia. The façade of the church has more than a passing resemblance to the twin towers of the cathedral in Santiago de Compostela, except on a more modest scale.

'Come on then,' I said, leading the way.

The front door was an open invitation to enter. One by one we stepped inside.

'It's a bit dark,' said Janet.

'Over there,' said Melanie, pointing at a light switch.

Bob skipped between two rows of pews and flicked it on.

'It's not a bomb, is it?' he asked.

'A bomb?'

'It's ticking.'

'No, it's on a timer.'

Flicking the switch had flooded the apse with light, illuminating its golden gilding. An intricately embroidered pall or altar cloth was draped over the central altar which was covered with a host of eucharistic objects fashioned from precious metals. Beautifully painted biblical scenes, mounted in gilded frames, decorated the walls. Looking around this palatial temple I questioned the wisdom of allowing the general public unfettered access. I couldn't decide if it was an act of faith or one of stupidity.

'Look at that,' said Bob, pointing at the ceiling.

'What is it?' asked Janet.

'It's a Spanish galleon,' I replied.

Hanging from the ceiling of the nave was a scaled replica of a three-hundred-year-old Spanish galleon complete with sails and rigging. From stem to stern the model ship looked about a metre and a half long. Its fascinating history was detailed on an information plaque. On the 23rd of September 1702, a local man and mariner, Pedro Centeno, fell overboard during manoeuvres at sea. Unable to swim, he trod water for over three hours before another vessel was able to pluck him from a watery grave. As a sign of his appreciation, Pedro crafted the vessel as an offering to the Almighty.

'It says here that these types of models are quite common in coastal churches.'

Just as I'd finished reading the plaque the timer ended, plunging us into darkness.

'I think that's our cue to leave,' I added.

'Is it lunchtime yet?' asked Melanie.

'That sounds like a good idea,' replied Janet.

'Right then, let's mount up and head on to Viana do Bolo,' said Bob.

From the church we drove through the village. The steep incline took us back onto the main road. The sign read, "Viana do Bolo 16.5 km". Twenty minutes later we entered the outskirts of this small inland town. At first glance the place is quite unremarkable and rather neglected, but dig a little deeper and you'll find a charming town with a rich history and some outstanding views. Legend has it that the town was founded by migrants from the Trojan War around 1119 BC, but history would have to wait; we were starving.

'Have you eaten at A Nosa Casa restaurant?' I asked.

'Restaurant! The last time we were here we brought a picnic,' replied Janet.

'You'll love it,' added Melanie.

The restaurant serves a three-course *menú del día* which includes wine, bread, and coffee for the princely sum of ten euros per head. What sets this establishment apart from others in the area is the quality of the food.

Bob drove past the restaurant and parked in a side street nearby. Even in the shade it felt comfortably warm. We strolled into the restaurant and found a table. The menu was delivered orally and the selection was mind-boggling. We made our choices and devoured each course as it arrived. As usual the food was excellent. We settled the bill and wandered outside.

'Let's walk up to the *torre*,' suggested Bob.

After such a filling lunch, the stroll would do us good.

Opposite the restaurant is the town's main square, the Plaza Mayor. To my mind, it has quite a French feel to it. It reminded me of a school trip I went on to St Malo in Brittany. I think I was twelve at the time. On the final day of our stay I went shopping for souvenirs. I'd enjoyed the freshly baked French sticks so much I decided to take one home for Mum. You wouldn't believe the trouble I had getting the half-metre-long bread stick back to England in one piece. I handed Mum the gift and couldn't believe it when she burst out laughing. Unbeknown to me, the exact same loaf could be bought from Thurston's Bakery in the centre of Huddersfield. Now there's gratitude for you!

Having wandered through the Plaza Mayor we headed towards the *torre*. Ambling through this part of town was like stepping back in time. At a fork in the road we turned left. The lane rose steadily and before long we came to a small park with outstanding views of the confluence of the rivers Bibei and Camba. From there the going got much tougher. Stone steps climbed past a church and all the way to the *torre* at the top of the hill.

'That's quite a climb,' I said, gasping for breath.

'I need to sit down,' said Melanie.

The *torre* is all that remains of a castle, built by Ferdinand II in the 12th century. It too was partially destroyed during the Irmandiño revolt. By the end of the 18th century only the *torre* remained. For a short time it was used as the town's prison. If the ascent doesn't take your breath away the view will. A 360-degree panorama over the surrounding countryside of rolling hills, forests and pastures, and below us the cool blue water of the Bao reservoir. This was one trek worth the effort.

'So, where are we heading next?' asked Bob.

'La Cruz de Santa Cruz,' I replied.

'Santa Cruz? That sounds exotic,' remarked Janet.

'Hmm, I'm not sure exotic is the right description but it's certainly interesting.'

The walk back to the car was almost as testing as the climb to the *torre*. By the time we reached the Plaza Mayor my calves were begging for mercy.

We left Viana do Bolo and headed back along the same route we'd come. After seventeen kilometres a road sign read "Santa Cruz".

'OK, slow down. There's a slip road coming up on the right.'

'There it is,' said Melanie, pointing towards the cross.

Standing on the hillside was an eight-metre-tall concrete cross, hand-painted in brilliant white emulsion. The Mirador de Santa Cruz was the brainchild of Manuel González Rodriguez, a resident of the village. As a young boy, Manuel spent hours on the hillside staring out across the landscape and dreaming that one day he would share his special place with the rest of the world. On the 30th of August 1990 his dream came true when he opened the site to the public.

'Turn off here,' I said to Bob.

He pulled off the main carriageway and climbed a short track leading to the entrance.

'Here is fine,' I said, as we came to a stop.

The path to the *mirador* was steep, rough, and narrow. As it climbed, it twisted and turned through an unusual collection of artistic exhibits ranging from strange wind chimes, made from recycled rubbish, to weird, prehistoric-inspired rock paintings. Janet looked less than impressed but we scrambled up and eventually reached the cross.

'It's a bit spooky,' remarked Janet.

'I know but look at that view.'

It was easy to see why Manuel was inspired to share his special place with as many people as possible. It's one of those locations that takes your breath away and leaves you contemplating the meaning of life.

'If you think the ascent is spooky, just wait until you meet the man himself,' said Melanie.

'Where is he?' asked Janet.

'He lives somewhere in the village and suddenly appears as if by magic,' she replied.

Janet looked uneasy.

'There's nothing to worry about. He's just a bit eccentric,' I added.

'How does he know we're here?' she asked.

'Doo, doo, doo, doo. Doo, doo, doo, doo.'

I teased Janet by humming the theme tune to the cult TV series, *The Twilight Zone.* She was not amused.

'Come on, let's go and introduce ourselves,' I said, heading back down the hillside.

As we reached the final stretch of the dusty footpath, Manuel appeared right on cue.

'Told you,' I whispered.

'*Hola, buenas tardes*,' he called.

He recognised Melanie and me from our visit earlier in the year.

'These are our friends,' said Melanie.

He greeted them warmly and handed Janet a few tourist leaflets about local places of interest.

'*Gracias*,' she said, nervously accepting his offerings.

'Come again whenever you like,' he said.

'We will,' I replied.

We said goodbye and strolled back to the car.

'He seemed very nice,' commented Janet.

'Told you,' I replied.

'Are we heading back now?' asked Bob.

'Unless you'd like to stop at the Pazo do Castro Hotel for afternoon tea,' I suggested.

'Oh yes, can we Bob?' asked Janet.

'Of course.'

What better way to end a fabulous day than with a pot of Earl Grey on the terrace of a luxury hotel overlooking the vineyards of the Valdeorras wine region.

4

Competitive Streak

There was a time when eating Indian cuisine was as easy as picking up the phone and ordering a takeaway. Nowadays, it requires a lot more effort.

'Can you find me a recipe for a Peshwari naan?'

Melanie had brought me another cuppa to help blow the cobwebs away. I was in the office, checking my inbox before doing some research for my next blog post.

'A naan you say?'

'That's right, a Peshwari naan.'

For those unfamiliar with this variety of the famous Indian flatbread, a Peshwari naan is filled with dried fruit and coconut, and is one of my favourites.

'OK. And thanks.'

Within minutes I'd found a host of recipes. I thought it best to let Melanie decide which was most suitable. If anything went wrong, I didn't want to be blamed.

'There's loads of different recipes. You'd better come and choose one,' I announced.

Melanie followed me into the office.

'That one looks alright. Can you print it off and then take me into town?'

'Town, what for?'

'To get the ingredients.'

An hour later Melanie had worked her magic.

'What do you think?' she asked.

'Erm, the word calzone springs to mind.'

Melanie glared at me.

'But looks aren't everything, take me for example,' I added.

That brought a smile to her face. I tore off a piece.

'Ow, ow.'

'Be careful, it's only just come out of the frying pan.'

'Frying pan?'

'In the absence of a tandoori oven, the recipe suggested using a frying pan.'

I blew on it, impatient to have a taste.

'Mmm, that's really good. It might not look like a Peshwari naan but it certainly tastes like one.'

'Are you sure?'

'Try some.'

Melanie tore off a piece and took a nibble.

'Ooh yes, it's not bad at all. Right then, I'll make some more.'

'Do you want to share this one?' I asked.

'Of course.'

'Are you sure?' I teased.

'Certain.'

Not every day in June begins with bright sunshine and a cloudless sky, but if it's grey and overcast in the morning it's usually gone by lunchtime.

'Have you seen the weather?' asked Melanie, as she nudged open the bedroom door.

Jazz waddled in behind her, always willing but no longer able. She'd recovered well from the spinal injury she'd suffered last year, but the vet made it clear at the time: no more jumping. Thankfully, Jazz recognised her limitations and was more than happy to wait for me to lift her onto the bed to receive her morning treats.

'We might be grateful of a bit of shade,' I replied.

We'd arranged to meet Bob and Janet, and Carol and Gerry, outside the post office in Escairón to see what the *feria* had to offer before heading back to Carol and Gerry's for lunch.

'What time are we meeting the others?' I asked.

'We said eleven. How long will it take us to get there?'

'About twenty minutes.'

The bi-monthly *feria* in Escairón attracts people from far and wide. Within minutes of arriving we'd found a parking space and made our way to the pre-arranged meeting place.

'We're a bit early,' I said.

'Let's have a wander around before they get here.'

'OK.'

The *feria* in Escairón is one of the biggest in the area, but can still be covered in less than ten minutes.

'Hang on a minute,' said Melanie, as I walked swiftly past another stall.

'We can come back after we've met the others,' I replied.

By the time we got back to the post office, everyone was waiting for us.

'What time do you call this?' joked Gerry.

'We arrived early so we've had a quick look around.'

'Come on then,' said Carol, leading the way.

Rural markets aren't really my thing. If I'm honest, shopping is not really my thing. Don't get me wrong, I like spending as much as the next person but I prefer to know what I want and where I'm getting it from. For me, retail therapy involves online browsing and one click ordering. That said, I did find a stainless steel bolt I needed for one of the wine vats and nipped into a nearby jeweller's to get a replacement watch battery. Bob and Janet bought a garden rake and three bath towels and Carol badgered Gerry into buying some tea towels from the same stall.

'What do we need tea towels for?' asked Gerry.

'So we don't have to bring them all the way from England every time we come.'

Begrudgingly, Gerry put his hand in his pocket.

At the next stall, Bob bought himself two leather change purses. They weren't exactly "on trend" but practical nonetheless, although why he bought two was a bit of a mystery.

'Stops you getting holes in your pockets,' he said.

I couldn't argue with that, but surely he wasn't planning on having one in each trouser pocket.

The prize for the day's most popular stall went to the one selling handcrafted wooden toys.

'Look Bob,' said Janet, pointing at a wooden train pulling five lettered carriages spelling the name María.

'We don't know anyone called María,' he joked.

'Tsk! You can choose whatever letters you want.'

Carol was next to take an interest.

'Look Gerry,' she said, grabbing his arm.

Gerry wasn't getting away that easy.

'Let's get one for Oliver,' suggested Janet to Bob.

Oliver is their grandson.

Bob picked up the engine to take a closer look. Bad move. Like the strike of a king cobra, the hint of a sale brought the stallholder leaping to his feet.

'They're a very good price. What name would you like? I can do you a special price.'

Janet would usually recoil from such enthusiasm, but she was really enamoured with the wooden train set. Bob, on the other hand, was more interested in the special prices.

'How much?' he asked.

The negotiations had begun.

Carol listened with interest as prices went back and forth. Bartering is an activity most Brits shy away from, but not me. I love a good haggle, much to Melanie's embarrassment. Janet was keen to seal the deal and quickly agreed to a small reduction. While the price was low, Carol placed her order. Letters were chosen, money changed hands, and everyone left happy.

'What now?' asked Carol. 'It's too early for lunch.'

We'd ambled around the market at a snail's pace and feigned interest in goods we had no intention of buying, but I defy anyone to make a trip to Escairón *feria* extend beyond an hour.

'Let's grab a coffee,' suggested Janet.

'Or a beer,' replied Gerry.

'Now you're talking.'

On the street adjacent to the town hall, two bars had commandeered a section of the pavement with tables, chairs, and parasols. The sun had been working its magic all morning and only a few wispy clouds remained. Temperatures had risen and my fair skin demanded shade. We took a seat and waited to be served. Service was noticeably swift. On *feria* day it's all about maximising your opportunities and getting customers in and out as quickly as possible. We ordered our drinks. Everyone except Carol opted for a lunchtime beer. It's surprising how quickly time flies when you're laughing, joking, and people watching.

'Right then, let's settle the bill and go back for something to eat,' said Gerry.

I glanced at my watch.

'What time is it?' asked Melanie.

'A quarter to one.'

'Perfect,' said Carol.

We each went our separate ways to wherever we'd parked and met back at Carol and Gerry's.

The curry was delicious and Melanie's Peshwari naans went down a treat.

'What do you think to these?'

Gerry was holding a moth-eaten golf bag containing a half set of worn and rusty clubs. He'd pulled out a seven iron and handed it to Bob.

'I think they've seen better days,' he replied.

The faux leather hand grip was peeling off the chrome-plated shaft which was pitted with spots of rust. As for the club head, that was scarred and chipped from years of abuse.

'Vintage clubs can be worth a few quid,' said Gerry.

Bob raised an eyebrow.

'Vintage? These are ancient and I'm not talking Royal and Ancient,' I replied.

Gerry ignored my remark.

'And look at this,' he said, handing Bob a three wood. 'You don't see many wooden woods these days.'

'I think there's a reason for that, Gerry,' replied Bob.

Don't get me wrong, when it comes to secondhand golf clubs I'm no expert, but this set should have been thrown away years ago.

'Do they still work?' I asked.

'Of course they do.'

'Come on then. Grab your balls and let's have a knock-about,' I said, getting to my feet.

'Alright, come on ladies,' said Gerry.

'I don't play golf,' replied Carol.

'It's only a bit of fun,' I said.

Back in my teenage years, I'd taken quite a shine to the game of golf, but I hadn't held a club for over thirty years, never mind swung one. Golf was one of the few activities Dad and I had done together. We used to travel from Huddersfield to Thornes Park in Wakefield, some thirteen miles away, to play on an eighteen-hole pitch and putt course. Neither of us was very good but we both enjoyed it. Some years later, my friend Mark and I joined Crosland Heath Golf Club as junior members for the princely annual membership fee of nineteen pounds. That course was built on the moors above Huddersfield on the edge of the Pennine Hills. It was a desolate, windswept place, fashioned from moorland and a disused quarry. My playing days ended rather abruptly when employment called. Storage space in my East End bedsit was at a premium to say nothing of the lack of opportunities. Dad suggested I sell the clubs and that was that. By the time circumstance afforded me a second chance, long hours, hard work, and a much older frame had caught up with me. Striding out over uneven terrain was too much to ask for, but every cloud … golf's loss was writing's gain.

Bob and Gerry are both keen golfers and were off their seats in a flash. The ladies were less eager but they came along for moral support. Either that or to have a giggle.

'Which club shall we take?' asked Gerry, as we walked past the moth-eaten bag.

'That seven iron should do,' replied Bob.

He pulled it from the bag, picked out a dozen practice balls, and marched outside.

Gerry has quite a sizeable field adjacent to his house. It's about seventy metres long by forty wide and enclosed with drystone walls.

'Go on then Bob, show us how it's done,' said Gerry, handing him the club and dropping a ball on the ground.

Like a seasoned pro, Bob limbered up with a few practice swings before addressing the ball. With his feet firmly in position he shifted his weight from left to right until he was completely happy with his stance. He stared down the field before fixing his eyes on the ball. In one smooth pendulum-like stroke he raised the club and brought it sweeping down, *thwack!* It was obvious from the sound he'd hit the sweet spot. We stared into the powder blue sky and watched in admiration as the ball travelled the length of the field and landed just short of the boundary wall.

'Look at that. Straight as a die,' I said.

'Let's see if I can beat that,' said Gerry, taking the club from Bob. 'Mind you, it's a long time since I've played. I'm sure to be a bit rusty.'

'Gerry, just get on with it,' said Carol, sensing he was preparing his excuses in advance.

'I'm just saying. And I'm not sure this grip is as good as it should be; the club might twist in my hands and the ball could go anywhere.'

'Stop making excuses and hit it,' urged Carol.

'Yes Gerry, stop making excuses,' I teased.

'It's your turn next,' he replied.

That shut me up.

'Gerry!' Carol's impatience was mounting.

To give him his due, he certainly gave the impression of knowing what he was doing. After a quick hip shimmy, he raised the club and brought it crashing down. His swing wasn't as smooth as Bob's but he hit the ball and managed to get a little air on it before it bounced off down the field.

'Not bad Gerry,' I said, suitably impressed.

'Here you go then,' he said, handing me the club.

I found a tuft of grass and carefully placed the ball on top of it before stepping back.

What now?

My mind went blank. I hadn't a clue where to position my feet or how to address the ball. Everything I'd learnt was gone, lost forever in the annals of time. Everyone was watching. Gerry was talking to Bob about what went wrong with his shot, but all eyes were trained on me. I had no choice but to hope for the best and (s)wing it. Perhaps I'd find my natural rhythm, if I ever had any.

Somewhere in the back of my mind a little voice was telling me that the position of my feet in relation to the ball was crucial, as was the distance from my feet to the ball, and the position of my hands on the grip, and the direction of my toes on the lead foot. In short, everything was critical to me hitting this tiny white ball straight and true, but what use is a little voice if all it has are the questions? Failure seemed inevitable. Oh well, it wouldn't be the first time I'd made a fool of myself and I doubt it'll be the last; and to think, this knock-about was my idea.

I took a few practice swings and felt as stiff as a board. Slowly, I addressed the ball. The one thing I knew for sure was that I had to keep my eyes trained on the ball until I'd hit it. Slowly I raised the club before whipping it down, *clunk!* A dull hollow sound meant one thing. I lifted my eyes skywards, more in hope than expectation. Where the hell was it? Out of the corner of my eye, I caught a flash of white scampering down the field. My heart sank. I'd done one of two things: hit the ground before the ball or hit the top of the ball before the ground. Either way, I'd made a complete pig's ear of it.

'That was rubbish,' said Melanie.

True, but not exactly encouraging.

'I think you hit the ground first,' said Bob.

Bob's critique would have been extremely useful if only I'd known what adjustment to make in order to remedy the problem, but I hadn't got a clue.

'Here you go. Let's see what you can do,' I said, offering the club to Melanie.

'I can't do it.'

'How do you know until you've tried?'

Melanie has many wonderful attributes but hand-eye coordination is not one of them. Neither is rhythm, and both are essential for playing golf. She took the club and wasted no time in making a less than enthusiastic attempt to hit it. Having failed to connect, she kicked the ball into the grass and handed the club to Carol. If Melanie can't do something at the first time of asking, then as far as she's concerned, she can't do it.

'I can't play golf,' said Carol, passing the seven iron to Janet.

Janet was a bit of a dark horse. She'd been quietly watching proceedings and was not in the least bit intimidated by Carol passing on the baton. I doubt even Janet would describe herself as a golfer, but shortly after Bob took up the sport, she decided to have some lessons with a view to sharing his interest. It wasn't until Bob's hobby became his passion that Janet's love for the game waned. However, those tutorials were still fresh in her mind.

She took the club from Carol, and Bob handed her a ball. She found an unused patch of grass and placed the ball carefully on the ground. Her preparations were methodical and meticulous. I watched her every move and made mental notes of her approach. Dormant memories came flooding back. She calculated the distance between her feet and the ball by placing the club head behind the ball and leaning the grip into her groin. She opened her stance and was very deliberate in the placement and angle of her feet in relation to the ball and the alignment of those two to the target: an imaginary green seventy metres ahead.

Preparation was one thing, but the proof of the pudding was in the execution. I once followed Lee Trevino around a few holes at Gleneagles. His stance broke all the rules, but when it came to competing, he was up there with the best of them.

Slowly and precisely, Janet raised the club through a sweeping arc and brought it careering down with all the might she could muster. The ball's sweet spot yelped with joy as it flew into the air like the round from a Howitzer. More power and she would easily have matched Bob's shot. A ripple of applause followed her effort.

'That was brilliant, Janet,' I said.

'Have you had lessons?' asked Gerry, knowing full well she had.

Lessons are one thing; learning is another.

Janet's effort had unleashed the competitive beast in all of us. She handed the club to Bob whose next effort cleared the wall at the end of the field.

'Great shot sir,' said Gerry.

Even course etiquette was rearing its ugly head.

Gerry's next effort mirrored his first, as did his excuses. Now it was my turn. Had I learnt anything from Janet's methodical approach?

I mimicked her every move. Raised the club slowly and brought it crashing down. This time the projectile launched into orbit and flew over the boundary wall. I could hardly believe my eyes. Given the deafening silence, neither could anyone else. The one problem I needed to address was direction. Although I'd cleared the wall with ease the ball had veered off to the right. A minor adjustment on my next effort saw the ball veer off to the left. Such is the frustration of the game of golf.

My suggestion to hit a few balls had been a great idea. Bob had reinforced his status as the best of a bad bunch. Melanie had reaffirmed her commitment never to pick up another club. As for me, I'd really enjoyed the afternoon's event but with one caveat: trying to find wayward golf balls is as much fun as harvesting a field of wheat with nail clippers. Still, at least the sun was shining.

5

Water Works

All good things must come to an end. On Saturday morning we were back at work, albeit briefly. Robert and Shirley were halfway through their two-week stay. We needed to change the linen and I wanted to run the mower over the lawns.

'What are you doing with that?' asked Melanie.

I was holding one of the framed pencil sketches.

'I thought we could leave it at the house.'

'Aren't we going to invite them to a Wine and Tapas night?'

'We will if they're there.'

'But if not, you're going to leave it anyway?'

'Why not? It doesn't cost much and if they book to come again it'll be worth it.'

'I suppose so.'

As it turned out, Robert and Shirley were at home when we arrived. They greeted us warmly and I wasted no time in inviting them.

'We'd love to come, wouldn't we Robert?' said Shirley.

It seemed Robert didn't have much say in the matter.

'Yes darling. Will there be any more of that Pantón wine?' he asked. 'I really enjoyed it.'

'Robert!'

Shirley's reprimand didn't go unnoticed.

'I'm only asking.'

'I'm afraid not, but I'm sure we'll find something else for you to try. Which reminds me, we've got a gift for you. We usually give it to people after the tapas night, but we didn't know if you'd be home,' I explained, handing the wrapped sketch to Shirley.

'Oh, thank you. Can I open it now?'

'Yes, of course. It's not much, just a small souvenir of your stay here.'

Shirley opened the parcel and pulled out the frame.

'Look Robert, isn't it wonderful?' she said, offering it to him.

For such a small outlay, our idea was going down a treat.

'That's really nice. Thank you,' said Robert.

'You're very welcome. Right then, we'll make a start. I'm going to mow the lawns while Melanie changes the bed. We won't be long,' I said.

'Leave the sheets, Melanie. I can change the bed, and we don't actually need fresh towels. I've only just washed the ones we've got,' said Shirley.

Melanie stayed chatting while I ran the mower over the grass. Within half an hour we were heading back home.

'Perhaps we ought to try that again,' I suggested, on the drive home.

'Try what?'

'Handing out the picture on the proviso guests make their own bed,' I joked.

'Tsk!'

The Wine and Tapas night went well. I pulled the cork on a bottle of Ribera del Duero which Robert found particularly agreeable, and they loved the tapas.

On the morning of their departure, we drove to *Campo Verde* to ready it for the new arrivals. We ask departing guests to vacate the house by 10:00 am; that gives us ample time to get the place looking spick and span. I pulled into the entrance and Melanie hopped out to open the gate. Seconds later she was back.

'They're still here,' she whispered. Their car was parked in the drive.

Tardy departees are the last thing we need on changeover day. The morning is one long sprint to finish cleaning before the next guests arrive.

'Be polite but don't keep them chatting,' I said.

Time was of the essence.

As I rolled down the driveway, Robert and Shirley stepped outside. I pulled up alongside their car and we went to say hello.

'We won't keep you. We know you're busy, but we didn't want to leave without saying thank you,' said Shirley.

'You're very welcome and please come back and stay again,' I replied.

Their Visitors book comments expressed their appreciation.

Robert and Shirley Panton – Elviria

If you are fond of quality, style and good taste, this house will provide you with all three in abundance – we loved it. Added to the appeal of the house, there is the beauty of the Galician landscape and cities which taken together with the friendly, helpful welcome of the owners, makes for the perfect holiday.

Over the next two and a half hours, hard work and rising temperatures sapped our energy. By the time we headed home we were tired and sticky, but the stage was set for the next guests. That night we set the alarm clock, just in case. Thankfully we didn't need it and another summer's day began with a chorus of songbirds.

'What are these people called?' asked Melanie, as we sat up in bed sipping our morning coffee.

'I'm not sure. The diary is in the office.'

'I'll get it then, shall I?'

Melanie was joking. She knows full well that once I've pulled on my orthopaedic boots that's that, I'm set for the day. It's not a question of laziness, more of comfort. If I take them off and then tie the laces again, they're either too tight or not tight enough. Either way, they're never as comfortable the second time around. It's for that reason Melanie always makes the morning coffee and why, if she wanted to know the names of the incoming guests, she'd have to fetch the diary.

'Where is it?' she asked.

'On the office desk to the left of the computer.'

Melanie slid out of bed and wandered through into the office. Moments later she handed me the diary.

'Let's see, here it is, Date,' I said.

'I think it's the 27th.'

'What is?'

'The date, it's the 27th of June.'

'I know what date it is.'

Melanie glowered at me and raised an eyebrow.

'Well why did you ask?'

'I didn't. Date is the name of the new guests, Donald and Julie Date.'

'Tsk!'

The quality of Galicia's road network, and the low volume of year-round traffic, guarantees the travel time from home to Vilatán is always fifteen minutes. When we arrived at *Campo Verde*, the gates were open and a two-seater roadster was parked on the drive. To our surprise, the Dates were outside, sitting under the gazebo. On closer inspection the roadster was a Mazda MX5 painted British racing green, a curious mix of East meets West.

'Remember, happy faces and nothing is too much trouble,' I whispered.

'Yes darling.'

We stepped out and strolled over to introduce ourselves.

'You found us OK then?' asked Melanie.

'Your written directions were excellent,' said Donald.

'And is everything alright?' I added.

'Perfect.'

'Do you have any questions?'

'No, your Guest Information book seems to cover everything.'

Their replies were polite but short. It was time to go.

'Right then, if there's nothing else we'll leave you to it. Enjoy your stay and if there's anything at all, our phone number is in the Guest Information book.'

We shook hands and left.

'You didn't invite them to a Wine and Tapas night,' said Melanie.

'No, I don't know about you, but I got the distinct impression they wanted to be left alone.'

'I think you're right. If only we'd known we could have had a lie-in.'

'It doesn't harm to have a shave and a shower every once in a while.'

'Speak for yourself.'

We'd arranged to meet Bob and Janet later in the day to wish them bon voyage, or *buen viaje*, as we say in Spain. Their stay in Galicia was drawing to a close and they were heading back to Blighty first thing in the morning.

When it came to saying goodbye, Janet was almost in tears. They'd really enjoyed their extended break.

'I do have one thing to ask,' said Bob.

Bob's final day requests usually involve me getting my hands dirty, not that I'm complaining. We'd looked after their house for over three years and even though they weren't letting it any more, we were happy to help out if we could.

'Fire away.'

'Would you be interested in relocating the ventilation pipes for the septic tank?'

Now there's a question you don't get asked every day.

'We'll pay you, of course,' he added.

I probably earned more per hour as a paperboy than I charge nowadays but every little helps; and besides which, if I didn't do it Bob would have to.

'Sure, no problem.'

Bob showed me what he had in mind and I promised to keep him informed.

'There's no rush. Just do it as and when,' he said.

Two days later we received the phone call every rental owner fears.

Ring, ring! Ring, ring!

Melanie picked up the receiver.

'It's for you,' she said, handing me the phone.

'Hello.'

'Hello, is that Craig?'

'Yes.'

'This is Donald, Donald Date.'

For a second my mind went blank.

'We're staying at *Campo Verde*,' he added.

'Oh yes, of course. How are you?'

'We're fine but we've got a problem.'

A short statement that filled me with dread.

'What's wrong?' I asked.

'There's no water. I've checked the circuit breakers, but they're all in the upright position. Do you have any suggestions?'

The water supply to the house comes from a borehole in the middle of the garden. It took the drilling company two attempts and several days to find an aquifer and when they did, it wasn't exactly gushing. The borehole is nearly 200 metres deep (650 feet). Unlike shallow wells, which have a small surface pump, the pump for a borehole is far more powerful and is lowered to the bottom of the hole. This allows the water to be pushed to the surface rather than sucked. If it had stopped working, it would have to be hauled out and sent away to be repaired. That could take days if not weeks. If the water had run dry, I didn't know what we were going to do.

'I'm sorry Donald, I don't, but don't worry, we'll be right there.'

My optimism was as much to reassure me as it was him.

'What's matter?' asked Melanie, after I'd replaced the receiver.

'They don't have any water.'

'What does that mean?'

'I'm not sure.'

Melanie and I jumped into the car and we set off to Vilatán. My mind was racing. What could it be?

'Have they checked the circuit breakers?' asked Melanie, as we sped through the Galician countryside.

'Yes.'

'What else can it be?'

'I'm not sure. It could be the pump or the water has run dry.'

'It had better not be the pump. It cost a chuffing fortune.'

There was a long, reflective pause as the implications of her statement sank in.

'What are we going to do if there's no water?' she added.

I hadn't got a clue. With the exception of the last week in July, the diary was fully booked from now until mid-

September. If we'd run out of water, we might have to cancel the whole season. The financial implications would be catastrophic.

No sooner had we arrived at *Campo Verde* than the Dates stepped outside. Graciously, they accepted our apology, even insisting that it wasn't our fault, which directly it wasn't; but it was our responsibility.

'If you don't mind, I'll just take a look at the fuse box?' I said.

'No problem, do whatever you've got to do,' replied Donald.

I began my investigation by checking the circuit breakers. It wasn't that I didn't trust Donald, I just wanted to be sure. All of them were in the on position. Next, I checked the hot water. That wasn't working either which suggested a lack of pressure. The only supply that was independent from the house fed two outside taps and the automatic sprinkler system. If either of those was working the problem was probably a burst pipe. If that was the case, repairing it might involve digging up the driveway. Things were going from bad to worse.

'Anything?' asked Melanie, as I stepped outside.

Donald, Julie, and Melanie were relaxing in the garden furniture under the gazebo. I thought it best to put on a brave face.

'Nothing yet.'

One of the outside taps was mounted on the wall above the upper lawn. I turned it on. My heart skipped a beat as a stream of water flowed onto the lawn.

'Is it working?' called Melanie, with a bounce in her voice.

Within seconds the flow slowed to a dribble, and then a drip, and then stopped altogether. My optimism drained away as quickly as the water.

'I'm afraid not. That was water left in the system,' I replied.

'What now?' asked Melanie.

'There's only one thing left to check, the sprinklers.'

The control panel for the watering system was mounted on the wall inside the *bodega.* I set the switch to manual and pushed the start button. A hiss of water and air signals the beginning of a cycle. Silence spoke louder than words.

'Nothing,' I said, emerging from the *bodega*. 'You'll have to ring Ramón.'

Our hopes now rested with the plumber, Ramón, and his willingness to drop everything and come to our rescue. Melanie made the call and explained the situation.

'What did he say?' I asked, as soon as she'd finished.

'He's coming straight away.'

'Would you like a beer while you're waiting?' asked Donald.

Given the indifferent reception we'd received at the Meet and Greet, Donald's hospitality took me by surprise but was nonetheless welcome.

'Thanks, that would be lovely.'

Donald and Julie turned out to be good company and before we knew it Ramón had turned up. I glanced at my watch. Fifteen minutes was quicker than I'd expected. I went to say hello and explain what I'd checked.

Ramón is a man of few words, which is just as well. His first language is *galego* not Spanish. When he does speak Spanish, his northern accent is so thick, it's a struggle to understand a word. Before doing anything, he double-checked everything I'd done. Thankfully, I hadn't missed anything. He moved swiftly on to the wellhead located in the middle of the bottom lawn. Removing the manhole cover revealed the pipework and electrical relays that control the pump.

'Hmm.'

I hate hmms. They're rarely good news and range from a hmm of curiosity to a hmm of disaster.

'Is there a problem?' I asked.

'Look,' he replied, pointing at one of the relays in the junction box.

Charred terminals didn't bode well.

'What's caused that?'

'Hmm.'

There he goes again.

He'd identified the reason the pump wasn't working but not the cause. I feared the worst. A lack of water would certainly cause the pump to overheat. He checked the other relays for signs of damage but found nothing untoward. To make doubly sure, he tested each terminal with a voltmeter. Everything seemed in order. I looked on, hoping for a breakthrough. He turned his attention to the sprinkler system. Adjacent to the wellhead is the subterranean valve box for the three-zone watering system. He took out a screwdriver and jemmied off the lid.

'Oh my word. Come and look at this,' I called to Melanie.

While I'd been watching Ramón, Melanie and the Dates had downed their beers and started on a bottle of white wine. She placed her glass on the table and came to take a look.

'You're doing a great job occupying the guests,' I whispered.

Melanie ignored my sarcasm and peered into the void.

The valve box is a four-sided container with a lid, which sits on a bed of gravel. Removing the cover had revealed a major problem. One of the three copper valves had fractured, causing a catastrophic leak. The ensuing torrent had washed away most of the gravel and the earth below and created what can only be described as a cavernous subterranean sinkhole, slap-bang in the middle of the lawn.

'What on earth!' exclaimed Melanie.

'How has that happened?' I asked.

Ramón did his best to explain. The fractured valve had acted in exactly the same way as an open tap. The pump had kept pumping water until the relay couldn't take any more, and burnt out. Only then did it stop.

'I've never seen anything like,' he said, referring to the fractured copper valve. 'I think you've been very lucky.'

'Lucky!'

'Yes. A new relay will only cost a few euros, but if the pump has overheated you could be talking hundreds.'

'Do you think it has?' I asked anxiously.

'I don't think so. I won't know for sure until I've replaced the relay, and I can't do that until I've swapped this broken valve.'

For the time being, Lady Luck was placed on hold.

'What now?' I asked.

'I'll get the parts and come straight back, and don't worry, I'll soon have it sorted,' he added.

Why is it when tradesmen tell you not to worry, they seem to imply the opposite?

Ramón left and we ambled over to Donald and Julie.

'What did he say?' asked Julie.

We explained the situation.

'But don't worry, we won't leave until everything is sorted,' I reassured them.

'In that case, I'll open another bottle,' said Donald.

Over a glass of wine, the conversation flowed. It turned out that Donald was interested in veteran cars, a term I was unfamiliar with. My first thought was a redundant army vehicle. If ex-soldiers are veterans perhaps their vehicles are too.

'Excuse my ignorance, but what's a veteran car?' I asked.

'Any car built before the First World War. The sort of thing you see on the London to Brighton Run.'

'Before 1914.'

'That's right, but to qualify for the London to Brighton they have to be even older. The cut-off point for that event is 1905.'

'Crikey, 1905! It must be a devil getting hold of spares,' I quipped.

'You're not kidding, and they're always breaking down. I make most of my own,' he replied.

'You actually own one of these cars?'

'I've got a couple at the moment: a 1905 Iden and a project car I'm trying to finish in time for our daughter's wedding.'

I'd never even heard of an Iden, never mind seen one.

'And you manufacture your own spare parts?'

'Yes, I've got a small workshop at the bottom of the garden.'

Donald was something of a dark horse.

'They must be worth a fortune,' I commented.

'People think so but most aren't. The last one I bought only cost six grand.'

It was clearly a labour of love.

Every year they participated in various rallies and shows including the London to Brighton Run.

'It's great fun,' said Julie, 'but I prefer cold and dry to warm and wet.'

'And what about this little thing?' I asked, pointing at the Mazda.

'That's mine,' said Julie. 'Although Donald has been doing most of the driving on this trip.'

'It handles great on the twisty bits but it gets a bit hard on the backside after a while,' he admitted.

I wasn't surprised; that part of the anatomy was less than six inches above the tarmac.

The conversation moved on to how often we travelled back to England.

'We missed the flight home on our last trip,' I confessed.

When Julie found out we'd gone back to watch a football match, she confessed to being a lover of the beautiful game.

'Huddersfield, do they have a professional team?' she teased.

It was good to know that football banter was alive and kicking, even in the backwoods of Galicia.

'Go on then, who do you follow?' I asked.

'The Sky Blues, of course!'

The sale of Manchester City FC to the Abu Dhabi United Group in 2008 gave the club access to unlimited funds and they'd wasted no time in strengthening their squad.

By the time Ramón returned, an hour had passed.

'Did you get everything?' I asked.

'Yes.'

That was a relief.

Within ten minutes he'd fitted the new parts and the system was ready to test. The consequences of failure were unthinkable. I followed him into the downstairs lobby and he isolated the power, plunging us into darkness.

'When I tell you, flick this switch on. If I shout stop, flick if off again,' he said, before hurrying outside.

I waited nervously with one finger on the circuit breaker. My only companion was a shaft of light from the open door.

'OK, now!' he called.

I held my breath and switched on the breaker. I was literally in the dark, not knowing if his fix had worked or not. The wait was agonising.

'OK!'

Melanie had poked her head around the door and almost given me a heart attack.

'Don't do that when I've got my finger resting on two hundred and thirty volts,' I said.

'Ramón says it's fixed.'

Thank heavens for that.

We thanked him for coming to our rescue and asked him to drop the bill off when he was passing. Donald and Julie had been such good hosts we invited them round for a Wine and Tapas night, an invitation they gratefully accepted. The evening went well and despite a lukewarm start to our relationship we parted as friends, a fact recorded in their Visitors book entry.

Donald & Julie Date – Coventry, England

Peaceful – Sheer bliss in the morning.

Enjoyable – Surroundings and countryside.

Relaxing – With wine and tapas, magical.

Friendly – Can't get nicer than Mel & Craig!

Enlightening – The Galician countryside.

Comfortable – Furnished fabulously.

Totally – A paradise in Galicia.

We will tell all and remember always. Thank you for making our holiday so special. x

Safe to say, it was "a job well done".

6

Older and Wiser

Solving the water crisis had left us with another problem. Between the Dates departing and the next guests arriving we had just four hours to clean the house, ready the gardens, and fill in the subterranean sinkhole.

'Any ideas?' asked Melanie.

'What about getting a trailer-load of soil from over the back?' I suggested.

A few years ago, when the main arterial road through the area (the N-120) was widened, our neighbour Nemesio allowed the contractor to tip their unwanted hardcore into the disused clay pits at the back of our house. The mounds of earth had grassed over since then, but with a bit of elbow grease, I felt confident we could excavate enough dirt to fill the hole.

'That's a good idea.'

'Come on then.'

'What, now?'

'There's no time like the present.'

Two hours later, we'd filled the trailer.

On the morning of the Dates' departure, I hitched it to the car and we headed off to Vilatán. A plume of red dust shadowed our journey. The sinkhole turned out to be a bit bigger than I'd estimated. To make up the shortfall, I used some gravel from the base of the gazebo. Once I'd replaced the valve box lid, no one would have ever known.

The next guests to arrive at *Campo Verde* were the Comerford family from Singapore: husband Edward, his wife Roberta, and their two children Daniel and Poppy. We'd met them three years ago when they stayed at *Casa Bon Vista*, the house we'd managed for Bob and Janet. That was one booking we'll never forget. During their stay, Edward had accidentally closed the self-locking front door. To get back inside, I'd had to scale the roof terrace and smash a window.

You can imagine our apprehension when he rang to book a stay at *Campo Verde*. Edward couldn't wait to tell me they'd bought a property in the area with the intention of creating a European base. He liked to express himself in such flamboyant terms.

'Are you ready for off?' I asked, as we readied ourselves for the Meet and Greet.

'I'll just nip to the loo.'

I should have known.

Five minutes later we were on the road to Vilatán.

'Let's hope they don't break anything this time,' remarked Melanie.

'Technically, it was me who smashed the window.'

'You wouldn't have had to if they'd read the instructions.'

I wasn't going to argue.

Fifteen minutes after leaving home I pulled into the entrance. Melanie hopped out and opened the gate.

'They're here,' she mouthed. Their rental car was on the drive.

As I drove in, Roberta came out to meet us. We exchanged greetings and she invited us inside.

'This is beautiful,' she said, as we climbed the stairs to the first floor. 'You've done a fantastic job.'

'Thank you.'

'Edward is in the lounge. Go through and I'll make you a coffee and you can tell us all about it.'

Edward was slouched on the sofa reading a copy of *The Times*. He looked up and put the paper to one side. He seemed pleased to see us and was keen to hear how we'd transformed our ruin into a luxury home. Two minutes later, Roberta brought the coffees through.

'I don't know what it's like. It's supposed to be cappuccino. Now tell me, what have I missed?'

Her tone was unusually apologetic. One sip explained why.

'How is it?' she asked.

'Different,' I remarked.

I quickly recapped and continued. They were eager to learn what difficulties we'd had during the renovation. I explained some of the issues we'd faced. Edward expected to have no such problems. It didn't surprise me and I wasn't offended. When we first moved to Galicia, I was confident of getting things done my way. I was wrong, and as much as I wished them every success, I knew exactly what lay ahead.

'The place we've bought is in Taboredo, do you know it?' asked Edward.

'It doesn't ring a bell.'

I glanced at Melanie who shook her head.

'It's close to Monforte de Lemos,' he added.

'Which estate agent did you use?' I asked.

'Galicia Real. Do you know them?'

'Ah yes. Carlos Manuel.'

'The man who showed us around was called Mano.'

'That's right, he sometimes goes by that name.'

Roberta stared at Edward who looked quite uneasy.

'He's an excitable chap. Lots of wild hand gestures and nothing is ever a problem,' I added.

'That's him,' said Roberta.

'Is he alright?' asked Edward.

It seemed a little late to be asking now.

'He's an estate agent,' I quipped.

People have forgotten that before the financial crisis, estate agents were disliked more than investment bankers.

'You know what it's like? Some people swear by them; others swear at them. Personally, I like him. He can be a bit pushy at times, but he knows when to stop,' I added.

'Does he own a building company?' asked Edward.

I had a good idea what was coming next so deflected the question.

'Why do you ask?' I replied.

'We're having some plans drawn up and Mano is going to quote for the building work.'

I knew of one other English couple who had used his aftersales services and to my knowledge nothing untoward had happened.

'I'm not sure. I think he's more of a facilitator than an actual builder,' I replied.

They hadn't yet laid a brick and cracks were beginning to appear in their plans. It's not the problems you foresee that catch you out, it's the ones you don't.

'We're picking up the plans and the quote later in the week. Would you mind taking a look at them and telling us what you think?' asked Edward.

'Not at all. When will you have them?'

'We're going to see him on Tuesday.'

'In that case, why don't you come round to ours for lunch on Wednesday? The kids can play in the pool while we talk.'

'That would be great. Thank you,' said Roberta.

'No problem. We're not difficult to find. I'll email you directions.'

I glanced at my watch.

'What time is it?' asked Melanie.

The clock had ticked around to 1:00 pm.

'Time we were making a move.'

'What time would you like us on Wednesday?' asked Roberta, as we got to our feet.

'Come for one and we'll eat about two.'

On that note, we said goodbye and left.

'Well, that was interesting,' commented Melanie.

'Wasn't it.'

'What do you think?'

I didn't know what to think. Edward and Roberta were at the start of their Galician property adventure. They were doing things their way, and there was nothing wrong with that, but asking our advice at this stage seemed a little like closing the stable door after the horse had bolted.

'I think it's lunchtime,' I replied. 'Let's eat out.'

'Where did you have in mind?'

'What about Melgaço?'

Melgaço is a Portuguese border town about an hour's drive from home. It's a charming place with a number of fine eateries.

'Yes please.'

An hour later we were strolling through the narrow streets en route to our favourite restaurant, Cantinho do Adro. Bright sunshine bathed the town's picturesque cottages whose walls radiated the midday heat. In comparison, the restaurant's interior felt cool and refreshing.

'Do you have a reservation?' asked a friendly waitress.

'No.'

'One moment please.'

The establishment is divided in two by a central wall of exposed stonework. We'd entered the bar area which was also packed with hungry diners. The waitress walked to the end of the room and disappeared into the dedicated dining room. Seconds later she reappeared and gestured us to follow. She'd found us a table. We took a seat, ordered refreshments, and perused the menu.

'What are you going to have?' asked Melanie, flicking from one page to the next.

'I'm going to have the steak dish topped with ham, cheese, and a fried egg.'

'Oh yes, I think I'll join you.'

As usual, the food was delicious. We skipped coffee and asked for the bill.

'Let's wander around to the far side of the castle and get an ice cream from that café below the walls,' suggested Melanie.

'Why not?'

The café was busy when we arrived. People of all ages were taking advantage of the fine weather on a lazy Sunday afternoon. We found a table on the terrace and ordered two Magnum ice creams. On such a clear day the panorama was beautiful. Beyond the town lies an undulating patchwork of differing shades of green, hemmed in by an overlapping collage of blue and grey mountains. We nibbled our ice creams in silence, soaking up the scenery.

'Right then, is it time we were making a move?' I asked.

Melanie agreed.

On the outskirts of town, we made one final stop before heading home. A trip to Portugal wouldn't be complete without stocking up on our favourite wines. Unlike Spain, supermarkets in Portugal are allowed to open on Sundays.

By the time we got back to Canabal, we'd been away from home for almost eight hours. As ever, Jazz was pleased to see us.

'Is it time for a Teatime Taster?' asked Melanie.

'I don't see why not. I'll just check the emails before we sit out.'

I booted up the computer. Outlook indicated four new messages: junk, junk, junk, and a new enquiry for *Campo*

Verde. I opened the email. To my surprise it wasn't an enquiry but a booking. Even in my wildest dreams I hadn't expected to be still taking bookings at this time of year. Not only that, but this one filled the niggling vacancy for the last week in July and brought our running total of weeks booked to fifteen. I couldn't have been happier. All our hard work and effort was being rewarded.

'Guess what?' I said, as I marched towards the end of the garden.

'What?'

'Guess?'

'We've got another booking.'

Melanie's flippant remark was right on the money.

'That's right.'

'You're joking?'

'No.'

'When is it for?'

'That spare week we had at the end of the month.'

'That's fantastic.'

'I know. I can hardly believe it.'

That evening we toasted our success with a fine bottle of Vino Verde.

'*Salud* (Cheers)!'

What a difference a year makes. This time last year we'd been agonising over what furniture to buy for *Campo Verde*. Choosing the suite had proved particularly difficult. A year on and we were enjoying the summer weather while guests were reaping the rewards of our decisions.

'Can I help you?'

Melanie had burst into the office, my office, and started rifling through the filing cabinet, my filing cabinet.

'No.'

That told me.

'What are you looking for?'

'Got it.'

She'd pulled out Jazz's pet passport and was flicking through the pages. The passport allows Jazz to travel between EU member states without the need for quarantine. It also contains a record of her vaccinations.

'What's the matter?' I asked.

'It's almost time for her annual health check. I'll ring the vet and fix up an appointment.'

The passport's validity is reliant on a continuous period of immunisation. The appointment was set for the following week.

We spent the next few days getting ready for the Comerfords. I cleaned the pool and mowed the lawns while Melanie tidied inside.

'Are we ready?' I asked.

'As ready as we'll ever be.'

We'd decided to have a barbecue of marinated chicken and pork sausages. What kids can resist a flame-grilled sausage?

Within half an hour of their arrival, Daniel and Poppy were splashing about in the pool. Roberta pulled the architect's plans from her bag and opened them out on the table. Edward wasted no time in eulogising about their grandiose design, the property's enormous dimensions, and how it would become a lasting family legacy. Roberta, on the other hand, was far more practical and down-to-earth. She asked serious questions about timescale and costs. I listened carefully and looked at the blueprint. The plans were nothing if not ambitious.

'What do you think?' asked Edward.

'It looks very impressive,' I replied.

Which was true, if somewhat diplomatic.

'We've got that quote from Mano, but it looks quite expensive,' admitted Roberta.

'How much do *you* think it should cost?' asked Edward.

'Without more information it's impossible to say,' I replied.

'A ball park figure.'

Renovating a house is a serious business, not a game.

'What has Carlos Manuel quoted?' I asked.

'Who?' asked Edward.

'Mano,' replied Roberta.

At least one of them had been paying attention.

Roberta plucked an envelope from her bag and handed it to me. I'd expected to see a detailed estimate with an itemised list of all the work required and a breakdown of the costs. All this contained was a general description and a jaw-dropping bottom line.

Stories of foreign buyers handing over huge sums of money in exchange for substandard work are not uncommon in Spain, but I'd never seen anything like this.

'What do you think?' asked Edward impatiently.

I paused to consider my response.

'What exactly is this for?' I asked.

'That's the total cost of all the building work,' replied Edward.

'And does it include the architect's fees?'

'I'm not sure. I don't think so.'

'What about plumbing?'

Edward looked at Roberta.

'He didn't mention plumbing,' said Roberta.

'What about electrics, and windows, and carpentry …'

'Carpentry?' interrupted Roberta.

'Internal carpentry such as doors and built-in wardrobes.'

'I don't think so.'

'What about a kitchen and the bathrooms?'

They looked at each other again. Their bewildered expressions were a telltale sign. The penny was starting to drop.

'I think we need to go back and ask Mano to clarify a few details,' said Roberta.

Edward looked somewhat deflated. I felt like the purveyor of doom, but it was better to ask these questions now than find out the answers later.

'Once you know what's included, or perhaps more importantly what's not, you'll have a much clearer idea if it's a fair price or not. However, I would make one comment, our architect once told us that we could build whatever we wanted for thirty million.'

The pair of them looked flabbergasted.

'That's pesetas, thirty million pesetas,' I added.

'How much is that in euros?' asked Roberta.

'One hundred and eighty thousand. And build costs haven't changed much since then,' I said.

To reinforce the point, I slid the quotation back across the table. Edward and Roberta stared at the bottom line, which was significantly higher.

'Will you make a start on the food?' asked Melanie.

Her timing was impeccable; while I watched the grill, Roberta and Edward digested the conversation. By the time we were ready to eat, they'd recovered from their initial disappointment and were keener than ever to get to the bottom of the costings.

The kids didn't eat as much as we'd thought but the adults more than made up for them. Before leaving they had one more favour to ask.

'Would you mind taking a look at the house and telling us what you think?' asked Edward.

'Of course, no problem.'

Edward gave us directions and scribbled a rough map.

'We should be able to find it with that,' I said.

'If not, we'll ask a neighbour which house the English have bought. They're sure to know,' joked Melanie.

'Thank you so much for your help. We've really enjoyed today,' said Roberta, as they walked back to their car.

'You're very welcome,' replied Melanie.

We didn't hear from the Comerfords again before they left. Changeover day came and went without any dramas and before we knew it, we were heading back to Vilatán for another Meet and Greet.

The new arrivals were a couple from Scotland called Lyanne and Hugh Mitchell. From the moment we stepped out of the car the conversation flowed. Lyanne was warm and friendly with a bubbly personality and a smile that could light up a room. Husband Hugh was more measured but his satirical sense of humour struck a chord and we hit it off straight away. They quizzed us about our lives in Galicia and the restoration of the house. We asked them about Scotland.

Lyanne was a professional illustrator who had recently illustrated the children's book *The Curious Mind of Young Darwin,* as part of his bicentenary celebrations. Hugh was a college lecturer.

'We've been inviting guests to join us at our home one evening for wine and tapas, if you'd like to come?' I asked.

'I don't know about that. What do you think, dearie?' joked Lyanne.

'Let me check my schedule,' replied Hugh. 'I think we can squeeze you in.'

Before we left Melanie gave them directions and a map.

'If it takes you longer than twenty minutes you're lost,' I quipped.

'That's useful to know. Barring a wrong turn, we'll see you on Thursday at seven,' said Lyanne.

'We look forward to it.'

On the drive home, Melanie noticed me smiling and shaking my head.

'What's the matter with you?' she asked.

'I can't believe it.'

'What?'

'All the dreary jobs there are in the world and we get to meet lovely people who pay us for the privilege.'

'They do get to stay in a beautiful house as well,' she replied.

There was no let-up in the hot, sticky weather. Temperatures skipped past thirty degrees Celsius, draining our energy. We spent the days relaxing in the sunshine. Working in the garden was restricted to first thing in the morning or last thing at night.

'Let's see if we can find Edward and Roberta's place,' I suggested after lunch one day.

If truth be known, we'd been dying to take a look ever since they'd left.

'OK.'

The car's interior was baking and the steering wheel was so hot I had to keep swapping hands. It wasn't until we'd reached Monforte de Lemos that the air conditioning began to work its magic. From there we took the LU-P-3202 and headed into the surrounding countryside.

'There should be a left turn around here somewhere,' said Melanie, reading from the instructions Edward had given us.

'What about this one?' I asked.

I slowed down to take a closer look. The lane was surfaced but a line of weeds had grown down the centre. Tall grasses on the roadside verges leaned inwards, giving it the appearance of being abandoned.

'I don't know. The instructions do say that if we reach a church we've gone too far.'

'I haven't seen a church, have you?'

'No.'

'I'll go a bit further.'

Wouldn't you know it, around the next bend was a village church perched on a hilltop.

'It must have been that one,' said Melanie.

I turned around and headed back down the hill.

'This is it coming up,' she warned.

I turned off.

'What now?' I asked.

'It should be around here somewhere. Park up and let's walk.'

I pulled onto a small patch of rough ground and stopped. A gust of hot, dry air entered the cabin as I opened the door. I stepped out and looked around but couldn't see a house anywhere.

'It might be up there,' said Melanie, pointing at an overgrown track ten metres further along.

'Are you sure?'

It looked like no one had passed that way in months.

'It must be.'

'Come on then.'

I went ahead to make sure nothing untoward was hiding in the undergrowth and to trample a path for Melanie. A droplet of sweat trickled down the back of my neck as we made our way along the track.

'What's that?' I said, pointing up ahead.

Hidden in a thicket of tangled brambles was a stone-built structure. On closer inspection it looked like a shed of some description. The masonry was poor quality and the roof looked ready to collapse.

'That can't be it. It's far too small and look at the roof,' said Melanie.

She had a point.

'You don't think this is the guest wing Edward kept banging on about, do you?' she asked.

'Wing? As in a wing and a prayer?'

'Exactly, but I bet it is.'

'Surely not. The only thing this is good for is demolition. Come on.'

A few metres further along I caught sight of a stone farmhouse set to one side of a field.

'That must be it,' I said, pointing at the house.

'I think you're right.'

We stared at the ruin for a while and then back down the track towards the lane.

'That's their first problem,' I said, tipping my head in the direction of the track.

Melanie knew exactly what I was referring to.

At this time of year the ground underfoot is baked hard, but come winter it would quickly become an impassable quagmire. Without proper access, building costs would soar. The alternative would be to surface the track but that would cost a small fortune, assuming they could get permission.

Even from a distance, the farmhouse looked in very poor condition. On closer inspection, our fears were realised. The roof slates indicated the property's age. They were thick and unequal, suggesting they'd been split by hand, and their large irregular form dated them prior to the introduction of circular saws. Over the years, their weight had taken a toll on the joists and created an undulating and sagging roofline. A heavy-duty chain and substantial padlock prevented us from entering but it didn't matter. Since moving to Galicia we'd seen lots of properties like this and knew exactly what to expect.

At a right angle to the house was an attached barn. It was a sizeable structure built from cheap prefabricated concrete panels. Sections of the roof had collapsed and broad beams of sunlight angled in through gaping holes. How anyone could have fallen in love with this dilapidated and ugly building was a mystery to us. Edward and Roberta were bright, intelligent people and this place screamed "money pit". Realising their dream would cost every penny that Carlos Manuel had quoted, and more besides.

'I can't believe it,' said Melanie.

'I know what you mean. Look at that barn, it's falling down.'

'What is it made of?'

'They're prefabricated concrete panels,' I replied.

'It's awful.'

'And look at the condition of those over there,' I said, pointing at a section that had been damaged by rainwater and was crumbling in front of our eyes.

'The main house isn't much better.'

'I know. It's rubbish.'

'What are you going to tell them?' asked Melanie.

The weight of responsibility was considerable. Yorkshire folk have a reputation for being forthright but this called for diplomacy.

'I'll stick to the facts and leave personal feelings to one side,' I replied.

'I think that's best.'

Perhaps wisdom does come with age.

7

A Corpse in the Attic

Visits to the vet are a hit and miss affair. Sometimes we can be in and out in a flash, on other occasions we're hanging around for ages. We were once told that waiting times get shorter towards the end of the month, the argument being that monthly paid employees are less likely to take their pets as payday nears. The observation might be true, but the hypothesis leaves a lot to be desired. On this occasion we were unable to test the theory as Jazz's annual check-up fell midway through the month.

'Come on lass. It's time for the doggy doctor.'

Jazz heaved herself up off her bed and toddled outside. She followed me to the back of the car and I lifted her in. She'd had a torrid time over the last four months. Her accident in March had almost left her paralysed. Slowly but surely her condition had improved, but her days of running and jumping were now behind her. Constant visits to the vet had made her something of a celebrity. Practice owner, Honario, could hardly believe his eyes when she walked into the waiting room wagging her tail.

Within an hour, they called her name. We wandered through into a treatment room where a thorough examination revealed no new problems. Her annual booster seemed painless and the bill, including a worming tablet and Frontline pipette, came to sixty-two euros.

'Here you go,' said Honario, handing her a treat.

She accepted it gratefully and the three of us headed home.

The following day was warm but overcast, ideal conditions for undertaking manual labour.

'I'm going to make a start on Bob and Janet's septic tank this morning,' I said, as we sipped our morning coffees.

'Will you need me?'

'I don't think so.'

'In that case, I'll drop you off and nip into town to get what we need for tonight's tapas.'

Our Braveheart Scots would be joining us this evening.

'OK.'

By the time Melanie dropped me off, the clock had ticked around to 10:30 am.

The septic tank was a relatively new installation after the previous, antiquated system was found wanting. Unfortunately, the flaws didn't come to light until paying guests were holidaying there. Unblocking it was a messy affair. Emergency measures involved me getting my hands dirty and led to an ultimatum, "update the system or find a new management team". Bob chose the former.

An adjacent plot was chosen for the site of the shiny new septic tank. It was a patch of unused and unloved land separate from the main house. Unlike a *pozo negro*, which is literally a pit lined with stones which allows liquids to filter into the surrounding earth, a modern septic tank is fabricated from non-porous material. To prevent explosive gases building up, and to help bacteria break down the solids, the tank is ventilated to the open air.

In the case of Bob and Janet's tank, this took the form of two ten-centimetre diameter grey plastic pipes, one and a half metres tall and capped with a right-angled elbow. At the time their location was unimportant, but now Bob and Janet had retired they were keen to create a garden on this hitherto unused plot. The sight of two grey pipes sticking out of the ground like U-boat telescopes was not the sort of garden feature they had in mind. To make matters worse, they were slap-bang in the middle of the plot. A simple solution was to dig down to the septic tank, cut them off and lay new, underground pipes to the edge of the garden before reattaching the breather pipes. Strategic planting would soon camouflage the offending tubes.

'What time do you want me to pick you up?' asked Melanie.

'Twelve thirty.'

I had no intention of letting work interfere with lunch.

'OK, I'll see you then.'

On Melanie's return, I'd completed most of the excavation work. One more shift would finish the job.

Hugh and Lyanne arrived at 7:00 pm, laden with gifts: a bottle of red Rioja, eight bottles of beer, six of which were non-alcoholic, and a box of chocolates.

'I've brought my picture diary for you to look at. I thought you might be interested,' said Lyanne.

I was fascinated. I hadn't heard of a picture diary before, never mind seen one.

'You should recognise some of the places from your Self-Drive Tour Guide,' she added, handing me her sketch book.

I opened the first page and was blown away. After the Meet and Greet on Sunday, Lyanne and Hugh had driven into Monforte de Lemos to get their bearings. Lyanne's first illustration was a beautiful interpretation of one of the town's most iconic buildings, El Escolapios, a 16th century

Jesuit college repurposed as a public school. Each page was dated and contained short notes and descriptions. On Monday they'd taken the self-drive tour around the river Sil. On it, we suggest a walk to Pena do Castelo, one of the area's most stunning *miradors* (viewing points). It presides over a landscape too vast for the naked eye to absorb. Lyanne's illustration had certainly done it justice. On Tuesday they'd visited the walled city of Lugo, but my personal favourite was Wednesday's entry: *Campo Verde* in all its glory. Her watercolour sketches were bright and vivid, a mixture of architectural drawings, fine art, and animation.

'These are fantastic,' I said, handing the book to Melanie. 'I'd love some copies if you wouldn't mind?'

If you don't ask, you don't get.

'No problem, I've got your address. I'll send you some as soon as we get home.'

'That would be great.'

Hugh had agreed to drive which allowed Lyanne to let her hair down. As the wine flowed the conversation became more animated and we ended up having a whale of a time. Lyanne was a proud Scot and ardent nationalist, but we didn't hold that against her.

The following morning, I felt surprisingly sprightly. That said, I was pleased to be filling in the trenches at Bob and Janet's rather than excavating them. As I expected, one more shift finished the job. I'd kept a photo log of the work and emailed it to Bob that afternoon.

The day after, we were back at *Campo Verde.* Owning a rental property was certainly keeping us busy. Hugh and Lyanne had left when we arrived.

'Come and look at this,' called Melanie from the kitchen window.

I'd made a start in the garden.

'What is it?'

'Their Visitors book entry.'

I left what I was doing and went inside.

Lyanne's comments were as unique and lovable as her personality. She'd left a colourful illustration and a creative little ditty. The picture was a self-portrait. She had her one arm around Hugh and was waving goodbye with the other. He was naked with a copy of her sketch book covering his modesty with the word "Censored" across it. The topic of nude sunbathing had cropped up at the Wine and Tapas night and given all of us plenty to laugh about. Overhead was a blazing yellow sun and within the outline of a fluffy cloud she'd written, "Toodle loo the noo!", with the blue and white Saltire (Scottish flag) fluttering in the opposite corner. The poem went as follows:

Lyanne & Hugh Mitchell – Glasgow,
Scotland

Campo Verde – Sturdy, strong
You've made us happy, all week long
Private space for peace and food
(And Hugh's sunbathing in the nude!)
Your guided driving tours were BRILL
Amazing views down to the Sil
We're moving on – a fond farewell
To perfect hosts ... Craig and Mel.
Thank you for a lovely week
And "LANG MAY YER LUMS REEK!"
(that's Scottish for "Long may your
chimneys smoke!")
El Sueño & Campo Verde!

'That's brilliant,' I said.

'Isn't it. They also left this.'

Melanie handed me a handwritten note which read:

Dear Craig and Mel,

We have thoroughly enjoyed our week at Campo Verde – and have much appreciated your directions / information / and especially "guided tours" – which "unlocked" the area for us and gave us access to places we would never have found on our own.

We loved the house – the quality of its interiors & finish. Favourite room – the bedroom. The outside areas are lovely – so private and spacious. Campo Verde is an outstanding holiday accommodation.

We enjoyed our evening with you both very much – delicious tapas and good conversation. Thank you both so much for a lovely week. I hope we shall keep in touch.

Best wishes,
Lyanne & Hugh

'I don't know what to say.'

'It almost had me in tears,' admitted Melanie. 'It's so lovely of them to take the time to tell us.'

We'd put our hearts and souls into renovating this ruin, and our love and affection into creating a home. We'd gone that extra mile to ensure visitors could find their way around and discover the places and people that make this corner of Spain so special. To read these comments made all that effort worthwhile. Right at that moment, I couldn't have felt prouder.

'Come on then, we'd better make sure it's ready for the next guests,' I said.

We spent the rest of the day with our heads in the clouds, as proud as punch and chuffed to bits that our efforts were appreciated.

The next guests were Michel and Brigitte DeVille from Belgium, but they weren't the only visitors we were expecting. The Kershaw family were due to arrive at *El Sueño* for their annual summer getaway: dad Richard, mum Yvonne and the two kids, Mason aged nine, and Melanie's goddaughter Erren, who was now six.

On Sunday morning the Meet and Greet was quite a swift affair. Michel put us to shame with his language skills. His native tongue was French, but he also spoke Dutch, German, and Flemish, none of which were much use to us. Melanie has an O level in French, gained at the tender age of sixteen. As for me, my French vocabulary consists of "*S'il vous plait*", "*Merci*", and "*Avez-vous un cuppa?*", a line immortalised by a chimpanzee in the 1970s TV advert for PG Tips teabags. And wouldn't you know it, one of the few languages Michel didn't speak was Spanish. Thankfully, we found a common tongue in English.

Having completed our paid responsibilities, we drove home to ready the house for the invasion of the Kershaws. As soon as we got back, I checked the inbox for any new messages. One email caught my eye. The sender was Tony White.

Tony and his wife Margaret had twice stayed at *Casa Bon Vista*, but as Bob and Janet were no longer letting, we had hoped they'd choose to stay at *Campo Verde*. Before retiring, Tony had travelled the world selling printing presses to the newspaper industry. When he discovered I used to own a small printing company, we found a topic of common interest.

'Guess who we've had an email from,' I said, as I walked into the kitchen.

'I don't know.'

'Tony.'

'Tony?'

'Tony White.'

'That's nice, how are they both?'

'They're fine and they're thinking of taking a break.'

She stopped what she was doing and looked straight at me.

'At *Campo Verde*?'

'That's right.'

'That's great news. When are they coming?'

'The 28th of September until the 5th of October.'

'That's late.'

'I know. I hope the weather stays fine.'

'How many weeks does that take us to?'

'Sixteen.'

'That's amazing.'

It was indeed. Dare I dream of doubling our original ten-week target?

Over the next few days, we worked tirelessly to make sure the house was ready for our guests. I toiled in the gardens, mowing the lawns, cleaning the pool, and even found time to wash the car. Melanie cleaned inside.

'What time are we expecting them?' I asked, on the morning of their arrival.

'Yvonne said she'd text once they'd landed.'

'I see, land o'clock?'

My sarcasm prompted a response.

'Sometime around noon, probably.'

'Where are they flying to?'

'Porto.'

'Is that noon our time or theirs?'

Portugal is an hour behind Spain.

'I don't know, ours I think.'

Porto isn't the obvious choice for a trip to Spain but flights from the north of England to Santiago de Compostela are few and far between. In the end, it boils down to a long drive on UK roads or a stress-free journey through northern Portugal. I know which I'd prefer.

'What are those for?' I asked.

Melanie was busy peeling potatoes.

'I thought I'd make a tortilla for lunch.'

'That's a good idea.'

'Is there anything you want me to do?'

'No, everything's done.'

I wandered outside and took a seat in the shade. Ten minutes later Melanie joined me. By the time she went back inside to flip the tortilla, the clock had ticked around to 11:30 am. Time passes slowly when you're waiting. I'd just about dozed off when Melanie's text message alert sounded. I looked at my watch: 11:50 am.

'They've landed,' she announced.

Two hours later it chimed again.

'They're driving through Ourense.'

Not long now and they'd be with us. At 2:45 pm the doorbell rang. Jazz dragged herself to her feet and trotted around the side of the house.

'Slow down,' I called.

By the time I'd caught up with her, Mason had opened the gates, Richard had driven through, and Yvonne and Erren were opening their car doors. Melanie had wandered through the kitchen and appeared at the French doors. Erren leapt from the car and ran into her arms.

'I'll get them,' I called to Mason.

By the time I'd reached him the gates were all but closed.

'Good afternoon young man,' I said.

'Hiya Uncle Craig.'

With each passing year the spontaneity of youth diminishes. Where seconds once counted the time from car to pool, the minute hand now sufficed.

'Seven minutes,' remarked Melanie, as Mason sank his alabaster frame into the water.

Erren was one step behind.

Lunch was put on hold for an hour. Once fed, the sounds of excitement filled the garden again. It wasn't until 9:00 pm that calm prevailed. The kids had reluctantly given way to Mum's calls for bed.

A routine of early rising and late nights had its compensations when Melanie and I returned to work. We'd heard nothing from Michel and Brigitte, which was always a good sign. Their Visitors book comments confirmed that Michel's English wasn't perfect, but anyone who can joke in a second language has my respect.

Michel & Brigitte – Belgium

We had a very fine week in Galicia, even with a "Belgian" weather some days. Galician people are very kind and with the kindness of yours, Craig and Melanie, you have become very alike them. We will recommend the place.

On the drive home we stopped at the bakery for two *barras*. The *barra* is a delicious artisan loaf, baked in a wood-fuelled oven with a thick crust and doughy, aerated centre. Today's lunch was self-service. Chunks of crusty bread, cured ham, chorizo, salami, various different pâtés, a selection of cheeses, tuna, green salad, homemade pickled beetroot, and a bowl of tinned sweetcorn just for Erren.

'How are things going with the house?' asked Yvonne over lunch.

'We're really pleased. Our target was ten weeks and we've already got sixteen.'

'It's hard work though,' added Melanie. 'And the washing machine never stops.'

Later that afternoon the kids persuaded Dad to join them in the pool. Ever since they could swim, their favourite game has been the shooting star. Dad launches each one in turn as high as he can out of the water and they form a perfect four-pointed star before splashing back into the pool. Richard does his best to keep up with them, but growing kids take their toll.

'One more, Dad,' pleaded Erren, but Richard had to concede defeat.

Ring, ring … Ring, ring!

On any other day a ringing telephone is of little consequence, but on a Saturday it takes on a whole new significance.

'I'll get it,' said Melanie, rushing inside.

I waited with bated breath. Moments later she stepped outside.

'That was Emilio,' she said.

Her face said it all. Something was wrong.

Emilio Alfonso Alvar and his family were the latest guests to arrive at *Campo Verde.* They lived in Murcia on the Mediterranean coast.

'What's matter?'

'Well …'

She paused, and then all of a sudden, her face lit up. She was teasing.

'Nothing. He just rang to say they'd arrived and the house is *preciosa* (beautiful).'

'Thanks, you nearly gave me a heart attack.'

That evening I fired up the barbecue. Having a full house gives me the opportunity to test my cooking skills on a fully loaded grill. There were sausages sizzling, chicken fillets turning, pork medallions oozing, and beef steaks gently browning. Melanie rustled up a mixed salad, and homemade coleslaw and potato salad. A veritable feast.

'Does anyone want that last sausage?' asked Richard.

Everyone was stuffed.

'It's all yours,' I replied.

Ring, ring … Ring, ring!

I glanced at the time: 8:47 pm. Who could that be at this hour?

'I'll go,' said Melanie.

She hurried inside. Seconds later she was back.

'That was Emilio.'

Once bitten ….

'Really.'

'Yes really. They've got a problem.'

I didn't believe a word of it.

'What kind of problem?'

'An infestation kind of problem.'

Unbelievable.

'Infestation?'

'Infestation!'

She wasn't giving in.

'What kind of infestation?'

'Hundreds of tiny flies in the back bedroom.'

She was either very good at keeping a straight face or they really did have a problem.

'Are you sure?'

'That's what he said. I told him we'd come straight away.'

That confirmed it. We definitely had a problem.

'Right then, we'd better go.'

We jumped in the car and raced up to Vilatán.

'What do you think it is?' asked Melanie.

'I've no idea. They must have left the window open.'

'He said there were hundreds.'

'That's what I can't understand. Even with the window open you wouldn't get that many.'

'What about the loft, could they be getting in from there?'

Images of a decaying corpse swinging from the rafters and infested with flies flashed through my mind. "Get a grip", I told myself, as I exited the main road and drove cautiously through the narrow village lanes.

I pulled into the entrance and Melanie jumped out. She rang the doorbell and opened the gates. No sooner had I entered than Emilio, his wife, and their two daughters stepped outside. An apology competition ensued. Try as I might, Emilio was winning. Melanie joined the contest but even her contribution failed to win the day.

'I'm so sorry to have to call you out,' said Emilio.

'Please, don't worry about that. I'm sorry you've had to,' I replied.

'What's the problem?' asked Melanie.

'My girls are frightened otherwise I wouldn't have disturbed you,' he replied.

His comment sent a chill down my spine. Perhaps there was a body in the attic.

'Where are they?'

'In the girls' bedroom, come,' he said, leading us into the house.

We followed him up the stairs. The bedroom door was closed. Emilio grabbed the handle and slowly opened the door. I held my breath and squinted, anticipating a swarm of flies would come flooding out, but they didn't. Perhaps it wasn't as bad as he was making out. He stepped inside and we followed. That's when we saw them. Emilio wasn't exaggerating. There were hundreds of tiny black flies floating silently in the air; others had landed on the beds, and even more were climbing up the walls. I couldn't believe it. Melanie continued apologising while I took a closer look.

The tiny insects weren't flies but flying ants. During spells of hot humid weather, common garden ants develop wings and take flight in search of a mate. We sometimes get them in the garden but I'd never seen them inside. The perfect conditions only occur a few times a year but when they do, the little blighters make the most of it.

Killing the ones we could see wouldn't be enough. I needed to find the nest and destroy it. Watching ants copulate isn't my preferred pastime, but needs must. I scanned the room searching for the source. The highest concentration seemed to be on the wall near the window. I searched the frame looking for any gaps, and that's when I noticed a tiny hole in the mortar close to the window. During the renovation we'd kept as many of the natural stone walls as was practical. The builder had cleaned the stones, removed the old mortar, and replaced it with new. Ants were coming and going through the hole as if it were a revolving door. This had to be the gateway to the nest.

'That's it,' I announced.

Melanie and Emilio were still apologising to each other.

'What is it?' asked Melanie.

'There must be a nest inside the wall. Look!'

Another cheeky chappie poked his head out and took flight.

'Do we have any terminator spray?' I asked.

'That stuff in the red can?'

'That's the one.'

The aerosol in question is six times more expensive than standard fly spray but worth every penny. One treatment along a threshold is enough to deter insect invaders for up to twelve months. If there was a nest inside the metre-thick stone wall, Armageddon was heading their way. Genocide is nothing to be proud of. I eased my conscience by convincing myself another exit was possible.

'I think there's a can in the *bodega*. I'll just take a look,' said Melanie.

A few minutes later she returned armed with the deadly poison. A thin straw is supplied with the aerosol which attaches to the spray nozzle for pinpoint application.

'We're going to need a dustpan and brush, and it's probably better if you and your family wait outside,' I suggested to Emilio.

Melanie fetched the dustpan and Emilio ushered his family into the hall.

'Pull that door closed,' I said to Melanie.

As if by design, the straw fitted perfectly into the hole in the wall. I pressed the nozzle and the hiss of death escaped into the cavity. I held it for several seconds to ensure maximum penetration. We stared at the hole; nothing emerged.

'That's done it,' I said.

Any survivors would have to find an alternative escape route or perish. Now for those stranded in the bedroom. Their days were numbered. A few approached the hole but couldn't breach the invisible barrier. All we had to do now was slaughter the remaining stragglers and it was job done. A few quick bursts and all that remained was to sweep away the evidence.

'That's it, they're all gone,' I announced, as we stepped into the hall.

'Thank you so much,' said Emilio.

'You shouldn't have any more problems but we'll leave this with you just in case, and if there's anything else, anything at all, just let us know,' I said.

On that note, we walked back to the car. Emilio and his family followed us downstairs.

'Just one minute,' he said, before dashing back inside.

Daylight was fading fast and we were keen to get back to our guests. Seconds later he reappeared.

'Please accept these as a thank you.'

Melanie and I were speechless. As a sign of his gratitude he presented Melanie with a handful of Saturn peaches and a large bunch of grapes. He gave me a bottle of fine red wine: Jumilla Reserva.

'The fruit is from our garden and the wine is local to Murcia,' he said.

It was time for us to express our gratitude.

Driving home we couldn't quite believe his generosity. As for Richard and Yvonne, they were gobsmacked. Every nation has its good people and its bad, but in our experience, Spain seems blessed with more than its fair share of good.

8

Culture and Caricatures

Sunday's Meet and Greet became redundant following Saturday's meet and massacre. Had it not been for the energy of youth, we might even have enjoyed a lie-in. As it was, we made the most of our reprieve and took it in turns to entertain the kids. Periods of activity were interspersed with eating, drinking, reading, and bathing. All in all, a thoroughly enjoyable way to spend a lazy Sunday, or any other day, for that matter.

Given the choice, the kids would have happily spent the remainder of their stay in this state of euphoria, but Mum had other ideas. No Kershaw holiday would be complete without Mum's day of culture. She'd waited patiently, biding her time for the perfect opportunity. At breakfast on Monday, she spotted her chance and seized the moment. The kids were sitting at the table devouring a breakfast of fresh fruit, cereals, and yogurt, oblivious to her intentions.

'You know that bridge in Ourense, did you say you can walk around it?' she asked.

Yvonne was referring to the Puente del Milenio (Millennium Bridge).

'That's right,' I replied.

The city of Ourense is divided in two by the great river Miño. Six bridges connect the two halves: three road, two pedestrian, and a railway bridge. There are also two footbridges on the outer limits of the city which link a riverside promenade that stretches for more than fourteen kilometres. It's a popular walkway with great river views, but if you're looking for something more challenging, scaling the Puente del Milenio is a must.

Designed by Álvaro Varela de Ugarte in a style reminiscent of the architect Santiago Calatrava, construction was completed in 2001. It marries contemporary design with modern engineering to produce a dynamic, four-lane suspension bridge. In doing so, it has created an iconic and inescapable city landmark. Incorporated within the design is a hammock-shaped pedestrian walkway, suspended from the structure like a carriageless rollercoaster.

Yvonne turned to the kids who were still munching away. 'How would you like to go for a walk around that bridge?'

'What bridge?'

'That funny looking bridge we drove past in that city by the river?'

The kids looked thoughtful.

'Was it white?' asked Mason.

'That's the one.'

'Up that really steep path?' asked Erren.

'Yes, up that really steep path.'

'Yer!' they chimed in unison.

That was a surprise; Mum's day of culture usually goes down like a lead balloon.

'Does that mean we can't go in the pool?' asked Mason.

It hadn't taken long for the penny to drop.

'You can spend all day in there when we get back. Now come on, eat up and let's get ready.'

Their initial enthusiasm had soon waned as they sloped off to prepare for the day ahead.

'What time do you want to set off?' I asked.

'Half an hour?'

'That's fine.'

More than enough time for me to check the inbox.

'We've got another,' I whispered, as Melanie entered the bedroom.

'Another what?'

'Booking.'

'How many does that make?'

'Seventeen.'

'It's amazing. I can't believe it. Who is it this time?'

I glanced at the email.

'Eloise Brodeur from France, plus three adults. They've booked for one week, 10th until the 17th of October.'

'October!'

'I know. At least we'll be able to test the heating.'

On the drive to Ourense we stopped at the viewing point, high above the river Miño. The Kershaws hadn't been before and the kids needed no encouragement to pose for the camera; they were naturals.

Mason and Erren are as close as any siblings I've ever known. It must be a real joy for parents when that happens. My sister and I ran Mum and Dad ragged. We didn't have a civil word for each other and on the rare occasions we did play together, it always ended in tears. Melanie and her brother Charles were exactly the same.

'Come on then,' I said.

Yvonne had put away the camera and the kids were getting restless.

'Just follow me, Richard. We'll drive across the bridge and try to find a parking space on the approach road to the railway station.'

Twenty minutes later we entered the city. Richard hadn't let me out of his sight as I negotiated the busy streets. Having crossed the Puente del Milenio, we headed towards the station. We were in luck. There were two parking spaces within metres of each other.

The morning clouds had all but disappeared as we stepped onto the pavement. A few stubborn patches provided brief respite from the fearsome heat of the midday sun as they floated overhead. Daily temperatures in Ourense are usually two degrees warmer than Canabal due to its geographic location, and boy, could we feel it. We'd parked within sight of the bridge's towering white steel columns. The hanging walkway is accessed at two entry points in the middle of the bridge.

'Up or down?' I asked as we reached the entrance.

One by one we stepped from the pavement and onto the walkway. Heads turned this way then that: decisions, decisions. Looking down from our current position, the walkway looped below the level of the road before climbing, steadily at first and then more acutely as it neared the top of the suspension tower. At the summit it swung around the tower and descended on the other side of the carriageway before climbing to the top of the opposite tower, looping around that one and descending to our current position.

'It's as broad as it is long,' remarked Richard.

'Can we go down?' asked Erren.

Decision made.

The walkway consists of a series of steps. On the less steep sections they were long and shallow. As the slope steepened, they became shorter and taller. Heading downwards gave us an easy start. As the walkway dipped below the level of the road, the hustle and bustle of the city was replaced by the rushing water of the river Miño, and the sound of traffic was drowned out by the raging rapids below. The water looked close enough to touch but was tens of metres away. A cool breeze drifted upwards from the river as thousands of gallons of water slipped past. From here we could see the walkway on the other side of the bridge, but to get there we had quite a trek.

'Right then, up we go,' I said.

The kids marched on ahead without a care in the world. Us oldies brought up the rear. The higher we climbed the steeper it became.

'I'm sure the air is thinner up here,' huffed Melanie.

'Thinner? Your problem is you're out of condition,' I joked.

I wasn't about to let on how much I was struggling.

'It doesn't half take it out of your knees,' said Richard.

'What was that?' Fear rippled through Melanie's voice.

'What?'

'That.'

Our efforts to scale the bridge had translated into minor tremors from the suspended pathway.

'It's a suspension bridge,' I replied.

'So?'

'So, it's designed to flex.'

'I don't like it. I feel sick.'

Melanie's dislike of fairground rides is legendary, but this movement was barely discernible. Unfortunately, her confession only served to encourage mischievous minds.

'What's wrong Aunty Melly, don't you like it when it moves?' asked Mason, who'd started bumping his body into the handrail.

'No, I feel sick.'

Not to be outdone by her brother, Erren started jumping up and down on the step. What started out as an indiscernible vibration had become a noticeable shake.

'Stop it you two. Aunty Melly's not feeling very well,' said Yvonne, in a less than convincing tone.

'Come on. We're almost there,' I said, encouraging her to continue.

'I'm going to have to sit down.'

Melanie perched herself on a step with her head in her hands. The kids stopped messing around and continued upwards. After a short break, so did Aunty Melly.

'Wow! Look at that,' I said, in an effort to tempt her to the summit.

The bird's eye view was worth the effort. Immediately upstream was the Ponte Romana or Roman Bridge. Its history can be traced back to the 1st century, although the structure we were looking at was rebuilt in the 17th. Its form, that of an upturned v, is typical of the medieval period. Nowadays it's closed to traffic, but during the summer months the road-going tourist train uses it to ferry passengers from the Plaza Mayor, in the centre of the city, to the municipal hot springs downstream. Behind that was the Pasarela Río Miño, a modern footbridge allowing people living north of the river direct access to the Ponte Vella shopping centre. The next bridge upstream is the Puente Nuevo road bridge, although why anyone would name anything "new" is beyond me, and towering over that is the Viaducto railway bridge. Downstream the river races below another road bridge, imaginatively called Ponte Novisimo or Newest Bridge. I wonder what they'll call the next one, Even Newer Bridge, perhaps?

Both riverbanks are lined with public walkways, parks and recreational spaces, and downstream are the famous natural hot springs which are open year round to the public. Surrounding this beautiful natural landscape is a modern urban skyline set against a backdrop of rolling hills and forested peaks.

Nothing creates a thirst like scaling two thirty-six-metre-tall towers and circumnavigating a twenty-three-metre-wide bridge in the baking midday heat.

'Let's find a café before we head home,' suggested Yvonne.

We strolled into town and called at the first bar we stumbled across. We ordered our drinks and relaxed in the shade of a large parasol.

'Is there anywhere else you'd like to visit before you leave?' asked Melanie.

'Did you say that hotel on the hill is worth a visit?'

The kids looked devastated. More pool time lost to boring adult stuff.

Yvonne was referring to the Parador Hotel in Monforte de Lemos. Paradores de Turismo de España is a luxury chain of hotels owned by the Spanish government. The name comes from the Spanish word *parar* meaning to stop or stay. Many of the hotels are located in buildings of historic importance such as castles, palaces, and monasteries. The one in Monforte de Lemos is housed in the former palace of the Counts of Lemos and sits on top of a hill in the centre of town.

'It's stunning Yvonne. No expense was spared during the renovation work, and it shows. There's the tower next door as well. The views from the top over the town and surrounding countryside are quite something,' replied Melanie.

The Torre da Homenaxe or Homage Tower is the town's landmark building. It was built between the 13th and 15th centuries, and with the exception of a few unimpressive sections of wall is all that remains of the town's castle.

'Let's go there then. How does tomorrow morning sound?'

'OK. I think the tower opens at eleven.'

'Perfect.'

As soon as we got back to *El Sueño* the kids were stripped and in the pool. With yet another excursion planned, there was no time to waste.

Predicting the July weather is not difficult. It's either warm and sunny or even warmer and sunny. Perfect weather for fun and games in the pool, but the less said about that the better. To their credit, the kids readied themselves in a timely fashion and didn't moan once. Twice, perhaps, but definitely not once. The sun had got its hat on, and by the time we left home the mercury was on the rise, but there was no need to worry; the *torre's* three-metre-thick walls keep its interior refreshingly cool. When everyone was ready, we drove into town and parked next to the Parador.

'This way,' I said.

Richard bent down and rubbed the back of his leg.

'What's matter?' asked Yvonne.

'My calf muscles are killing me.'

'So are mine,' said Melanie.

'That's strange, mine are too,' said Yvonne.

All of a sudden, the penny dropped.

'I bet it's from walking up and down that bridge,' said Richard.

'I'd wondered what it was. I think you're right,' replied Melanie.

As the one person least equipped for scaling a suspension bridge it seemed ironic that I felt fine, and I wasn't about to let it go unnoticed.

'I feel great. It must be my general level of fitness,' I joked.

Melanie turned to Richard and Yvonne. 'He must have started pulling corks out with his feet.'

The three of them laughed. I ignored them and marched off with the kids. The others hobbled after us.

Beyond the entrance to the Parador stands the *torre.*

'Is it closed?' asked Melanie.

I looked at my watch: 11:08 am.

'Either that or someone has overslept.'

We perched ourselves on a nearby wall and waited in the warm sunshine. The kids became restless. Richard took them for a scramble over the few remaining ramparts of the medieval castle. Five minutes later they returned.

'What time is it now?' asked Richard.

I glanced at my watch.

'It's almost twenty past.'

'Perhaps it's closed today,' suggested Yvonne.

'Wait here and I'll ask in the Parador.'

Melanie walked off in search of information and returned a few minutes later.

'According to the receptionist, it opens at eleven o'clock and if no one is waiting it closes again.'

'You're joking. Don't they even wait ten minutes?'

'Apparently not.'

'Do you see what we're up against?' I said to Richard. 'Can you imagine the Eiffel Tower closing for the day if no one was queueing, or the London Eye, or any tourist attraction for that matter?'

'Let's have a look around the Parador and decide what to do next,' said Melanie.

Unlike many luxury hotels, Paradors welcome the general public although access is restricted to certain areas. These include the restaurant, cafeteria, and some reception rooms. We climbed the stone steps to the front door and the hiss of hydraulics invited us into the opulent surroundings of the palace of the Counts of Lemos. We wandered past the reception desk and into a covered walkway surrounding a central square terrace. Works of art adorn the walls and period furniture gives the impression that the counts could return at any moment. It provided a fabulous photo opportunity and the kids were happy to oblige.

'Shall we take refreshments?' I asked, in my Jeeves the butler accent.

'Why not,' replied Yvonne, in the Yorkshire equivalent of the Queen's English.

We ambled around to the cafeteria and took a table overlooking the terrace. Refreshments were ordered and we relaxed in the luxurious surroundings. The closure of the *torre* had left a gap in our schedule, but I had a suggestion for filling it.

'Would you like to go to a viewing point before lunch?' I asked.

'The one in Doade?' asked Melanie.

'That's what I was thinking.'

'It's really beautiful Yvonne, you'll love it,' she said.

'How far away is it?'

'About a fifteen-minute drive and then a ten-minute walk to the viewing platform. It's worth it though.'

'Why not?'

We settled the bill and made our way back to the cars. Fifteen minutes later we'd reached the hilltop village of Doade. Access to the viewing point at Pena do Castelo is through a forest trail. We left the village lane and made our way slowly along the rutted track. Two hundred metres in, we parked the cars and continued on foot.

'It's this way,' I said, heading out in front.

The forest footpath provided patches of shade, but there was no such relief on the open heath. At the end of the path the panorama opened out on a landscape so vast it exceeds one's field of vision.

Below us the river Sil snaked its way through the valley, dark and mysterious. A tourist boat glided silently down the river leaving white-fringed ripples in its wake. Downstream the river cuts through a dramatic canyon forged millennia ago by a ferocious earthquake. Rising from the riverbank are row upon row of terraced vineyards hugging the contours of the land and climbing over a thousand feet to the summit of the valley. At this time of year, their foliage provides a shimmering blanket of vivid shades of green.

'Wow! How on earth did you find this place?' asked Richard.

'Some friends own a house in the village. They brought us.'

Having exhausted every possible photo opportunity, we made our way back to the cars.

'We'd like to take you out for a meal tonight,' said Richard, as we strolled along the dusty track.

'There's no need.'

'No, we want to. Where would you like to go?'

'What about that bistro we've been to before, La Maja?' I suggested.

'That's good for us.'

Back at *El Sueño* the kids made up for lost time and spent the whole afternoon in and out of the pool, exhausting Richard in the process.

That evening we drove into town. It was just as well we'd made a reservation as the restaurant was busy with diners. We took our table and a waiter handed out menus.

'What would you like to drink?' he asked.

'Are you going to tell him?' I asked Mason.

On a previous stay Mason had learnt how to order his own drink and taken great pride in doing so.

'What is it?' he whispered, sheepishly.

'*Una coca cola lite*,' I whispered.

Mum overheard.

'*Por favor*,' she said.

The addition of "please" threw his concentration and he melted into the chair.

'What do you want, Mason?' asked Mummy, encouraging a response.

'*Una coca cola lite … Por favor.*'

The waiter smiled and replied, '*Sin favor*.'

'What does that mean?' Mason asked.

'That means you don't have to say please.'

'But we're English Mason, so we do,' replied Yvonne.

I gave him a sly wink and smiled.

As usual the food was excellent and the atmosphere buzzing. Yvonne had let the kids bring their Nintendo Gameboy consoles; even the best-behaved kids get bored at their age. They played with them sparingly and switched them off when asked.

'Smile,' said Erren, pointing the console at Melanie.

'Does it have a camera?' I asked.

Erren nodded and then nudged her brother. The pair of them stared at the screen and burst out laughing.

'What are you two up to?' asked Mummy.

'Nothing,' replied Erren.

Which is a standard reply when the opposite is true.

'Give it to me.'

Erren handed it over. Yvonne looked at the screen and also started laughing.

'I'm not that ugly, am I?' asked Melanie.

'Just look at this.' Yvonne handed the console to Melanie.

'Oh … Perhaps I am,' she said, with a smile on her face.

Her reply sent Erren and Mason into uncontrollable fits of laughter. What on earth was so funny?

'Let's have a look,' I said, holding out my hand.

Melanie passed it to me and I stared at the screen. Erren had used image manipulation software to distort Melanie's portrait and the result was hilarious. If you've ever stood in front of a warped mirror at the fairground, you'll know exactly what I mean. What fun Picasso would have had with such a device. Her face was contorted almost, but not quite, beyond recognition. She looked like a cross between Quasimodo and the Elephant Man. I couldn't help but laugh.

'You think it's funny, do you?' said Melanie. 'Perhaps you ought to take one of Uncle Craig, Erren.'

Erren took aim.

'Smile,' she said, which seemed a little unfair.

It wouldn't matter how I posed; I was going to end up looking like a freak. I gave her the broadest grin possible. The result had everyone in tears, crying with laughter. Other diners were left wondering which asylum we'd escaped from. Erren had captured the frame perfectly. Forget about all mouth and no trousers; this was all teeth and no hair.

By the time we got back to *El Sueño* the clock had ticked around to 12:30 am.

'If you ask Uncle Craig nicely, he might switch the pool lights on and you can take a dip,' said Yvonne.

A well-deserved end of holiday treat. The kids had been great since the moment they arrived. Energetic, without a doubt, but overall they'd been as good as gold.

'Yer! Will you Uncle Craig, will you?' they chimed.

'What do you say?' instructed Yvonne.

'Please, Uncle Craig.'

I turned to Mason and winked, '*Sin favor.*'

Yvonne glared at me.

The kids stripped off and stepped gingerly into the pool. Cool air and warm water sent clouds of steam rising into the night sky. They splashed about as if it was the middle of the afternoon. Had it not been for Mum, I think they might have stayed there all night.

'Just a bit longer, Mum,' pleaded Mason.

'Yer Mum, just a bit longer,' echoed Erren.

'Come on now, it's time for bed.'

Mum had spoken and the kids had no intention of spoiling what had been a wonderful evening.

Even the kids had a lie-in the following morning.

'I'm going to have to nip into town,' said Melanie, over morning coffee.

'What for?'

'We haven't got anything for lunch.'

'Do you want me to come with you?'

'No, you stay here.'

There's a certain inevitability to the final few hours of a holiday. Everyone, including the kids, had their minds elsewhere. They went through the motions of jumping in and out of the pool but the clock was ticking and they would soon be on their way.

'I'm back,' said Melanie, as she stepped out of the kitchen.

'Where have you been, Aunty Melly?' asked Mason.

'To get something for lunch.'

Having satisfied curious young minds she turned to me. 'I bumped into Ian and Kathy in town. Their daughter Rachel is here as well.'

We'd met Ian and Kathy through a mutual friend and hit it off straight away. It was they who had introduced us to the viewing point at Pena do Castelo.

'Are they well?' I asked.

'Yes. I invited them round for lunch.'

'Today?'

'No. This coming Monday. Is that alright?'

'Of course.'

Melanie did a great job with lunch and the kids had a final hour in the pool before readying themselves to leave. At 4:00 pm we said our goodbyes and waved them off. As usual, we'd really enjoyed their visit. It had been chaotic at times, but kids have a way of putting life into perspective.

'What's that?' I asked.

'What?'

'Listen.'

'I can't hear anything.'

'Exactly.'

9

Paella à la Briggs

Operating a holiday rental was child's play compared to hosting a young family for a week. Readjusting to the quiet life would take time. Even the dog seemed a little subdued. Thankfully, it wasn't long before we were heading back to *Campo Verde* to clean for the next guests.

'Can you believe this weather?' I said, as we drove through the village.

We'd woken to the pitter patter of raindrops dancing on the roof tiles. Grey sky and puddles were the last thing we wanted to see on the first day of August.

'Let's hope it improves. Have you looked at the forecast?'

'I didn't think I'd need to. I'll take a look when we get back.'

The Alvar family had left when we arrived. The first thing Melanie did was check the Visitors book.

'They haven't written anything,' she said.

Given their lack of English, it was hardly surprising. The house, however, was spotless.

'It's almost as clean as we left it,' remarked Melanie.

Mowing the lawns was out of the question as the grass was far too wet. They'd have to wait until the mid-stay linen change.

'What do you want me to do?' I asked.

'Make a start in the twin bedroom; I'll begin in the master bedroom, and we'll meet in the middle.'

An hour and a half later we were heading home.

'That must be the quickest clean ever,' remarked Melanie.

On this occasion, the rain in Spain made life less of a pain.

Beep! Beep! Beep! Beep!

The sound of the alarm clock jolted us into a new day. Melanie slid out of bed and went to put the kettle on, while I crossed my fingers and pushed open the window shutters. It wasn't exactly tipping it down, but everywhere looked damp and miserable. Before we left for the Meet and Greet, I booted up the computer and checked the forecast.

'Well?' asked Melanie.

'It's set to improve.'

'That's good. When?'

My absence of clarity hadn't gone unnoticed.

'From tomorrow … ish, but it should be back to normal by the end of the week.'

Normal in August is sunny, hot, and sticky.

'Perhaps they won't notice.'

'Won't notice!'

'They do live in England.'

She had a point, and if they'd chosen to holiday in the Lake District it might even be true, but they hadn't. They'd chosen Spain, where the sun always shines.

The new arrivals were Wallis Law, his partner Tina and her daughter Emma from Horsham in Surrey. Wallis met us at the front door and invited us in.

'I thought we'd left this behind,' he remarked.

Bang goes the not noticing theory.

Tina and Emma were waiting for us in the dining room. As soon as we entered, Emma hid behind her mother.

'Is everything alright?' asked Melanie.

'Oh yes, this is lovely,' beamed Tina.

Things were looking up, and she wasn't just being polite. Tina really did love the place. We chatted for a while and went through our list of things to mention: location of the village bins, places of interest, the self-drive tours, and restaurant reviews.

'How far away is the nearest beach?' asked Tina.

Emma poked her head out from behind her mum.

'It's about an hour and a half to the coast,' I replied.

Emma looked devastated.

'But there's a river beach less than twenty kilometres away,' I added.

'What's a river beach?' whispered Emma.

I explained that the beach at A Cova was a popular hangout during the summer months. The imported sand was clean and well maintained. There was also a bar and restaurant, and visitors could even hire a pedalo if they chose.

'That sounds great, doesn't it Emma?'

'Can we go today?' she asked quietly.

We all stared out of the window.

'Perhaps tomorrow.'

'Intermittent showers are forecast for the rest of the day but it should start to improve from tomorrow onwards. By the end of the week it'll be glorious,' I reassured them.

'If there's nothing else, we'll let you get on with your holiday. We'll call back next Saturday to change the linen and mow the lawns. If there's anything you need before then, don't hesitate to call. The number is in the Guest Information book,' said Melanie.

By the time we left the rain had almost stopped.

'They seemed nice,' I remarked, on the drive home.

Melanie agreed.

'What are we going to do if it's like this tomorrow?' she asked.

'Tomorrow?'

'Don't tell me you've forgotten.'

'Forgotten what?'

'That Ian, Kathy and Rachel are coming for lunch.'

'Of course I haven't,' I replied, which of course wasn't true.

'So?'

'Don't worry,' I said in a Spanish accent.

This annoying phrase is uttered by almost everyone, from builders to plumbers, bank managers to accountants, and when it is, you can be sure that the opposite is true. Melanie didn't dignify it with a response.

Chattering birds eased us into a new day. I held my breath and flung open the window shutters. Visibility was less than a hundred metres, but at least it wasn't raining. I hopped back into bed and waited for Melanie to return with our morning coffee. Jazz was first to appear.

'Come on lass.' I bent down and picked her up. 'Crikey! I'm sure you're putting on weight.'

'Don't say that, you'll hurt her feelings.' Melanie had arrived with the coffees.

Jazz seemed none the wiser and tucked into her morning treats oblivious to my remark.

'Have you seen the weather?' asked Melanie.

'It could be worse. It'll probably clear up before lunch.'

It couldn't do any harm to sound optimistic, and besides which, at this time of year it doesn't take long for the sun to burn away the morning mist.

We sipped our coffees in silence, pondering our next move. An empty mug signalled a call to arms.

'I'm just going to check the inbox before I make a start.'

'OK.'

I nipped into the office and booted up the computer.

'You're not going to believe this,' I said, as I walked into the kitchen.

'We haven't got another booking, have we?'

'We have.'

'That's brilliant. How many weeks does that make?'

'I'm not sure. Hang on a minute.'

I went back into the office and checked the diary.

'Eighteen, we're up to eighteen weeks.'

'That's fantastic.'

Toot, toot!

I looked out of the window just in time to see the postlady reversing out of the entrance and driving off into the village.

'I'll go,' I said.

Melanie was busy kneading dough for the bread rolls that would accompany today's lunch. We'd decided to treat our guests to the house speciality: Paella à la Briggs. It's similar to Spanish paella but without all the nasty bits, and definitely no shellfish. Melanie's allergy sees to that.

As I stepped outside, I couldn't help noticing a few patches of blue sky. The sun was working its magic. I opened the mailbox and lifted out a brown C5 envelope addressed to Mr and Mrs Briggs. What could it be? Carefully, I peeled back the adhesive flap and pulled out the contents.

'Look what I've got,' I said, as I stepped inside.

'What is it?'

'Copies of the illustrations Lyanne promised me. Look.'

'They're wonderful. I must write and thank her.'

'Right then, I'd better make a start in the garden.'

I began by cleaning the garden furniture, a task which

had become all too familiar since *Campo Verde* opened for business. It felt as if I spent half my life scrubbing and polishing. I shouldn't complain; we'd sunk a sizeable chunk of our savings into our new venture and needed to earn a return, but we hadn't expected to be this busy. If we weren't careful, we might lose what we came here to find: a chance to walk a different path, free from the stresses and strains of modern living. Our new venture had set us on a different course. We were sailing in uncharted waters in an unknown direction. For the time being we'd keep a tight grip on the tiller and see where the trade winds blew us. One thing was certain, if we were going to work throughout spring, summer and autumn, then winter should be ours.

By the time I'd finished philosophising, bright sunshine had dissolved the morning mist. We couldn't have asked for better weather.

'I think we ought to go off for the winter,' I announced, as I stepped into the kitchen.

Melanie was busy preparing the ingredients for the paella.

'We are going off.'

She was referring to the clifftop cottage we'd booked near Nerja on the Costa del Sol. A four-week stay starting on the 12th of December.

'No, I mean for the whole winter.'

'The whole winter?'

'Yes. Perhaps until the end of February. What do you think?'

Melanie said nothing. It seemed wise to drop the matter for now. I'd sowed the seed and felt confident that with regular watering my idea would blossom.

At precisely one o'clock our guests arrived. After much umming and arring Melanie had decided not to make a dessert which was just as well; Kathy arrived carrying a white chocolate torte. We served drinks on the terrace and caught up on each other's news.

'Right then, I'll make a start,' I announced.

Preparing a paella is more than cooking, it's a theatrical event. It seems a little unfair that I take all the plaudits because the real work goes on backstage. Thanks to Melanie's efforts, my job was a piece of cake. I'd set up the gas burner on the terrace for maximum exposure. I began by pouring a generous measure of extra virgin olive oil into the ten-person paella pan and turning up the heat. To that I added chopped onions and crushed garlic. The aroma of sizzling onions grabbed my audience's attention. I left them to sweat and fetched the remaining ingredients from the kitchen.

Next, I tipped in diced, boneless chicken, enough to feed the five of us. Turning fifty or more pieces of chicken was the trickiest part of the operation. A droplet of sweat trickled down my back as I flipped the last chunk.

'Is the stock ready?' I asked.

'Yes. Do you want it now?'

'Not just yet.'

The next stage is critical. Timing is everything. I added a sachet of saffron to the chicken, onions, and garlic. Ounce for ounce, this oriental spice was once the most expensive commodity on earth. Abracadabra and my magical wooden spoon transformed everything into a rich golden yellow. Speed was of the essence. I added large chunks of fresh, peeled tomatoes, followed swiftly with a bowl of frozen garden peas. Now for the main event. When it comes to rice, quality is everything. I use a brand called La Cigala. It's a short grain rice specifically designed for making paella. I've tried others but they always fall short; no pun intended. I find it's better to be generous and have a little left over than hungry guests; besides which, it's Jazz's favourite.

Any delays at this point and you'll end up with a pan of savoury chicken flavoured popcorn.

'Right love, I'm ready for the stock.'

My indispensable assistant jumped to her feet and dashed into the kitchen.

While she fetched the stock, I added two heaped teaspoons of sweet paprika to the mix. Melanie dashed back outside balancing two one-litre jugs filled to the brim with chicken stock.

'Just a minute,' I said, as she prepared to pour.

Frantically, I stirred the contents to ensure an even coating of paprika.

'OK, pour.'

One jug at a time, the chicken stock flowed onto the back of the spoon and into the pan.

'More?' she asked, having emptied the second jug.

'Some boiling water will be fine.'

A kettle of hot water topped up the pan.

I turned up the heat and brought it to the boil before lowering the flame and leaving it to simmer. To add a touch of artistic flare, I placed alternating strips of red and yellow bell peppers in a sunburst pattern on top of the bubbling ingredients. It adds nothing to the taste but looks great.

It takes between twenty minutes and half an hour to cook. Plenty of time to top everyone's glass up and enjoy the company. When all the liquid had evaporated, I checked the pan at regular intervals. As soon as it starts to catch, it's ready to serve. Voilà! Paella à la Briggs, sunny side up.

'Lunch is served,' I announced, as I turned off the burner and placed the large pan in the centre of the table.

The proof of a paella is in the eating and with all but a spoonful left, it's safe to say everyone enjoyed it. We let it settle for a while before making a significant dent in Kathy's white chocolate torte.

'You really shouldn't do that in front of guests,' I said, as Melanie placed the pan on the lawn.

Jazz looked a little disappointed at the miserly portion we'd left her, but wasted no time in tucking in. She'd learnt from experience that the best bits are baked to the bottom of the pan. To extract them, she placed a paw in the pan to stop it moving around and scraped it clean with her front teeth. Comical doesn't come close.

'That'll save on the washing up,' I joked.

Rachel's eyes widened. Her mum knew better.

'Did you bring your trunks?' I asked Ian.

'Under my shorts,' he replied. 'Rachel's got her cossie on as well. Do you mind?'

'Not at all. You have a swim.'

Ian and Rachel enjoyed a dip in the pool. We spent the rest of the afternoon lounging about in the sun. At 8:00 pm they headed home. And to think we'd been worried about the weather.

Wallis, Tina and Emma were at home when we called for the mid-stay linen change. They'd spent most of the week at the river beach and were full of praise.

'It's just like a normal beach and the sand is really clean,' remarked Tina.

'And the water is crystal clear and so safe. There's not a hint of a current,' added Wallis.

I explained that the river was in fact a reservoir, created to produce hydroelectricity.

'I went in the water,' said Emma, who seemed far more confident.

In the space of a week, she'd gone from hiding behind her mum to joining in the conversation. Perhaps Galician life is infectious.

'We've eaten at the restaurant most days, haven't we Wallis?' said Tina.

Wallis nodded.

'The food is really good and it's so cheap, isn't it Wallis?'

He nodded again.

We couldn't have been happier for them. Owning a holiday rental property is far more rewarding than simply banking the money. We were part of an industry that aims to provide unforgettable experiences. Surpassing other people's expectations had become our goal. A trip to Galicia wouldn't be everyone's destination of choice, but for those who took the plunge, we were determined to do everything we could to ensure they left with positive memories that would last a lifetime.

Before we left we invited them to a Wine and Tapas night, an invitation they were delighted to accept.

'If you come for about 6:00 pm, Emma can play in the pool if she'd like to,' I said.

Emma's eyes lit up and she turned to Mum for approval.

'I don't see why not,' said Mum.

Mad dogs and Englishmen go out in the midday sun. While Jazz relaxed in the shade, this mad dog, and Englishman, picked up his mattock and walked. Gardening is not really my thing, but when Melanie's enthusiasm for growing her own had waned, I suggested transforming the would-be vegetable plot into a vineyard. She was delighted to hand it over, along with the task of weeding.

As for the fledgling vineyard, I couldn't have been happier. With a few exceptions every grapevine was well over a metre tall and looked as fit as a fiddle. It had kept me busy, removing secondary canes and nipping off *nietos* or grandchildren (a colloquial term for shoots that spring up at the junction of a leaf and the main fruiting cane), and the prospect of drinking our own wine was a great incentive.

Weeding is a thankless task. Hour after hour I'd toiled in the vineyard, wielding my twin-forked mattock like an axe into the unforgiving ground. Every so often I'd hit a stone which sent a shockwave up the handle, through my hands, and rattled my elbows. This was hard labour at its most brutal.

At 1:00 pm Melanie called lunch. A break at last. We sat under the back porch and nibbled our sandwiches.

'Have you thought any more about winter?' I asked.

'Winter?'

'Yes, about going away for longer.'

'Where were you thinking of going?'

'I'm not sure, perhaps further down the coast. It would all depend on what price I can negotiate,' I said.

'It can't harm to make some enquiries.'

That was all the encouragement I needed to begin my search.

Within the hour I was back at it, determined to tame this defiant land.

'How's it going?'

Melanie had crept up behind me.

'It's chuffing hard work. This ground is rock hard. What time is it?'

'About three thirty. I thought you might like a drink.'

Melanie held out a glass of cold water which was exactly what I needed.

'Thanks.'

'How much longer?'

'I'm nearly there. What I really need is a rotavator,' I added.

'Perhaps you ought to have a look for one online.'

A sympathetic reply which didn't need repeating.

That night we went to bed early, and I slept like a dog.

The Wine and Tapas night with Wallis, Tina, and Emma was quite different to previous ones, and made a refreshing change. They arrived on time, which is always a good start, but came empty-handed. I was quite pleased, in a strange kind of way. They gave me the impression that daily life in England didn't include invitations to someone else's home. It made our offer feel special.

Tina made herself at home and plonked her, not unsubstantial, frame down where Melanie had been sitting. Wallis was a little less forward and waited to be asked. Emma had come prepared and with Mum's encouragement was splashing about in the pool in no time. The evening flowed and the tapas went down almost as quickly as the wine. At one in the morning, they finally made a move. I think it's safe to assume they'd enjoyed the evening.

'If we don't see you on Saturday, have a safe trip home,' I said as they left.

Job done and another satisfied customer.

10

Milestone

Wallis, Tina, and Emma had already left when we arrived at *Campo Verde* for the changeover day clean. Melanie was a little disappointed they hadn't left a comment in the Visitors book. I wasn't surprised. They seemed a little self-conscious in unfamiliar situations. What else didn't surprise me was the condition of the house. They'd gone to a lot of effort to make sure it looked as loved when they left as it did on their arrival, well almost.

Today's guests were the Lecoq family, originally from France but currently living in Barcelona. They were a party of four adults and two babies. During the booking process they'd requested a cot. After much consideration we'd decided to buy one. The choices in Monforte de Lemos were limited to two: a very large and ornately carved wooden prison-like structure, or a nifty travel cot. The latter folded neatly into its own carry case, and the sales assistant made assembling it look like child's play.

'Before you start mowing the lawns can you set up the cot?' asked Melanie.

'Where do you want it?'

'In the master bedroom?'

I carried it through and unzipped the carry case. Velcro straps held it all together. I ripped them open and stared at a heap of brightly coloured interconnected tubes. I picked up one section and another flew open. I tugged on that one and the first section collapsed. Hmm, the girl in the shop had made it look so easy. More hands were needed.

'Can you remember how this thing goes together?' I called.

'I thought it just unfolded.'

'So did I. Can you give me a hand?'

Melanie dropped what she was doing and stomped into the bedroom.

'Can you hold these two?' I asked, handing her two of the four corner posts.

'And then what?'

'It should just lift up.'

Each corner was connected to a central hinge which allowed the sides to fold in half. I tugged at one set of corner posts while Melanie held the other two.

'Don't pull it so hard,' she complained.

'I have to, otherwise look.'

I let go and it fell to the floor.

'Well I don't know. You'll have to sort it out. I'm too busy,' and off she went.

Melanie is not good at these types of challenges, which is strange because she's a whizz with a Rubik's Cube. She also has a very low tolerance threshold. I, on the other hand, refuse to admit defeat, especially when it's something as straightforward as a travel cot.

There are times when two hands are better than four. This wasn't one. I felt like a solo competitor in a game of Twister. I propped one post up with my foot, grabbed the opposite two with both hands and nudged the remaining post with my spare knee. It was just about to click into position when my left knee slipped, leaving me and the cot in a tangled pile on the floor.

'What happened?' called Melanie.

'Nothing,' I replied, rubbing my knee.

Melanie poked her head around the door.

'Are you alright?'

I jumped up and pretended I was fine.

'Everything's good, except this chuffing thing.'

'Do you want me to help?'

'No!'

What I actually meant was yes, but I was determined this contraption would not get the better of me.

'Please yourself,' and off she trotted.

There had to be a better way. It was time to do what I should have done in the first place and study the problem. I stared at the pieces, searching for inspiration. In order for it to stand upright, all four hinges had to be locked. Attempting to lock them synchronously hadn't worked. Perhaps I should try locking them one at a time. I lifted the first hinge and the two connected posts stood to attention and the mechanism locked. I couldn't believe how easy it was. The opposite hinge did exactly the same, as did the two others: simple, or was that me?

'I've left it in the corner of the bedroom,' I said, as I wandered through the lounge.

Melanie looked stunned.

'Have you done it?'

'Piece of cake,' I replied, and marched off with my head held high.

Three hours after leaving home we arrived back, tired and hungry. Saturday siestas are becoming an important part of my changeover day routine. While I snoozed in the shade, Melanie fried in the sunshine with her nose in a book.

Ring, ring … Ring, ring!

If tension could make a sound, this would be it. I held my breath while Melanie ran into the house. Moments later she stepped outside.

'That was the Lecoqs.'

She paused.

'And?'

'They're en route and will be arriving at about eight thirty this evening.'

What a relief. Cardiac rhythm restored.

Having people ring us, either before arriving, as in this case, or upon arrival, as in the case of the Lucas family, was a new and unnerving experience. In the three years we'd managed Bob and Janet's house, everything had run smoothly. Guests would arrive unannounced, let themselves in, and we would welcome them officially the following day. Why people felt the need to contact us was a mystery to me.

Drama over, Melanie returned to her historical romance novel and I pottered about in the garden. As the sun began its slow decent into tomorrow, the heat subsided. Time for a Teatime Taster. We decamped to the far end of the garden and watched as it slipped behind the woody knoll, silhouetting the tall pine trees and leafy oaks. Patches of cloud reflected the sun's final farewell with a glorious display of colour ranging from white hot to golden orange before melting into pastel shades of lilac and blue. Dinner was served under the covered terrace. Melanie rustled up coleslaw and a tomato salad and I fired up the barbecue. Tonight's selection was grilled chicken marinated in a spicy sauce. I pulled the cork on a bottle of red and we enjoyed a leisurely meal in the warm, still evening.

Ring, ring … Ring, ring!

'Who's that at this time of night?' I moaned.

As soon as I'd said it, I feared the worst. Melanie jumped up and ran inside. I glanced at the time: 10:08 pm.

Surely it couldn't be the Lecoqs. By their own admission, they should have arrived over an hour ago. But who else could it be?

I pinned my ears back but couldn't hear a word. I waited impatiently. What was taking so long?

Melanie stepped outside clutching the phone to her chest.

'It's Jean-Pierre,' she whispered.

'Who?'

'Lecoq, Jean-Pierre Lecoq.'

'What's matter?'

'They're lost.'

'Lost?'

Melanie handed me the phone.

'What do they want me to do?' I whispered, holding my hand over the microphone.

I'd drunk far too much wine to go gallivanting around the Spanish countryside in the middle of the night searching for a missing Frenchman and his family. I couldn't believe it; without exception everyone had complimented us on the quality and accuracy of our driving instructions.

'It sounds like they're outside Ferrol's,' she added.

Ferrol's house is virtually at the end of the driveway.

'Hello, this is Craig, can I help?' I asked, in a chirpy, nothing-is-too-much-trouble kind of a way.

Jean-Pierre explained where he was. To my relief, they did sound to be outside Ferrol's.

'You're almost there. Take the left-hand fork and follow the lane around to the left. There should be a black gate on your left and a mailbox with the name *Campo Verde* painted on it.'

Muffled French voices echoed down the line.

'Can you see it?' I asked.

The line went quiet. Perhaps they weren't outside Ferrol's.

'Ah, yes, I can see it. Thank you.'

'You're welcome. Enjoy the rest of your evening and we'll see you tomorrow morning at ten thirty.'

What a relief.

On reflection, our arrivals procedure probably seemed as strange to them as theirs did to us. Talk about lost in translation.

The Meet and Greet went well. Jean-Pierre and his wife Magdalen spoke excellent English, which was just as well. I asked about the cot, as much to make sure it was still standing as anything, which it was. The other two adults were Magdalen's parents who didn't speak a word of English which begged the question, 'Where's the other baby?'

'Our friends will be joining us later in the week. They also have a baby,' explained Jean-Pierre.

My quizzical expression prompted a response from Magdalen.

'My parents will be flying back to France when they arrive,' she added.

Their arrangements didn't really concern us. Providing they stuck to our maximum occupancy rule of four adults, their comings and goings were none of our business. Before leaving we told them we'd be back on Saturday to change the linen and mow the lawns.

Wednesday the 19th of August marked a milestone in my and Melanie's relationship. Twenty-five years ago to the day, I asked Melanie to go out with me. Eleven years after that, we finally tied the knot. We now celebrate both events.

Melanie was working behind the bar at my local pub, The Sands House, when I popped the question. She swears blind I'd been pestering her for weeks but that's not how I remember it. Whatever the whys and wherefores, on Sunday the 19th of August 1984, I picked her up from home and we drove to the Hey Green Hotel in Marsden for Sunday lunch. This 19th century former mill owner's home sits on the edge of the beautiful Saddleworth Moor. Lunch was typical Yorkshire fare of roast beef, Yorkshire puddings and three veg, smothered in onion gravy. Pudding was a fruit crumble and custard. It was hardly a romantic candlelit dinner for two but the location was perfect, and the price wasn't bad either.

After lunch I took her to the Pennine Show, an annual agricultural fair held on the moors above the village of Holmfirth. There, we met friends and fellow pub patrons, some of whom had entered the inter-pubs drinking competition.

We couldn't have asked for better weather: bright, warm, and sunny, a rare occurrence in Yorkshire, even in August. The drink-a-thon had pulled in a decent crowd. We took a seat on the grass and cheered on our team. Unfortunately, they failed to impress, due in no small measure to our star performer, a certain Steve Harper, having drunk seven pints at lunchtime. In the end, one of our nearest rivals, The Bull's Head in Linthwaite, won the day.

What I hadn't realised, until we got up to leave, was that my cross-legged seating position had cut off the blood supply to my right leg. When I tried to stand, I collapsed to the ground. My embarrassment was compounded by the length of time it took the blood to recirculate sufficiently for me to stand. Twenty-five years on, I can only assume my antics left a lasting impression.

'Let's go to Chaves for a celebration lunch,' I suggested.

'Ooh yes. I could murder a Chinese.'

Not literally, you realise.

The Portuguese border town of Chaves is home to our favourite Chinese restaurant, the Jing Huà. The 280-kilometre round trip is a small price to pay for such delicious food and for those who believe only DeLoreans can travel back to the future, I'll let you in on a secret. With a full tank and a fair wind, a Renault Megane performs equally as well, arriving in Chaves minutes before we leave home. Which is more than can be said for the return journey, when the one-hour time difference between Portugal and Spain really eats into the day.

From home we took the N-120 highway to Ourense before joining the A-52, Autopista del Norte, southbound to the town of Verin. From there we crossed the border into Portugal and on to Chaves.

As usual, lunch was exceptional. We started with their unique spring rolls. The filling is traditional, thin slices of crisp vegetables with a smattering of mince, but the wrap is very different. It's made from a type of dough, thinly rolled and deep fried. For mains we shared *galinha con caju* (chicken with cashew nuts), and *pato da amizade na caçarola* (duck friendship casserole). The chicken is presented on a sizzling hotplate and is accompanied by chopped vegetables and cashew nuts. The sliced duck breast has crispy skin and is served on a bed of stir-fried vegetables in a sweet and sour sauce and presented in an earthenware casserole dish with matching lid, reminiscent of a Lancashire hot pot; that's the bowl not the contents. To accompany that we ordered egg-fried rice with three delights: diced ham, garden peas, and carrots. Melanie polished off the best part of a bottle of white wine, and the designated driver ended up with a bottle of icy cold water.

The old part of town is very picturesque and a great place to walk off the excesses of lunch, but I had other ideas.

'Let's stop at Allariz on the way home,' I suggested.

'Where?'

'Allariz, that town we drive past.'

'What town?'

'You know. Off the A-52.'

Her expression didn't change.

'Where that big monastery is.'

'Ah yes, I know where you mean. OK, let's do that.'

We returned to the car and headed back to Spain. Fifty kilometres after joining the A-52, we turned off and followed the signs to Allariz. The old town is perched on a hilltop overlooking the River Arnoia. We headed for the historic centre and found ourselves in the Plaza Mayor. The monastery and a church occupy one side of the square and residential properties line the rest. I rolled into a dusty, unsurfaced carpark and stopped.

'This is lovely,' remarked Melanie.

Many Spanish towns have an old historic centre, and with the exception of a few modern windows, the properties surrounding this square hadn't changed in the last two hundred years.

'Let's take a look around,' I suggested.

We left the car and headed towards the monastery. The day had turned into a scorcher. Hot, dry air filled our lungs as we walked towards the historic monument.

'Over there,' said Melanie, pointing at an information board.

The 13th century monastery was called Real Monesterio de Santa Clara and was built under the patronage of Queen Violante, wife of Alfonso X. A note on the door indicated the opening times: mornings only. We'd have to return another day if we wanted a closer look. We continued on, strolling clockwise around the square to the church of San Benito. Built in the baroque style, it dates back to 1770. From there we ambled down a tree-lined avenue where a group of old men were playing pétanque in the shade. Bursts of dust drifted through the air as the heavy metal boules landed on the ground. If we hadn't known better, we could have been strolling through a park in the Dordogne. Leading off the Plaza Mayor was a network of cobbled streets lined with quaint cottages. Since moving to Galicia we'd visited many towns and villages but Allariz was undoubtedly one of the most picturesque.

That evening we had a double celebration. As soon as we got home, I checked the inbox. One email caught my eye. The sender was Celeste Sellier. She'd written to confirm her reservation for a two-week stay over Christmas and New Year. I could hardly contain my excitement and dashed outside to tell Melanie.

'We've done it,' I announced.

'What have we done?'

'We've beaten our revised target.'

'What revised target?'

I'd decided not to mention it before just in case we fell short, but as soon as we'd secured our fifteenth week I'd set my sights on twenty. If you don't shoot for the stars, you'll never reach them.

'The twenty weeks target,' I announced.

'I didn't know we had a …' Melanie paused. 'Are you saying we've got another booking?'

'That's right.'

'That's great.'

'Isn't it? There is a slight problem though.'

'What?'

'It's for a fortnight over Christmas and New Year.'

'We'll be away.'

'A minor detail.'

'Minor!'

'Don't worry.'

Melanie rolled her eyes. Perhaps it was my accent.

The coming weekend marked the cut-off point for treating the grapevines with herbicide. The manufacturer recommends stopping four weeks prior to harvest. Knowing precisely when that would be was difficult. To err on the side of caution, I decided to leave at least six weeks. On Friday morning, the conditions were perfect for spraying, bright and sunny without a breath of wind.

'I'm going to give the vines their final spray of the season,' I said.

'OK.'

Carefully, I measured out the correct quantity of blue *sulfatar* powder, tipped it into my spraying machine, and filled it with water. Forty minutes later, I'd finished.

'This looks like being a bumper harvest,' I said.

'That's good.'

'Yes. I'd like to get a head start and estimate the yield. Could you give me a hand?'

'Doing what?'

'If I call out the weights will you write them down?'

'OK.'

I found a notepad and pen and handed them to Melanie.

'We'll start in the front garden.'

Melanie followed me outside.

'Are you ready?'

'Ready when you are.'

'OK. Palomino: two, six, four, four, eleven …'

I went from vine to vine naming the variety and estimating the weights. Nothing too technical, or accurate. At this stage, a cupped hand and previous experience would suffice. There's something quite satisfying about groping bunches of grapes. When we'd finished, I totted up the totals. If my guesstimate was anywhere near correct, the coming harvest would be a cracker.

'I make that over two hundred kilos.'

'Are you sure?'

'That's being conservative.'

Two hundred kilos would represent almost twice last year's crop.

On Saturday we drove to *Campo Verde* for the mid-stay linen change. To our surprise Magdalen's parents were still there. We went about our work as usual, but I couldn't help thinking that all was not as it appeared.

When we returned the following weekend, our fears were realised. The Lecoqs were long gone when we arrived, as was everyone else. What they'd left behind had Melanie in tears. When we saw the sofa cushions on the lounge floor we knew more people had been staying than our terms allowed.

'Look at them. They'll never come clean,' said Melanie.

'I'm sure they will. Let's take the covers off and pop them in the washing machine,' I suggested, trying to placate her frustration.

Removable and washable cushion covers were a high priority when we'd been searching for a suite.

'There isn't time.'

'There is, the next guests don't arrive until Thursday.'

'What if they shrink?'

I was about to say "Don't worry" but thought better of it.

'If they do, I'll complain to the manufacturer.'

Unfortunately, the condition of the cushion covers was only the half of it. The entire place was a tip. Everywhere was filthy. The bins were overflowing, every piece of crockery and cutlery needed washing, and all the kitchen utensils and appliances were dirty. We'd chosen not to ask guests for a security deposit to cover breakages or extra cleaning. We preferred instead to rely on trust. That trust had been shattered. Melanie's emotions flipped from upset to anger.

'Look at that,' she said.

Someone had dribbled cereal and milk down the back of the sofa and not bothered to clean it up.

'We shouldn't let one bad apple cloud our judgement,' I cautioned.

'But look at everything. It'll take ages to get it looking nice again.'

I suspected it wasn't the extra work that disappointed her as much as the lack of respect. Had they told us about the additional guests, I'm sure we could have come to some arrangement and made their stay as comfortable as possible. As it was, they'd deliberately misled us.

'Let's just get all the dirty laundry together, load the dishwasher, and come back another day to clean,' I suggested.

Melanie agreed and within an hour of arriving we were heading home to lick our wounds.

11

Daylight Robbery

By the time we'd driven home, Melanie had calmed down. Having unpacked the laundry bag, she set about restoring the cushion covers to their former glory. Thankfully, they came up looking like new, and with a little gentle persuasion I managed to squeeze the cushions back inside.

'See, what did I tell you? They're as good as new,' I said.

'Hmm.'

Most mishaps get funnier with the passage of time, but I doubt this one will. Thankfully, I knew we'd have no such problems with our next guests. June and Malcolm Whitney had previously stayed at Bob and Janet's rental home.

The four-day gap between bookings gave us plenty of time to get the place looking spick and span, and gave me the opportunity to begin my search for a suitable winter getaway.

I began my quest by trawling through the same online

rental sites we were using to market *Campo Verde* and making a list of every property that fitted our search criteria, regardless of price. My next task was to compose an enquiry letter.

'I've written an offer letter. Will you take a look and tell me what you think?' I asked.

Melanie was relaxing in the sunshine reading. She pulled on some clothes and followed me into the office.

Dear ...

My wife and I live in Galicia in the northwest corner of Spain. During the cold winter months, we travel to the Costa del Sol. In previous years we've stayed in an apartment in the castle at Pueblo Aida overlooking Mijas golf.

This year, due to unforeseen circumstances, we find ourselves looking for alternative accommodation. We have already booked a four-week stay in a house at Playa del Río de la Miel, just outside Nerja, but are looking to spend another seven weeks further south.

Your property appears to tick all the boxes. However, we are on a tight budget and will be travelling with our pet dog, Jazz. She's a small to medium-sized collie-cross, twelve years old, fully house-trained and very well behaved.

The dates we would want to stay are Saturday the 9th of January until Saturday the 27th of February. Our budget for the seven weeks is 900 euros.

Obviously, we are writing to a number of places in the area that fulfil our accommodation requirements, but hopefully we can fulfil your income expectation.

We look forward to your response.

Yours sincerely
Craig and Melanie Briggs

'You've got a cheek,' said Melanie.

'What do you mean?'

'Nine hundred euros?'

'They'll either want our money or not. Anyway, what do you think?'

'I think you've got no chance.'

'We'll see.'

One after another, I copied and pasted the message into the enquiry box of each property and hit send. All we had to do now was cross our fingers and wait for the offers to come rolling in.

Composing the letter brought a smile to my face as it reminded me how we'd first met June and Malcolm. At the time, we were managing Bob and Janet's rental property and I'd received a similarly cheeky offer from June. They were living in Mojacar at the time and looking for a summer getaway to avoid the hellish temperatures in Almeria. For those who don't know, the province of Almeria is famous for being the only place in Europe with a desert. Like me, June was a keen negotiator, which is fine when you're a renter but not as good when you're an owner, or in this case the manager. When asking for a discount it's important to hold all the cards. Trying to secure a peak season stay, well in advance, is hardly top trumps. When I refused to budge on price, June decided to go elsewhere. At the time, only eight rental properties plied their trade in Galicia and only two in this area. It didn't take a genius to figure out where they would end up. Had I known then what I know now, predicting what happened next would have been equally straightforward.

June's enquiry had slipped my mind, when, completely out of the blue, I received an email from her. In the message she asked to take a look at Bob and Janet's house with a view to renting it the following year. There were lots of reasons why this might be the case, but one stood head and shoulders above the rest: they didn't like where they were currently staying. If that was the case, the negotiating table had swung even further in my favour.

A few days later, when I met June to show her around, my suspicions were confirmed. Their current accommodation had fallen well short of the standards they'd expected. In a two-house race, Bob and Janet's was furlongs ahead. The negotiations began and ended with the advertised price. June went away content in the knowledge she'd reserved the finest rental property in the area, and I left happy knowing I'd secured the best possible price.

The Whitneys were due to arrive at *Campo Verde* on Thursday. We'd arranged the Meet and Greet for the following evening. Malcolm, who's a retired architect, was on the lookout for a property project of his own. When he saw what we'd done, he was full of praise and really impressed with the standard of workmanship. Before leaving, we invited them for lunch on the following Tuesday.

'We look forward to it,' replied Malcolm.

Melanie and I spent the following day catching up on household chores. We'd had a busy four days and housework was getting neglected. That evening the phone rang.

'It's for you,' said Melanie, handing me the receiver.

'Who is it?' I whispered.

'Julie.'

'Julie who?'

'Your sister.'

My surprise was understandable; Julie never phones unless she wants something.

'Hello.'

'Hello Spaz.'

That's her idea of humour. The word "spaz" is short for spastic: a person who suffers from cerebral palsy. It could be worse; she called our dad "R'don" for decades.

His first name was Donald; I'll leave you to figure out the rest.

'How can I help you?' I asked.

'We're going to come over on the 9th of October. You do know it's my fiftieth on the 7th, don't you?'

'Yes.'

I thought it was the 8th but it's good to be reminded every once in a while.

'Well, I'm not having a party so me and Jeremy are going to come to you. You'll have to pick us up from the airport.'

'We will, will we?'

'I'd like to go to that hotel in Chaves.'

'Really?'

Julie was referring to the Forte de São Francisco Hotel, a 16th century Franciscan convent which was converted into a fortress during the Portuguese War of Restoration (1640–1668), and is now a luxury hotel.

'Yes. Can you book it and let me know how much it is? I'll text Melanie with the flight details.'

'We've got guests arriving on the 10th.'

'Who?'

'I'm not sure. I think they're French.'

'They're not staying with you then?'

'No, at *Campo Verde*.'

'Well book it for the day after, Sunday.'

'I'm not sure they'll allow dogs.'

'Chuff me! We can't go because of a chuffing dog.'

'I didn't say that. I'll ring and find out. If they don't, is there anywhere else you'd like to go?'

'You'll have to find somewhere. Anyway, I've got to go. Bye for now,' and on that note she put the phone down.

'Yes, we're both fine. Thanks for asking,' I said to the wall as I replaced the receiver.

'What did she want?'

I told Melanie of her plans.

'And we've got to arrange everything?'

'That about sums it up.'

An internet search confirmed that pets weren't allowed. We rang the hotel to make doubly sure.

'What now?' asked Melanie.

'We'll have to find somewhere else.'

'Rather you than me.'

It seemed I would have to shoulder the responsibility, which was fair enough; she was my sister, after all.

Three days later, my paella making skills were put to the test again when June and Malcolm arrived for lunch. They came bearing gifts: a fine bottle of Banda Azul Rioja, an Albariño white from the Rías Baixas, and best of all, a box of Devon clotted cream fudge. Lunch was a great success and we all enjoyed getting to know each other a little better.

'You must come to us for lunch when you're staying in Nerja,' said June.

'That would be lovely,' replied Melanie.

'Yes, you must. It's not that far,' said Malcolm.

'We'll give you a ring when we get there and sort out a convenient day,' I replied.

On Saturday morning, June and Malcolm had already left when we went to clean, but we couldn't have wished for a better Visitors book comment.

Malcolm and June Whitney – Almeria, Spain

Yet again Craig and Melanie have produced an immaculate holiday home as a result of high quality building, superb finishes and an incredibly knowledgeable attention to detail. The ample outdoor spaces added to the extensive interior touches, ranging from historical family portraits to the antique collection of

cameras, contribute to making this a very special place that only people who really know and care, can provide. Even the clothes pegs are superior. This is five star and sets the standard. All this and the location in an authentic Spanish hamlet, provide a uniquely comfortable base from which to discover the beauties of Galicia.
Hope everybody enjoys their stay as much as us.

'I don't think it could have been more complimentary if I'd written it myself,' I joked.

'Comments like that make it all worthwhile. Speaking of which, we'd better get cracking.'

Melanie worked her magic inside and I readied the gardens. Three hours later we headed home.

'Oh, I found this in the bathroom,' said Melanie, pulling an electric cable out of the laundry bag.

'I'll email June and see if they want us to pop it in the post,' I replied.

On Sunday morning we readied ourselves for the next Meet and Greet. They were a party of two from Leicester, England, Andrew Davis and his partner Chloe. Upon our arrival, a man in his mid-twenties introduced himself as Andy and led us upstairs.

'Chloe is in the shower,' he said.

We chatted for a while and then asked if he had any questions. People usually want to know about recycling their rubbish or where the nearest restaurant is. Andy's enquiry caught us off guard.

'Do you know where I can hire a canoe?' he asked.

I looked at Melanie and she stared back at me.

'That's the first time anyone has asked us that,' I replied.

'It doesn't matter if you don't, we can look it up on the internet. I just thought if you did, it would save us the trouble.'

'I'm sorry, we don't, but if you get stuck, the tourist information office in Monforte de Lemos should be able to point you in the right direction,' I replied.

'Hello, I'm Chloe.'

The bedroom door had opened and a young woman entered.

'Hello, I'm Craig and this is my wife Melanie. Andy was just asking us about hiring a canoe.'

'Tsk! You and your canoe.'

'Is there anything else?' I asked.

'I have a question. Do we need to recycle the rubbish?' asked Chloe.

Now you're talking.

Melanie ran through the options. They were only staying a week so before we left, I invited them to a Wine and Tapas night.

'That would be lovely, thank you,' replied Chloe.

'Right then, if there's nothing else we'll leave you to enjoy your holiday and look forward to seeing you on Thursday. Any problems, and our phone number is in the Guest Information book.'

As soon as we got home, I checked the email account for new messages. I was a bit disappointed we hadn't received a single reply to my rental enquiry. Perhaps Melanie was right, maybe nine hundred euros was too low. When I opened the inbox, one email caught my eye.

From: Katherine Txxx
Sent: Sunday, September 13, 9:12 AM
To: Craig Briggs
Subject: Re: Holiday-Rentals enquiry – "Luxury apartment in award-winning development near Santa Maria Golf."

Dear Mr Briggs

Firstly, I must apologise for not getting back to you earlier, but I have been away.

Thank you for your enquiry re the rental of my apartment for the period 9th Jan – 27th Feb. I wouldn't normally allow pets to stay in my apartment, so in view of this fact I feel that €995 is a price I would like for the 7 weeks.

I look forward to hearing from you again, apologies for the delayed reply.

Kind regards
Katherine Txxx

My heart skipped a beat. I couldn't quite believe it. I read it again to make sure. It wasn't exactly what I'd offered, but it was close enough. I opened the browser and went to the Holiday-Rentals website. I held my breath and entered the property's reference number.

Wow! This was one of my better choices. Melanie would be impressed.

'Melanie, have you got a minute?' I called.

She poked her head around the office door.

'What do you think to this place?' I asked.

She took a seat and stared at the screen.

'It looks really nice. How much is it?'

'It's a bit over budget.'

'I bet it is.'

I knew if I waited, she would have to ask.

'Go on then, how much over budget?'

'Ninety-five euros.'

'A week?'

'No, ninety-five euros.'

'You're joking.'

'Nope. The owner wants 995 euros for the seven weeks. Told you.'

Melanie scrunched up her nose. 'Are you sure?'

'Certain. Take a look at the email if you don't believe me.'

She grabbed the mouse and flicked through the online photos, each one better than the last.

'You'd better get it booked before she calls the police.'

'Police?'

'That's daylight robbery.'

I didn't know about that, but I was delighted with the price and even happier with the accommodation. Our winter getaway was sorted; all I had to do now was find somewhere suitable for big sis's birthday celebration. Just as I was about to start looking, an audible *ping* signalled an incoming email.

I opened the inbox and found another reservation, this time for *Campo Verde*. That brought our running total to twenty-one weeks. Never in my wildest dreams did I think we would get so many bookings, not in Galicia. I went outside to tell Melanie.

'Guess what?'

She looked up from her book.

'She's made a mistake.'

'Mistake?'

'With the price.'

'No, that's all booked.'

'What then?'

'We've got another booking.'

'Another?'

'That makes twenty-one weeks, and guess who it is?'

'Well it's not Santa Claus, those weeks are already booked, which reminds me …'

Before she had time to ask, I blurted out, 'It's W. Allan.'

'That chap who sent you the photos of an earthmover driving down the lane at the side of Bob and Janet's?'

'That's the one.'

My distraction had done the trick.

'How long have they booked for?'

'Nine days.'

'Nine days?'

'I bet he's got some cheap flights. Anyway, I've got a hotel to find,' I said, turning to leave.

'And don't forget to email June.'

'June?'

'About the cable.'

'Oh yes.'

I decided to do that first, otherwise I might forget, again. Her reply was swift. The cable belonged to Malcolm's rechargeable shaver, and could we post it to them as soon as possible. Her urgency was understandable. Malcolm sporting designer stubble was a scary thought. I shook the image from my mind and turned my attention to finding a hotel. The Pazos de Galicia website was my first port of call.

A *pazo* is a Galician manor house. Many are in private hands but some have been converted into hotels. One property caught my eye, Pazo de Eidián in a hamlet of the same name. Google Maps showed it nestling between the towns of Agolaga and Melide in the province of Pontevedra. It was described as a typical Galician manor house dating from the late 16th century. Interestingly, the *pazo* was built on land once owned by the Order of the Knights Templar. The website photos showed a well-appointed interior, and spacious bedrooms. There was a restaurant and most importantly, the establishment was pet friendly. In short, everything I was looking for.

'Come and take a look at this,' I said, stepping outside.

Melanie was lying face down on a sunlounger with her head hanging over the back and her book resting in the shade.

'What is it?'

'A possibility for Julie's fiftieth.'

Melanie hauled herself upright, and followed me inside.

'What do you think?' I asked.

'It looks alright.'

A little more enthusiasm wouldn't have gone amiss.

'What's wrong with it?'

'Nothing.'

'But?'

'But nothing. It looks fine.'

Fine is one of those annoying adjectives on a par with nice. There's nothing wrong with either, but you're unlikely to hear them in a motivational speech.

'Do you think I should book it?'

'I don't see why not.'

Melanie's lukewarm response was hardly the endorsement I'd hoped for, but the hotel did tick all the boxes and without breaking the bank. On that basis, I bit the bullet and confirmed the reservation. On my head be it.

By mid-September, evening temperatures are less predictable than the preceding two months. A fact we were acutely aware of when inviting people to eat. *El Sueño* was designed for outdoor living. The last thing we wanted was to sit inside on the Wine and Tapas night. To make matters worse, strong winds at the start of the week had brought a period of cooler weather. Autumn was in the air, but between now and then we intended to make full use of the garden.

'It feels cold outside,' remarked Melanie.

'It might warm up.'

'What if it doesn't?'

'Don't worry. They're from England. They might not notice.'

'If you say so.'

Melanie wasn't convinced, and neither was I.

Andy and Chloe arrived at 6:00 pm. Temperatures had improved steadily throughout the day which allowed us to sit outside on the terrace.

'Did you find a canoe?' I asked.

'We did, but it was quite a trek. What was the place called, Chloe?'

'Something like Rabacallos. Have you heard of it?'

We shook our heads. It was a new one on us.

'It's on the other side of the Canyon de Sil. It took nearly two hours to drive there,' said Andy.

'But was it worth it?' I asked.

'Oh yes. Paddling up the river was fabulous. I've left the details at the house in case anyone else is interested,' he replied.

Melanie brought the first tapas, *chorizo al infierno*. As equally delicious as it is dramatic.

'Did you fly to Santiago?' I asked, in an effort to keep the conversation flowing.

'No, we came by train.'

I smiled; Andy didn't. Was he serious? Was it even possible?

'Train?'

'Yes. Only as far as León and then we hired a car.'

'You got a train from England to León?'

'That's right.'

'I didn't even know you could do that.'

'Oh yes, we took the intercity from Leicester to London St. Pancras, the Eurostar from there to Paris; caught the TGV to the Spanish border, stayed overnight in a hotel in San Sebastián, and travelled to León the following day.'

'Crikey! That's what you call a journey.'

'Not really. Last year we went trekking in Morocco and took the train all the way to Cádiz.'

'Don't you like flying?' I asked.

'I don't mind, but I hate the whole airport experience.'

Me too, but travelling by train seemed a little extreme.

'And trains have much less impact on the environment,' he added.

I couldn't argue with that.

'Isn't it expensive?' asked Melanie.

'A little more than flying, but if you book well in advance it's less than you might think. A return ticket from Leicester to León was about three hundred pounds,' he replied.

Andy and Chloe were an interesting young couple. They were full of endeavour and positive about the future. It made a refreshing change to interact with the energy of youth, and despite the falling temperatures, they didn't head home until 11:30 pm.

Who knows, perhaps we were interesting too?

12

Well Well

The departure of Andy and Chloe marked the start of a nine-day break in bookings. It coincided with the return of Bob and Janet for their second extended visit of the year. Retirement was really suiting them. They'd invited us for dinner which we'd gratefully accepted but before then, we had work to do.

'I'll run the mower over the lawns while we're here,' I said.

Melanie unlocked the front door and went to collect the dirty laundry. I was just about to pull the starter cord when she poked her head out of the kitchen window.

'Come and take a look at this,' she said.

What now?

I climbed the steps to the first floor. Melanie was standing next to the open Visitors book.

'Read this,' she said.

Andy and Chloe – Leicestershire, UK

A truly special place to stay, unfortunately only for a week. The weather was mostly good, save for one cloudy day. We were delighted to have a day's kayaking on the Rio Sil, but a real effort to find Rabacallos, where we started off. Thank you for making us feel very welcome. No drawings, sorry! Hope to come back one day.

That evening we dined on chilli con carne accompanied by Janet's magical garlic bread. Pudding was a deliciously creamy chocolate mousse.

'You did a great job on the septic tank,' said Bob.

Hardly dinner conversation, but I was pleased they were happy.

'The breather pipes are exactly where we wanted them,' he added.

'With the right plants you'll soon have them camouflaged,' I replied.

'Yes. We've decided to create a border using the old roof joists, and seed the rest of the plot.'

Creating a lawn might prove problematic, especially as they weren't planning on installing a watering system, but Bob was keen to tidy it up and keep the maintenance as low as possible.

'We'd also like to renovate the water well,' he said.

'That's a good idea and the sooner the better.'

The old water well was in a terrible state. If something wasn't done soon, it was in danger of collapsing.

'Talking about doing something soon, you couldn't give me a hand to fix it up, could you?'

'No problem, just let me know when.'

'How does Monday sound?'

I smiled. Bob really was keen.

'Monday is fine. Can we say ten o'clock?'

'That would be great, and thank you.'

I was glad they'd decided to restore it. The well had a quaint, picture book appeal and would form a great focal point. The circular wall surrounding the top of the well was about a metre high. Above that, two ancient grapevines had grown across a chestnut framed arbour which rested on four tall granite posts. Throughout the summer, when the vines are in full leaf, I could imagine someone relaxing in its shade, sipping lemonade and writing romantic poetry. Alas, I doubt it would be any of us: Bob plays golf, Janet's a reader not a writer, Melanie prefers sunbathing, and I don't know the first thing about poetry.

Wishing on a well was all well and good, but our first priority was to make the structure safe. At the moment, a brick and render cap prevented animals from inadvertently falling in. Given its current condition, I was surprised it could withstand the weight of autumn leaf fall. As for the wall circling the hole, sections of that would have to be replaced and the whole thing pointed. Bob seemed relieved I'd be around to help.

'We've got some news,' I announced.

Melanie stared at me as if to say "What news?"

'We've decided to extend our winter getaway,' I added.

'For how long?'

'Seven weeks.'

'Another seven. How many does that make?'

'Only eleven,' I joked.

'Are you going to stay at the same place?' asked Janet.

'No, we've found a cracking apartment on the Costa del Sol, at a great price. Why don't you come and stay with us for a week?'

Bob and Janet glanced at each other.

'Yes, why not?' said Melanie.

'Can we think about it?' asked Bob.

'Of course. We'll be there whatever. Just let us know if you want to join us.'

'OK, and thank you.'

'Shall we have our coffee in the lounge?' suggested Janet.

'Why not?'

Bob had saved the best until last. A night in front of the telly watching the highlights of every Premier League football match on the BBC's *Match of the Day*. It's times like these I question the wisdom of not owning a TV. It seemed ironic that we'd gone to the expense of installing a state-of-the-art satellite system at *Campo Verde*, but we still didn't have one. We weren't that bothered. Throughout spring, summer, and early autumn we were happy to live without the distraction; but as the nights draw in, watching DVDs on a fifteen-inch laptop can become quite tedious. Oh well, perhaps one day.

By the time we headed home the clock had ticked around to 1:45 am.

'I've been thinking,' I said, as we drove home.

'At this time in the morning?'

'Yes.'

'What about?'

'Pazo de Eidián.'

'Where?'

'That hotel we've booked for Julie's fiftieth.'

'*You've* booked!'

'OK, I've booked, but you said it looked alright.'

'I suppose. Anyway, what have you been thinking?'

'I've been thinking we ought to take a run out there tomorrow, just to make sure.'

'It's a bit late for that, isn't it?'

Melanie had a point. I was sure it would be fine, but it couldn't harm to take a look, could it?

Yesterday's late night resulted in the new day making a start without us. Bright daylight flooded the bedroom as I rolled over and checked the clock.

'Have you seen what time it is?'

Melanie yawned.

'What time did we go to bed last night?' she asked.

'I'm not sure, but it was after two.'

We'd been in bed for over eight hours and my back was starting to complain. By the time we'd wiped the sleep from our eyes and finished our morning coffee, lunch was in the offing. Baked beans on toast topped with a fried egg. What better way to start the day?

'What time are we setting off?' asked Melanie.

'Setting off?'

'To the *pazo*.'

Melanie's reminder sent a shiver of anxiety rippling through my body. Second guessing Julie's preferences was impossible. The best we could hope for was that we liked the place.

'Half an hour?' I suggested.

'OK.'

I used the time to check the route on Google Maps and scribble down directions. The estimated driving time was about an hour.

From home we drove towards Monforte de Lemos before following signs to Chantada. From there we picked up the CG-2.1 to Monte de Faro and on to the village of Rodeiro. It's a route we'd taken many times before when travelling to Santiago Airport. Halfway through the village we deviated from our usual route and turned right onto the PO-212. At the town of Agolada, a quick left then right took us onto the PO-840.

'You've written "Turn left after 6.4 kilometres",' said Melanie.

I kept one eye on the mileage.

'That's six kilometres, so keep your eyes peeled.'

'There,' said Melanie, pointing at a sign. 'Next right.'

Exiting the main road brought us to within two and a half kilometres of our destination. The tension was palpable.

'This is nice,' said Melanie, as we drove slowly through the village of Eidián.

'I guess this must be it,' I said.

'Wow!'

Wow indeed. We'd entered a gravel parking area adjacent to the most impressive entrance to a *pazo* we'd ever seem. The property was surrounded by a high wall. Entry into the grounds was through an impressive gatehouse seven metres tall and eight metres wide. We stepped out of the car and made our way towards the entrance.

'Do you think you're allowed to just wander in?' whispered Melanie.

'Of course. Come on, let's find someone and ask if we can have a look around.'

The gatehouse was as deep as it was wide and paved with granite flagstones. Through centuries of use, two parallel grooves had been worn into the flags, presumably by horse-drawn carts. As if to emphasise this, two large wooden cartwheels, shod in iron, were leant up against the walls, one on either side of the doorway. The gatehouse led into a picturesque courtyard. Directly opposite was a sitting area where guests could relax in the shade of leafy grapevines growing across an arbour. To our right and left were a number of geometric-shaped flowerbeds featuring neatly trimmed dwarf hedges, lawns, and shrubs. Enclosing the courtyard to the east were the old coach houses and barns. These had been converted into rooms. The footpath took us west.

'Where is everyone?' whispered Melanie.

The place was deserted. I glanced at my watch. The time was almost three.

'They're probably in between times,' I replied.

Melanie looked bemused.

'Departing guests have probably left and they're waiting for the new arrivals,' I added.

To our right was a two-storey building and straight ahead the restaurant. The reception desk was in one corner but nobody was at home.

'What now?' asked Melanie.

'*Hola!*' I boomed. '*Hola!*'

Melanie glared at me.

'What?'

Her eyes widened, but before she could speak a door opened and a young woman entered. I explained who we were and why we were there, omitting the part about my sibling anxiety.

'You're very welcome to take a look around. Unfortunately, I can't show you the rooms as we have guests staying,' she said.

If the rest of the place was anything to go by, we had no concerns about the standard of the bedrooms, and besides which, we didn't want to spoil the surprise.

'That's fine,' I replied. 'But would you mind if we wandered around the grounds?'

'No problem, go right ahead. If you want anything just let me know.'

We thanked her and walked back outside.

'Let's see what's through there,' suggested Melanie.

She'd spotted a doorway leading out of the covered courtyard. We walked through into a landscaped pasture with flowerbeds and more outdoor seating.

'Look at that,' she said, staring out across the rolling hills of central Galicia.

'Let's order a drink and sit for a while,' I suggested.

'Ooh, yes.'

'Beer?'

'Yes please.'

'You take a seat and I'll ask at reception.'

I wandered back to the desk and ordered two beers. For the next forty minutes we sat in the garden soaking up the scenery and sipping Estrella, the beer of Galicia.

We couldn't have been happier with our discovery. Melanie had gone from lukewarm to boiling hot, and I felt confident Julie would approve.

'Have you seen the weather?' asked Melanie, as she bumped open the bedroom door.

She'd taken Jazz out for her morning constitutional and brought two cuppas back with her. While she'd been away, I'd scooted to the foot of the bed and flung open the window shutters. The morning looked grey, damp, and misty, which was hardly surprising considering tomorrow was the first day of autumn.

'It looks like it might clear up,' I replied.

'What time did you tell Bob you'd be there?'

'Ten o'clock, but I've got to pick some building materials up before then.'

I downed my coffee, wrapped up warm, and hitched up the trailer.

'Right then, I'm off.'

'What time will you be back?'

'I'm not sure, but I should be home for lunch.'

'OK.'

My first port of call was Ramón Otero builder's merchant on the outskirts of Monforte de Lemos. I bought half a dozen bags of ready-to-mix cement and some steel reinforcing rods. When I arrived at *Casa Bon Vista*, I had a decision to make. Should I attempt to reverse down the lane, or would it be better to unhitch the trailer and roll it down? Despite an unparalleled record of failure, I decided on the former. Carefully, I lined up car and trailer and began my manoeuvre. No sooner had I started to move than Bob stepped out into the lane, adding extra pressure to an already tense situation.

The gradient at the top of the lane was relatively steep.

A third of the way down it curved slightly to the right and levelled out. Try as I might, the slightest movement on the steering wheel sent the trailer veering off in the opposite direction. If I wasn't careful, I was in danger of making a bad situation worse and crashing into the neighbour's wall. After five frustrating minutes, I conceded defeat and tugged on the handbrake.

'I think it'll be easier if I unhook it and push it down,' I called to Bob.

To his credit he'd managed to keep a straight face.

'Here, let me give you a hand,' he replied, marching up the lane.

Carefully, we rolled the trailer into position. While Bob wedged a stone under each wheel, I collected the car.

'Right then, where do we start?' he asked.

'I think we should renew this cap before we do anything else,' I suggested.

The metal reinforcing rods would ensure a safe top for decades to come. While I cut them to size, Bob tied them together with wire to form a lattice. Cutting the rods with an angle grinder sent Catherine wheels of sparks flashing through the air.

'That should do it,' I said, as Bob tied the final cross section.

The early morning mist had all but disappeared by the time we'd finished. I glanced at my watch: 11:30 am.

'It's warming up,' I said, removing my fleece. 'See if you can find some stones, about this size.'

I handed Bob a stone and he went rummaging around the plot. While he did that, I mixed the first batch of cement, damp enough to fall between the spaces but firm enough not to run off the top of the well. The stones lifted the reinforcing rods off the old cap, allowing the cement to sit below and above.

'We'll leave that to cure overnight, but it'll need dampening down every so often.'

'How often?'

'Three times should be enough. About four o'clock, eight o'clock, and then before you turn in. Gently mind, you don't want to wash it away. We'll take the day off tomorrow. That'll give it time to harden,' I said.

'OK.'

'I'll see you on Wednesday then, at ten.'

When I arrived home, Melanie was in the kitchen doing some mixing of her own.

'Look what Meli gave me,' she said, pointing at an enormous leek and half a dozen beef tomatoes.

Meli is always giving us something. Lettuce usually, but we've had all sorts of things, from freshly laid eggs to Padrón peppers. Melanie was making today's offerings into tomato and leek soup.

'Isn't a bit warm for soup?'

'It wasn't when I started.'

The weather improved throughout the day. Come dinnertime, I fired up the barbecue and we enjoyed our evening meal on the terrace.

When I arrived at Bob's on Wednesday morning, preparations were well under way. He'd dragged a hosepipe from the courtyard into the garden and brought out all the tools and buckets from the *bodega*. The cap had set solid and watering it ensured there wasn't a single crack.

'Right then, let's make a start on this wall,' I said.

Over time, the more porous stones had disintegrated leaving cavernous holes.

'If the gap is this size, we can fill it with cement, but anything bigger we'll need to wedge some new stones in,' I said, pointing at the relevant sections.

Bob took note.

'Tap them in with a hammer, but don't hit them too hard or they'll go straight through.'

Bob watched while I demonstrated and then made a start on the other side. Having plugged all the holes, we could begin pointing.

'Have you done any pointing before?' I asked.

'No.'

'OK, no problem.'

During the renovation work at *Campo Verde*, I'd become something of an expert in the art.

'Use the back of the trowel to pick up the cement, like this, and then flick it into the joint, like that.'

Bob watched while I demonstrated the technique.

'And then smooth it in, like this,' I added.

I'd made it look easy, but it isn't.

'Don't worry about it being too smooth. Once it starts to dry, we'll feather it in with a sponge.'

Bob watched me for a while then made a start on the other side.

'Bugger!'

'What's matter?' I asked.

'How do you get the cement to stay on the back of the trowel?'

I stopped what I was doing and went to watch.

Bob dipped his trowel in the cement and picked up a dollop, exactly as I'd shown him. Carefully, he lined it up with the section he wanted to fill, but just as he was about to flick it into the hole the cement slipped off and fell to the ground.

'I've done it again,' he said.

'Try picking up a smaller amount until you get the hang of it,' I suggested.

Bob tried again. This time he managed to keep the cement on the trowel but as he went to flick it into the hole it started slipping off and splattered onto the stones.

'Nearly,' I said, trying to encourage him. 'A bit more practice and you'll have it cracked.'

A few minutes later, success.

'Done it,' he said, pleased as punch with his effort.

Two minutes later, 'Bugger!'

Whoops, he'd spoken too soon.

By the time we'd finished, Bob was starting to get the hang of it.

'Right then, feathering.'

'Would you boys like a coffee?' called Janet from the roof terrace.

Perfect timing, and even the sun had come out to play.

'Yes please,' we called.

The three of us sat in the morning sunshine sipping our hot drinks.

'Right then, we ought to get back to it,' I suggested.

Feathering is a much easier skill to master and Bob was quickly up to speed. He even seemed to enjoy it. By 12:30 we'd finished. We stood back to admire our handiwork. Fresh pointing on old walls looks quite odd at first, but over time it would blend in beautifully and, most importantly, prevent this charming centrepiece from falling into ruin.

'Will you be home this afternoon?' asked Bob, as I prepared to leave.

'I think so.'

Melanie hadn't mentioned going out.

'Would you mind if we came down to use the internet?'

'No not at all. Come whenever you like.'

Melanie was outside in the garden when I got home.

'How did it go?' she asked.

'OK. They're going to call in this afternoon. Bob wants to check his emails.'

'What time?'

'I said anytime, why?'

'I've got a dental appointment, but I can go on my own.'

'Are you sure?'

'Yes. It's only for a check-up. By the way, do you remember me saying I'd write to Lyanne and thank her for the illustrations?'

'Yes.'

'Well, I heard back from her this morning.'

'Oh yes, how are they both?'

'They're fine and you'll never guess what.'

'What?'

'Her and Hugh are going to Frigiliana for a week before Christmas.'

'You're joking!'

'No.'

'At the same time as we'll be in the area?'

'Yes. I was wondering if I ought to ask them if they'd like to meet up for lunch or something. What do you think?'

'Why not? It would be lovely to see them again.'

'OK, I'll ask. Anyway, what would you like in your sandwiches, tuna or egg mayo?'

'Egg, please.'

While Melanie prepared lunch, I had a quick shower. After a misty start, things were shaping up into a perfect autumn day: a cloudless, powder blue sky, bright warm sunshine, and not a breath of wind. We made full use of the weather and sat outside to eat.

At 4:00 pm Bob and Janet arrived. He set up his laptop on the dining room table and we went outside.

'What can I get you to drink?' I asked.

'Is it too early for a glass of red?' asked Janet.

'It's never too early. Same for you, Bob?'

'Yes please.'

At 5:30 pm, Melanie made her excuses and drove into Monforte for her dental appointment. By the time she returned, we were on our second bottle.

'I see you've missed me then,' she joked.

'What's that?' I asked.

Melanie was holding a slip of paper.

'It's a flyer. Someone had left it on the windscreen.'

'What's it for?'

'I don't know. Here.'

I opened it out and browsed the advert.

'It's announcing the opening of a kebab house.'

'A kebab house!'

Melanie's surprise was understandable. Galicia has a reputation for great gastronomy, but the closest they get to international cuisine is a pizza.

'I can't remember the last time I had a doner kebab,' I said.

'Me neither. They used to be delicious,' remarked Melanie.

'I've never had one,' said Janet.

'You've never had a doner kebab? Not even after a night on the lash?' I joked.

'No, and I'm not sure I've ever had a night on the lash either.'

The four of us laughed.

'You don't know what you're missing, they're delicious.'

'Really delicious,' repeated Melanie.

'Do you remember that one at the top of Chapel Hill?' she added.

'Do I. I used to walk past it after a night on the town.'

Bob and Janet hadn't a clue what we were reminiscing about.

'Let's give it a go,' I suggested.

'When?'

'Now.'

'Now!' exclaimed Janet.

'Why not? Have you got anything better to do?'

Janet looked at Bob.

'OK. Let's go.'

Somewhat by default, Melanie became the evening's designated driver.

The new eatery was situated in a previously vacant unit directly opposite the Escolapios in the centre of town. First impressions weren't great, but nothing ventured ...

'Come on,' I said, before anyone had a chance to change their mind.

The owners seemed as bemused by our presence as we were with their decor. I'd like to say no expense had been spared for their grand opening, but I can only assume they'd blown the budget on the flyers. What elbow grease couldn't revive had been left for dead. The tables and chairs were a mismatch of outdoor terrace seating, sporting faded brand logos. Some were that old the brands had long since disappeared.

'Did you make a reservation?' I quipped.

The place was deserted.

We took a seat in the middle of the room and one of the owners sauntered over. His enthusiasm was infectious, but whoever he'd passed it on to had long since left. We ordered a drink and read the menu. Janet looked a little nervous. By the time he'd returned, we'd made up our minds.

'Four doners,' I announced.

The kebab wasn't the best I'd ever had, but it was edible. Whether Bob and Janet will ever chance their arm again is another matter.

We returned to *El Sueño* for a nightcap and giggled at the evening's events. Spontaneity has its rewards. The food might not have been memorable, but the evening certainly was.

13

One Good Turn

We couldn't have wished for a better start to our new venture, but exceeding expectations had unexpected consequences. At this time of year, morning temperatures were more conducive to physical work, but Mother Nature had other tricks up her sleeve.

'Don't the trees look lovely at this time of year?' remarked Melanie, as I drove through the narrow lanes of Vilatán en route to *Campo Verde.*

'They're gorgeous.'

I pulled up in the entrance. Melanie hopped out and unlocked the gate. I could see she was struggling to open it and lowered the window.

'What wrong?' I called.

'Leaves.'

'Do you need a hand?'

'I think I've got it.'

When she eventually pushed it open, I could hardly believe my eyes. There were dead leaves everywhere.

'Look at the state of this. It's going to take me ages to rake up all these,' I said, as I stepped out of the car.

'I'll leave you to it then.'

Melanie's play on words didn't go unnoticed.

By the time I'd cleared up, mowed the lawns, cleaned all the garden furniture, and swept the paths and side terrace, Melanie had long since finished.

'Are you ready for off?' she asked.

I glanced at my watch.

'That must be a record. Three hours eighteen minutes.'

'Is that how long we've been here?'

'Yep.'

That afternoon Bob and Janet called in. We'd arranged to take them to the viewing point at Pena do Castelo and, like all first-time visitors, they were blown away with the views.

'How on earth did you find this place?' asked Bob.

'Ian and Kathy brought us,' replied Melanie, as we strolled back to the carpark.

'What time is it?'

Bob had caught me glancing at my watch.

'By my reckoning, it's time for a Teatime Taster.'

'That's a good idea,' replied Janet.

'Where to?' asked Bob.

'What about Club Fluvial?'

I was referring to the café bar Club Fluvial de Doade located at the bottom of the valley. To get there we would have to negotiate a twisting, five-kilometre stretch of road that descends a thousand feet in less than nine minutes. It's a drive that's as visually stunning as it is challenging.

'That would be nice,' remarked Janet.

Ten minutes later we were pulling up outside the bar. As usual there were more cars in the carpark than customers inside. We ordered a drink and took a table on the balcony overlooking the river Sil. During the summer months, the café is a hive of activity with passengers embarking and disembarking from the cruisers that ply their trade on the river. At this time of year, it's an idyllic location with nothing but the birds for company. The only blot on an otherwise perfect canvas was the lack of a tapas menu.

'Would anyone like another?' I asked.

'Why not?' replied Melanie.

'In that case, let's call at A Cantina and see if they're serving tapas,' I suggested. A Cantina is a bar and restaurant in the village of Doade.

'OK.'

The ascent back up the valley is slightly more fun than the descent. It gave Bob the chance to put his foot down and slip up and down the gears.

A Cantina didn't have a tapas menu either, but the young barmaid offered to rustle up a platter of *embutidos* (a selection of cured meats and local cheeses), which we gratefully accepted.

That evening we turned in early. We'd had a busy day and were both shattered. Thankfully, Melanie remembered to set the alarm.

Beep! Beep! Beep! Beep!

Melanie had rolled over and hit the snooze button before I'd opened my eyes. Surely it couldn't be morning already? It felt like we'd only just gone to bed. Five minutes later the piercing tones reminded us of our responsibilities. This time, Melanie switched it off and slid out of bed. By the time I'd wiped the sleep from my eyes, she'd returned with two mugs of coffee. Jazz waddled in behind her and I lifted her onto the bed.

'Have you been a good girl?' I asked.

Instinctively she offered up a paw. I responded by giving her a treat. She wolfed it down and offered me another. I gave her a second one; try as she might, there is never a third.

The new arrivals at *Campo Verde* were Tony and Margaret White, a retired couple who had twice stayed at

Bob and Janet's house. They loved our latest project and happily accepted an invitation to lunch.

'We'll see you on Friday then, and if there's anything you need, just call.'

Jazz had been waiting patiently for our return. Either that or she was fast asleep. Melanie opened the gates and I pulled the car into the drive.

'Come on then lass,' I said, leading her into the lane.

She sniffed around for a while before finding the perfect spot.

Short wanders are the limit of her excursions since her accident.

'Good girl. Come on then.'

She waddled back towards me and stopped for a doggy shake. Until the advent of slow-motion photography, dogs were thought to shake their whole body simultaneously. What actually happens is the shake begins at their nose and runs the length of their body, ending at the tip of their tail. An action that's particularly spectacular when long-haired breeds are soaking wet. After her accident Jazz's gait had been much wider and her actions much slower, but she managed to get by. What I hadn't expected to see was her collapse.

'Melanie!' I shouted.

The tone of my voice brought her running outside.

'What's matter?' she called, as she ran towards the gate.

'Jazz has collapsed.'

As soon as I saw her stumble, I had gone to her aid. Her eyes were open and she seemed surprised to be on the floor. Her first instinct was to stand. Mine was to keep her prone.

'No, just wait,' I said, stroking her head.

'What did she do?' asked Melanie.

'Nothing, one minute she was shaking and the next she'd collapsed on the ground. It was almost as if she'd fainted,' I said.

She tried again to get to her feet but I kept her down.

'Just wait.'

'What do you think we should do?'

'I think we should take her to the vet's.'

'Right, let's go.'

'Come on then. Up you get.'

I kept my hands by her sides as she rose to her feet. She stared at me as if nothing had happened. After everything she'd been through over the last twelve months it seemed a shame to have to take her to the vet's, but better safe than sorry. I lifted her into the back of the car and we drove into town.

After a short wait, one of the practice vets called us into a treatment room. We explained what had happened and looked on anxiously as she gave her a thorough examination.

'She has a very weak heartbeat,' she said.

Melanie's eyes welled up and I felt a lump form in my throat.

'But we should be able to correct it with medication,' she added.

'So it's treatable?' I asked.

'Oh yes. I'll give her something now and enough tablets to see her through the weekend, but you'll need to get this prescription from the chemist,' she said, handing me the slip.

'Give her half a tablet every day.'

'For how long?'

'Forever, I'm afraid.'

Melanie seemed quite upset but Jazz looked none the worse for her ordeal.

'Don't worry. Taking half a tablet a day is a small price to pay for a beating heart,' I said.

The following day Jazz showed no ill effects from her experience.

'What's that?' I asked.

Melanie had been to check the mailbox and returned with a white envelope.

'I think it's from the council. It's addressed to you,' she replied.

I sliced across the top with my favourite letter opener and pulled out an A5 flyer.

As the former owner of a printing company, I was horrified with the quality. The photocopied leaflet had been produced on the flimsiest of A4 pink copier paper and then torn in half. To make matters worse, the original copy had been laid skewwhiff on the scanner resulting in a lopsided leaflet. Horrible didn't come close.

'What is it?' asked Melanie.

'Probably the worst leaflet I've ever seen.'

'Tsk, you and your printing. But what does it say?'

'It's from the council. There's a concert tomorrow night at the Casa de Cultura.'

'What type of concert?'

'A woodwind quartet, by the looks of it.'

Melanie's silence spoke louder than words. I placed it on the wine rack and went outside to set the table. Tony and Margaret would be joining us for lunch. They arrived on time and Jazz was as eager as ever to welcome our new guests. The paella was a great success and our resident pan scrubber confirmed her recovery by licking it clean.

Raking leaves became a daily task at *El Sueño*, not that I was complaining. Without the time pressure of changeover day, the job was quite relaxing and the colours were amazing.

'Bob's on the phone,' called Melanie from the kitchen door.

Thankfully, the morning was dead calm. I left the pile of leaves at the far end of the lawn and walked swiftly up the garden. Melanie handed me the receiver.

'Good morning, how are you today?' I asked.

'We're fine. I was just wondering if you have an electric drill I can borrow?'

'No problem. What are you doing?'

'I'm going to put up a curtain rail in the lounge. Janet bought some curtains last week and wants to get them hung,' he replied.

'Have you got a bit?'

'A bit of what?'

'A drill bit, and what about a spirit level?'

'A spirit level?'

'You don't want the curtains sliding off,' I quipped.

The line fell silent.

'Would you like me to give you a hand?' I asked.

'Would you mind?'

His relief was obvious.

'Not at all. I'll finish what I'm doing and then set off. I should be with you in about half an hour.'

'Hang on a minute,' said Bob.

I could hear Janet in the background.

'Janet said, "If Melanie's not doing anything would she like to come for a coffee?"'

'I'm sure she would. See you in half an hour.'

I finished raking up the leaves, and collected some tools. I'd learnt the hard way that when working away from home it's important to take everything you think you'll need and most of the things you won't. The number of times I'd started a job at *Campo Verde* only to discover I didn't have the right size thingamabob. With that in mind, I loaded everything into the back of the car and off we went. Ten minutes later we were pulling up outside their house.

Melanie and Janet sat outside on the roof terrace sipping coffee while Bob and I made a start. Actually, that's not strictly true, I made a start and Bob handed me the tools. Within twenty minutes the curtain rail was fixed to the wall, safe and secure, and straight and level.

'That looks great. Thank you so much,' said Janet.

Appreciation goes a long way.

'What have you got planned for the rest of the day?' asked Bob.

'*Vendimia* (Grape harvest),' I replied.

'Would you like a hand?'

'If you wouldn't mind.'

One good turn deserves another.

'How does two o'clock sound?' I asked.

'That's fine.'

We said goodbye and headed home for lunch. I was looking forward to this year's *vendimia*. Throughout the growing season the weather had been kind and the vines had thrived. Expectations of a bumper yield were high. After lunch I made sure everything was ready. At two o'clock Bob and Janet arrived.

'Would you like to pick or crush?' I asked.

'We'll crush,' said Melanie.

'I guess that means we're picking, Bob.'

Both jobs involved a similar amount of lifting and carrying, but crushing could be done in the shade. Bob had come prepared with gloves and secateurs.

When we bought *El Sueño* the property was surrounded by grapevines, but winemaking had been the last thing on my mind. That changed when our neighbour Meli offered to help. Even then, I wasn't that keen. Spanish wine is so inexpensive it hardly seemed worth the effort, but Meli had been quite persuasive. She even sent her son, Jesús, round to spray them. That's when I decided to buy my own sprayer and take control. True to her word, Meli showed me the ropes and piqued my interest, but it wasn't until I tasted that first vintage that I became hooked. Buoyed by my success I planted more grapevines. Five years on, those additional vines were the reason my expectations were so high.

'Here you go. We'll start in the front,' I said, handing Bob an empty twenty-five-litre bucket. 'If you make a start on the reds, I'll start on the whites.'

First up was our most prolific vine, a majestic Palomino that was here when we moved in. Through accident and design, it had grown along the training wires and now covered more than ten square metres. The bunches of grapes were enormous: a feature of this variety. Most weighed well over two kilos.

'Have you got any for us?' asked Melanie.

Her sudden appearance had caught me by surprise. For a split second I took my eye off the prize and snipped. The bunch slipped through my grasp and fell to the floor.

'Chuff me!' I called.

The impact sent marble-sized, green pearls scattering across the granite slabs. Others exploded on impact, leaving sticky flesh splattered on the driveway.

'Ugh, that looks disgusting,' said Melanie.

'Don't just stand there, pick 'em up.'

By the time she'd gathered the ones that could be salvaged, I'd half filled the bucket.

'Go on then, you might as well make a start on that one.'

Melanie lifted it and staggered off.

'And don't forget to weigh it,' I called, as she disappeared around the side of the house.

Two minutes later she was back.

'I can't weigh that bucket, it's too heavy,' she said.

I left what I was doing and marched off around the side of the house. Janet looked quite comical standing in an empty bucket in a pair of summer shorts and Melanie's knee-length wellies.

Through trial and error, I'd discovered the best way to weigh the buckets was with a set of handheld luggage scales. I hooked a U-shaped piece of wire through the bucket's handles, attached the scales to that, and held it out at arm's length. Holding it straight and level while reading the scale wasn't easy, especially with the heavier loads, but overall, it worked well.

'Twelve kilos,' I said, before lowering it to the floor with a bump.

Having recorded the variety and weight, Melanie and Janet started the process of crushing. Again, experience had taught us that little and often was the most efficient method. Melanie tipped about six kilos of grapes at Janet's feet. After stomping them into a pulp, she stepped from that bucket into an empty one to avoid standing on the floor. Melanie tipped more grapes into the second bucket and poured the must from the first into the vat, and so it continued. In one bucket and out the other, time and time again until all the grapes had been crushed.

'When you come for the next bucket, bring the scales with you. It'll save me wandering back and forth,' I said.

In my absence, Bob had been soldiering on and had almost finished harvesting the first vine.

'Do these want to go in the other vat?' asked Melanie on her return.

'No, put them in with the whites. When we start picking the Garnacha, they can go into a different vat,' I replied.

Mencía is a red grape with white flesh, unlike Garnacha which has red skins and red flesh. On previous occasions, I'd either mixed everything together or kept skin colours apart. If my winemaking skills were ever to improve, something had to change. I had no idea if this was the right decision, but nothing ventured …

Bob and I kept Melanie and Janet busy and vice versa.

'These aren't the same as those others,' said Melanie on one return visit.

'What do you mean?'

'I mean they're not the same.'

Melanie was referring to the difference between the old Mencía vines and the ones we'd planted. Her comment wasn't a complete surprise. Over the years, I'd asked a number of people to identify our grape varieties. We were initially told the whites were Alicante, only to find out they're Palomino. As for the reds, they were thought to be Mencía and Garnacha. It wasn't until the newly planted Mencía vines started bearing fruit that I had my doubts.

Melanie's observations needed further investigation, but that was a job for another day.

It took a little under three hours to pick the grapes. Ten minutes after that, Melanie poured the last bucket of must into the vat and the four of us set about cleaning the equipment. For the first time in years we had enough grapes to make both red and white wine. With a bit of luck, one of them might even be palatable. I totted up the figures for the final count.

'Well?' asked Melanie.

'Well, it's even better than we thought. We've got 163 kilos of whites, sixty kilos of Mencía (or at least what we thought were Mencía), and thirty-seven and a half kilos of Garnacha.'

'Mustn't forget the half,' joked Bob.

'That's another two glasses of wine,' I replied.

'So, how many altogether?' asked Melanie.

'Two hundred and sixty kilos.'

'And a half,' added Bob.

'Talking of halves, who'd like a drink?' I asked.

The consensus was unanimous. We retired to the end of the garden and relaxed in the warm sunshine.

'I think it's that concert tonight?'

My casual remark stirred everyone's interest.

'What concert?' asked Melanie.

'That woodwind quartet at the Casa de Cultura.'

'Do you want to go?' she asked.

'I wouldn't mind.'

'Have you got anything planned?' asked Melanie of Janet.

'No.'

'Why don't we all go and then you can come back here for dinner,' she suggested.

'That would be lovely, wouldn't it Bob?'

Bob agreed. While they went home to get ready, I jumped in the shower and Melanie rustled up a chicken Madras. A couple of hours later they were back.

The performance was outstanding. Four young female musicians made up the talented quartet: flute, oboe, clarinet, and bassoon. The only disappointment was the size of the audience. Only forty people had turned out to this free event.

The day had started with an unexpected phone call and ended with an impromptu concert. Isn't life wonderful?

14

Celebration

Blustery wind and an overcast sky highlighted the unpredictability of autumn weather. To make matters worse, Julie would be arriving on Friday and guests were due at *Campo Verde*. We could only hope the weather gods looked down kindly on us.

Ring, ring … Ring, ring!

Melanie beat me to the phone.

'OK, have a safe journey and we hope to see you again in the future,' she said.

I guessed from her response that Tony and Margaret had called to say goodbye.

'That was Tony, they're about to leave and he wanted to say thank you and goodbye. He said they'd really enjoyed their stay.'

'That's good. Do you want to collect the dirty laundry this morning?'

'Yes, and we need to pick up Jazz's prescription.'

'OK. I want to turn off the sprinklers and switch on the heating.'

After extensive research, and hours of deliberation, we'd opted for an electric heating system. Purchase costs were low and installing the radiators required no specialist skills. On the downside, running costs were slightly higher but, as we didn't expect to have many off-peak bookings, that didn't really matter. Each oil-filled radiator worked independently of each other which made the system flexible and efficient. The only real drawback was their thirst for energy.

Unlike the UK, every Spanish home is limited to a specific power input. For non-commercial properties this is usually 5.75 kW or less. What that means in reality is when too many appliances are used simultaneously the system will trip out, and I'm not talking about illegal substance abuse. During daylight hours it's an unwanted inconvenience, but after dark it's potentially life-threatening. The house would be plunged into darkness and the box for the circuit breakers was in the downstairs lobby. Having guests fumbling around in the blackness was the last thing we wanted.

To mitigate this risk, we'd opted for the more expensive, programmable radiators. Through a series of stop-start commands, I'd worked out how to keep the house warm and the lights on. In theory, at least. The only flaw in the plan was its reliance on a policy of do not touch, which is guidance guests regularly ignore. We'd gone to a great deal of effort to ensure the house and its facilities were as foolproof as possible; however, the heating system was its potential Achilles heel.

Twenty minutes after leaving home we were pulling up outside the house. I turned off the sprinklers and went upstairs to begin the complicated procedure of programming each individual radiator.

'They've left a lovely comment in the Visitors book,' said Melanie, 'and look at this.'

She passed me a handwritten note.

Dear Melanie and Craig

Having already spent two most enjoyable holidays at Casa Bon Vista our expectations were very high. We were not disappointed.

Your recommended tours are superb and the detailed distances between direction points are a tremendous help.

Restaurant recommendations are most helpful and make interesting reading. Although we didn't eat out very much your comments on the restaurant in Os Peares were very accurate. We had an excellent meal and all for an unbelievably low price.

Our visit to Canabal was a highlight of the week and homemade paella will be a firm favourite back home from now on. Thanks so much for your excellent hospitality and a wonderful afternoon. Thanks also for the picture it will have a good home in Morton.

Thanks to you both.
Margaret and Tony

Ps. We even had a full presentation (in Spanish) by Manuel Gonzalez Rodriguez at Santa Cruz

'That's really nice. It sounds like they had a good time,' I said.

'Doesn't it? Are you going to be long with the heating?' asked Melanie.

Earlier in the year I'd tested the system and formulated a switching schedule. A more pragmatic person would have calculated the output of each electrical appliance, created a spreadsheet based on probable usage, and determined the most efficient use of the available kilowatt hours. I'm more of a trial and error guy; if at first … What I had done was make a note of the switching times. Not only that, but I'd even remembered to bring it with me along with the operating instructions.

'I shouldn't be too long,' I replied.

My confidence was ill founded. In my haste to programme the first radiator, I cocked it up.

'I thought you weren't going to be long,' said Melanie.

She'd taken the linen bag out to the car and then waited outside.

'I've had a slight hiccup, but once I've done this one the rest shouldn't take long.'

'I might as well make a start on the cleaning then.'

By the time I'd successfully programmed all five radiators, the best part of an hour had passed.

'Ready when you are,' I announced.

'Don't forget, we need to call at the pharmacy in Escairón on the way home.'

I waited in the car while Melanie went to the chemist. Five minutes later she was back.

'Chuff me! Guess how much they were?' she asked, as she slumped into the seat.

'Expensive by the sound of it.'

'You're not kidding.'

'Go on then, how much?'

'Ninety-six euros.'

Did she just say ninety-six euros? Surely not.

'No, seriously, how much were they?'

'Ninety-six euros!'

Fortunately, I was sitting down.

'For how many?'

'Twenty-eight.'

'Ninety-six euros for twenty-eight tablets! Are they gold-plated or what?'

'It's a good job she only needs half a tablet a day.'

'Well she'll have to have them.'

'I know. It's just a bit of a shock, that's all.'

I took a few deep breaths before setting off, to let my heart rate calm down. As we pulled into the driveway, Jazz appeared at the French doors wagging her tail to welcome us home. Who can put a price on that?

Over the next few days an improvement in the weather gave us reason for optimism, and an internet search for Fortekor 20 made me feel even better.

'I've found it,' I announced.

'I didn't know you'd lost it,' quipped Melanie.

'Ha ha, very funny.'

'Go on then, what have you found?'

'Fortekor 20 for less than fifty euros.'

'I thought there were twenty-eight in a box?'

'There are.'

'You just said twenty.'

'That's what they're called, Fortekor 20.'

Melanie looked confused.

'I think the twenty stands for twenty milligrams of stuff,' I added.

'Stuff?'

'The stuff that keeps your heart beating.'

'I see.'

'Is that all you can say? That's less than half price.'

'No, I mean yes, that's really good.'

'There's one problem.'

'What's that?'

'They're only available on prescription.'

'We should be able to get one from the vet.'

'You have to use their online form and it's in English. I've printed one off but we'll need to get an official stamp.'

'I'm sure they'll do it for us. We can ask them later, when we go into town.'

'Town?'

'To get your sister's birthday presents.'

I'd almost forgotten.

We'd asked a local photographic shop to enlarge a photo I'd taken of Huddersfield's most iconic landmark, Victoria Tower on Castle Hill. Melanie had also suggested getting her a blouse. Neither item was particularly exciting, but what else do you get the girl who has it all?

The vet was more than happy to stamp the prescription, and the photo turned out great. We found a suitable frame without too much trouble, but a blouse proved elusive.

'I know what we can get her,' I said.

'What?'

'Pedras de Santiago.'

'That's a great idea.'

Pedras de Santiago are toasted almond pieces coated in milk or plain chocolate. They're one of Julie's favourites. We were planning to visit Santiago de Compostela after we'd picked them up from the airport, so we could buy them there.

Juggling Julie's visit around our work at *Campo Verde* was a challenge, but one we were up to. As well as an overnight stay at the *pazo* we had a few other activities planned. Julie hates to be idle. Their flight was scheduled to touch down on Friday at 11:15 am. With that in mind, we readied *Campo Verde* the day before. With the exception of Sunday's Meet and Greet, that left the whole weekend free.

On Friday morning we set off early to Santiago Airport. We'd decided to avoid the toll road and take the N-525 instead. Progress across country was slow.

'We're going to be late,' I said, as we hit the outskirts of Santiago.

'They'll wait.'

By the time we'd made it to the airport, the flight had landed but their passage through arrivals had been slow. No one would ever know we were late. Greeting Julie was as awkward as ever. She has a thing about physical contact so we kept our distance and smiled at each other.

'Hiya,' she said.

'Good flight?' I asked.

By the time we'd walked back to the carpark her mood had softened and she was chatting freely with Melanie. The drive into the historic centre took less than twenty minutes. We parked near the cathedral and made our way to the main square, Praza do Obradoiro. Thankfully, the rain clouds had lifted although it felt quite cool in the shade.

Julie is a creature of habit. We took refreshments in the Parador cafeteria before wandering around the cathedral. On her insistence we dined alfresco at lunchtime, from the *menú del día* at Os Croque Bar in the Praza da Quintana de Mortos. On our way back to the car we stopped at every confectioner on Rúa de San Francisco to sample their Pedras de Santiago, before treating her to a box.

'Would you like to visit a viewing point we've discovered after we drop the cases off?' I asked on the drive home.

'Is it far?' asked Julie.

'About a twenty-minute drive, but we can stop for wine and tapas afterwards, if you'd like?'

'OK.'

I thought that might swing it.

Ten minutes after getting home we were setting off again, this time for the village of Doade and the Miradoiro de Pena do Castelo. The milder temperatures made the stroll from the carpark to the viewing platform far more pleasant than earlier in the season. What greeted our arrival was a spectacular collage of autumnal colours. The terraced vineyards on the southern slopes of the valley had changed from vibrant shades of green to swathes of rich reds and golden browns. On the north facing slopes, deciduous trees and evergreens combined to create an ever-changing kaleidoscope of seasonal colours.

On the way home we stopped at the bar A Cantina in Doade and ordered a *tabla* of locally produced *embutidos* to accompany our glasses of local wine. Julie picked at a few pieces but Jeremy wasn't keen. Cured meats aren't really their thing. Oh well, all the more for Melanie and me.

Back at *El Sueño* we wrapped up warm and sat out on the back terrace. I popped the cork on a bottle of Cava and Julie opened the presents she'd brought with her from home. She even seemed pleased with the framed photo of Castle Hill.

That evening Melanie cooked: homemade pizzas and spaghetti carbonara. We ended the night in style. I'd been waiting for the right occasion to open a 1977 bottle of vintage port. It seemed ironic that it had travelled from Portugal to the UK and then on to Spain, to end up less than three hundred kilometres from where the grapes were grown. Both Julie and I love port, so I couldn't think of a better time to pull the cork.

The following morning no one showed any ill effects from the previous night's port tasting. Melanie had made homemade crumpets for breakfast which went down a treat.

'These would be delicious with Lurpak,' said Julie.

There's no pleasing some people.

'Not that they aren't already delicious. They'd just be even nicer with Lurpak,' she added.

Julie's addendum was her way of acknowledging an ill-judged remark.

'We thought we'd take you on one of our self-drive tours today,' I said.

'What's that?' she asked.

I told her about the book we'd compiled to help guests make the most of their stay at *Campo Verde.*

'This is it,' I said, handing her a copy.

'So, which one are we going on?' she asked.

'We thought you might enjoy the Sanctuary and Scenery tour.'

She flicked through the book and read the details.

'Is that alright?' I asked.

'It looks very interesting,' she replied.

High praise indeed.

The day went remarkably well. Both Julie and Jeremy liked the Santuario de Nuestra Señora de las Ermidas although neither of them enjoyed the winding road to get there. Jeremy treated us to lunch at the restaurant A Nosa Casa, in Viana do Bolo, and on the way back we called at Santa Cruz. I had hoped to introduce Julie to Señor Rodriguez, but he was nowhere to be seen. At O Bolo castle the kestrels had taken flight but Julie got into the swing of things in the museum. She donned the mock armour and posed for photos atop the static steed. On the way home we called at the Hotel Pazo do Castro for a pot of Earl Grey where Julie was in her element.

That evening Melanie cooked a tortilla and made a huge bowl of cheesy coleslaw, two of Julie's favourites. Tomorrow was the big day. We could only hope the weather was nice and Julie liked Pazo de Eidián as much as we did.

Once again, the alarm clock poked us into a new day. Before setting off to Eidián, Melanie and I had a Meet and Greet to attend. This morning's guests were a party of four from Bergerac in France.

'Big smiles but keep it snappy,' I said, as we trundled through the village.

We had a tendency to rattle on and time was of the essence. We'd scarcely introduced ourselves when they enquired about an extra blanket.

'Isn't it warm enough in the bedroom?' I asked, thinking my radiator programming skills might be to blame.

'It's too warm. We had to turn the radiator off.'

Bang goes my do not touch guidance.

'We prefer a cold room but a warm bed. Don't we, dear?' she added.

Her henpecked husband nodded his head subordinately. It was clear who wore the trousers in their relationship. I turned to Melanie.

'There's a blanket in the wardrobe,' she said.

'Yes, we found that one but we're still cold.'

'Oh, OK. I'll find another and bring it up later. If you're not here don't worry, I'll leave it downstairs in the lobby,' said Melanie.

'Right then, we'll leave you to it. If there's anything else don't hesitate to give us a call, our number is in the Guest Information book,' I said, in an attempt to get away.

'Actually, there was something else.'

I knew it.

'Do we need to recycle the rubbish?'

'It's entirely up to you,' said Melanie, before explaining the various options.

'OK, thank you.'

We turned to leave.

'Just one more thing.'

I resisted the temptation to look at my watch.

'Should we keep the driveway gate locked?' she asked.

'Only if you're out for the day,' I replied.

The things people ask.

'Right then, we'll be off and I'll pop up later with that blanket,' said Melanie.

Not only had we spent more time there than we intended, but we were committed to returning later to drop off a blanket. Fortunately, we'd be passing en route to Eidián.

'Why don't you leave the spare blankets at the house?' I asked, as we headed home.

'Because we haven't got any.'

'But I thought you said …'

'We're going to have to borrow one.'

'From who?'

'Bob and Janet. Which reminds me, it's Bob's birthday today.'

'What have we got him?'

'I don't know, what have we got him?'

Point taken.

'I know.'

'What?'

'Let's call at Aguas Santas golf course and get him some balls from the pro's shop.'

'Will it be open on Sunday?'

'Are you kidding! I bet it's their busiest day.'

I had no idea if it would be open or not, but we were short of options.

As luck would have it, the shop was open. Lady Luck was with us again when we arrived at Bob and Janet's. They were at home and happy to lend us a blanket. I only hoped we hadn't used up all our good fortune.

Julie and Jeremy were oblivious to our hectic morning. She'd even had a dip in the pool while we were out.

'Rather you than me,' I commented.

'What time are we setting off?' she asked.

'About three. It'll take an hour to get there,' I replied.

At three o'clock I loaded the overnight bags into the back of the car and lifted Jazz in alongside.

'Straight in and out,' I said, as I pulled into the entrance at *Campo Verde.*

Melanie hopped out and disappeared down the driveway. Moments later she was back.

'They must have gone out,' she said.

An hour later, we were pulling up outside Pazo de Eidián.

'This looks impressive,' remarked Julie.

So far so good.

We unpacked the car and wandered through the gatehouse into the courtyard beyond.

'This is lovely,' she added.

'The reception is this way,' I said.

The receptionist checked us in and showed us to the rooms. Ours was situated directly opposite the restaurant. Five stone steps led to the door. This would be our first look at the room and I felt a little apprehensive. I pushed it open and we stepped inside.

'Wow!' said Melanie.

We weren't disappointed. We could only hope Julie and Jeremy's room was as impressive.

'If this is a double, how big is a suite?' I remarked.

'It's enormous.'

A vaulted ceiling and exposed roof joists added to the feeling of space. There was a dining table and two chairs in one corner and a two-seater sofa, armchair and coffee table in the other. Two windows along the outer wall provided ample natural light and looked out across the landscaped pasture to rolling hills beyond. The centrepiece of the room was an enormous bed.

Julie and Jeremy had been shown to the room below ours. We unpacked and went to check it out. Theirs too was beautifully appointed, if somewhat smaller, but they seemed very happy with it. Seeing the two rooms, I did wonder if the receptionist had got her wires crossed. She'd asked who owned the dog and to my mind, a room on the ground floor would have been more suitable. Nevertheless, Julie seemed happy which was the most important thing.

'Let's have a look at your room,' she said.

I could only hope it stayed that way.

Julie had a good look around and did comment on its size but admitted she preferred theirs.

'Let's sit out in the garden and order a drink,' I suggested.

Julie jumped at the chance.

The weather had improved throughout the day and the gardens had benefitted from the showers earlier in the week. I ordered a bottle of Galicia's famous Albariño white wine and we took a seat in the garden.

The next hurdle was perhaps the most difficult: food. Julie loves food and in particular fine dining. Galicia is renowned for its gastronomy but less so for its high-end cuisine. The menu here reflected this: hearty, peasant-based recipes with large portions. The restaurant was situated in one of many outbuildings and featured a water well, bread oven, and an enormous old wine press. Neither Julie nor Jeremy gave anything away, but if I had to guess, dining was their least favourite part of the stay.

We ended the evening in the lounge, a lofty, two-storey sitting room with a huge *lareira* (a traditional open fireplace which is large enough to stand inside). We ordered a selection of Galician liqueurs and chatted for a while before turning in.

What could be worse than being woken by the piercing tones of an electronic alarm clock or the clanging bell of a mechanical one? Let me tell you, the sound of a dog retching. Melanie was first to react. I blamed my slow response on the previous night's liqueurs.

'Aw Jazz, that's disgusting. Come outside.'

Melanie opened the door and a new day illuminated the bedroom. I rolled over and checked the time. A few minutes later they returned.

'What's happened, and what's that smell?' I asked.

'It's the dog. She's been eating cow poo and thrown up.'

The thought almost had me following suit.

'What can I clean it up with?'

Most of it had landed on her bed. Melanie folded it up and dumped it in the farthest corner of the room. A small amount had slipped onto the stripped floorboards. If we didn't do something soon, it would undoubtedly stain.

'I don't know. Is there anything in the bathroom?'

Melanie had a look and returned with our facecloth. I didn't say a word; now was not the time.

We'd agreed to meet Julie and Jeremy in the dining room at 10:00 am for breakfast. By the time we met up, we'd ventilated the room and Jazz seemed back to her normal self. Hotel breakfasts are never the same without a full English on the menu, but freshly squeezed orange juice, toast, ham, cheese, preserves, homemade cakes, and plenty of coffee helped ease the disappointment.

Julie's fiftieth celebrations ended with Paella à la Briggs at *El Sueño* before a trip back to the airport. Later that evening she phoned to say they'd arrived home safely and enjoyed their weekend away. We'd done our best, and took her at her word.

15

Sunday Lunch

Steamy speech and icy-cold floor tiles are Nature's reminder that winter is on the way. Even the hinges on the bedroom shutters squealed a complaint when I flung them open. Clinging to the roof of the car was a crispy coating of sparkling diamonds, but at least the lawns were frost free.

'It's freezing out there,' said Melanie, when she returned with our morning coffees.

I was sitting up in bed with the duvet pulled under my chin trying to think warm thoughts.

'You're not kidding,' I remarked.

'Were you warm enough in bed last night?'

Admitting I wasn't would bring the curtain down on another Galician summer. We'd had a season to remember and I was reluctant to see it end.

'Were you?'

I'd let Melanie decide.

'Not really. I think it's time to swap the duvet.'

The decision was made and she wouldn't hear any complaints from me.

'What have you got planned for today?' she asked.

'I'm going to clean the pool. With a bit of luck, it'll be the last time this year.'

We finished our coffees in silence, mourning the passing of another wonderful summer.

Cleaning the pool with the Aquavac can be quite therapeutic: gliding it slowly across the bottom, back and forth, back and forth; and despite the frosty start, a clear sky and warm sunshine made it a very pleasant task. I hadn't long begun when Melanie stepped out of the kitchen.

'That was the postlady,' she said.

I hadn't heard a thing but tipped my head in recognition.

'We've had a letter from Lyanne,' she added.

'Oh yes, what did she have to say?'

'You know I'd written to ask if they'd like to meet up while we're in Nerja?'

'Yes.'

'Well, they'd love to. She said she'd ring once they'd got settled.'

We'd had a really enjoyable evening with them at their Wine and Tapas night and it would be nice to catch up.

We made the most of the weather and enjoyed an alfresco lunch, a treat that would become less frequent as the month rolled on.

The Indian summer continued into the weekend. On Saturday morning we racked (cleaned) the wine. The primary fermentation had ended and the young wine needed separating from the solids. It's an essential part of the winemaking process, but my least favourite. Invariably it's cold and damp, but not today. We couldn't have asked for better weather.

Clang, clang, clang, clang!

Jazz rose to her feet and trotted off around the side of the house, barking as she went. Gone are the days when she would jump up and race around. Melanie and I were about to decamp to the far end of the garden and enjoy a well-earned Teatime Taster.

'I wonder who that can be?' said Melanie, marching off after the dog.

'*Hola*,' I heard her call.

Curious to know who it was, I followed her. Melanie was standing at the gate chatting to Manolo and his wife, Julia.

'*Hola*,' I called.

Manolo was the main contractor on the restoration of *Campo Verde*.

'We've been fishing,' he said, pointing at his two lads who were sitting in the back of the car.

'It's a nice day for it,' I replied.

'We thought you might like some,' he said, holding out a bulging carrier bag.

Manolo's offer took us by surprise. He opened the bag and we peered inside. There were hundreds of tiny little fishes.

'What kind are they?' asked Melanie.

'*Pez*.'

His answer wasn't exactly helpful; *pez* is the Galician word for fish. I'd always assumed that budding anglers knew everything about their quarry. Manolo was proving me wrong.

'You can eat them,' he added.

'That's very generous of you, but we couldn't possibly eat all those,' I said, knowing full well Melanie wouldn't touch them.

'They'll freeze,' chirped Julia.

Get out of that one.

Julia's quick reply made me wonder if they were trying to palm them off on someone: us. I could feel the net closing and paused to consider my response.

'Could we take a few. Melanie doesn't like fish?' I said.

Manolo and Julia looked a little disappointed.

'I'll get another bag,' said Melanie, rushing off towards the kitchen before anyone could counter.

Pouring slippery fish from one bag into another was trickier than you might think, especially when one party is trying to resist the good intentions of the other. If Manolo wasn't careful, the day's catch would end up skating across the driveway.

'That's enough,' said Melanie, urging him to stop.

Manolo took the hint and the transfer was complete.

'Let us know if you'd like some more,' said Julia.

'We will, and thank you.'

Manolo, Julia and the kids headed off home. I totted up the day's catch: twenty-two.

That night Melanie gutted ten and I grilled them on the barbecue. To her credit, she did try one, but a small fish, full of needle-thin bones, was unlikely to win her over. I ate the other nine, but give me a sausage any day of the week.

'I think we ought to have the wine tested this year,' I said during dinner.

'Oh yes.'

'Yes.'

'What for?'

I knew she was going to ask that and I didn't really have an answer.

'Well … Now the new vineyard is producing fruit I think I ought to take winemaking more seriously.'

'And how will testing it help?'

My attempt to parry the question had failed. I would have to admit my ignorance.

'I'm not sure, but if we don't get it tested, we'll never know.'

I could see from Melanie's expression that she wasn't convinced, which didn't surprise me as neither was I.

'Where can we get it tested?'

Perhaps I wouldn't need a more convincing argument.

'I've seen people taking their samples to Otecoa.'

Otecoa is our go-to shop for all our agricultural needs.

'OK.'

That went better than I'd thought.

We ended the evening with a few games of backgammon. It was either that or the umpteenth showing of *Gladiator* on the small screen. As usual Melanie seemed to throw all the best dice, or am I just a sore loser?

When the routine of a working week comes to an end, some people find it difficult to adjust. One day is very much like the next, and weekends can lose their appeal. Over the last six months, we'd journeyed in the opposite direction, and I for one was looking forward to getting back to work-free weekends.

'Let's do something today,' I said, as we sat up in bed sipping our morning coffee.

The car was covered with a light frost and mist was clinging to the surrounding countryside, but mornings like this inevitably lead to a bright sunny day.

'Like what?' asked Melanie.

'Let's go out for lunch.'

'Where to?'

'What about Melgaço?' I suggested.

Restaurateurs in Portugal are less reluctant to switch on the heating than their Spanish counterparts. Besides which, there was the added incentive of Sunday shopping to consider.

'Yes please. Shall we see if Bob and Janet want to join us?'

'Why not.'

Melanie made the call and they jumped at the chance. Bob even insisted on driving. His eagerness was probably a consequence of our last trip to Melgaço. On that occasion I'd driven and decided to take the scenic old road out of Ourense. It's a real driver's road, twisting and turning, dipping and diving. On reflection I probably enjoyed it a little too much. By the time we'd arrived in Melgaço, Bob felt a little queasy.

My suspicions were confirmed when Bob chose the more sedate route along the A-52 Autovía de la Rías Baixas. After passing through Ourense the road climbs into the mountains of southern Galicia, a sparely populated wilderness of natural forests and moorland. The one constant is the river Miño which snakes its way through the valley below and marks the border between Spain and Portugal. We exited the highway at the town of A Cañiza. From there the road descends steeply to the river before crossing the border close to the villages of Correlo and A Estanción. Eight minutes after that we hit the outskirts of Melgaço.

The weather had been improving throughout the morning and a blazing autumn sun greeted our arrival. The buildings in the old town looked stunning in the sunlight. It was as if each property had been cleaned especially for our arrival. We strolled through the narrow lanes and alleyways towards our favourite restaurant, Cantinho do Adro. In stark contrast to the deserted streets, the restaurant was heaving. We weren't the only ones taking advantage of the fine autumn weather.

A young waitress guided us to an empty table. We ordered drinks and made our choices. Melanie and I opted for one of my favourite Portuguese dishes, *cabrita* (young goat, slowly roasted). Bob played it safe with *frango* (roast chicken), and Janet opted for *costelos de porco* (pork ribs). As usual, the food was delicious.

After lunch we went for a wander around the old town. It's the perfect mix of new and old, restored and ruined.

'Have you ever been there?' asked Bob, pointing at a signpost which read "Museo de Cinema de Melgaço".

'No. Why don't we take a look?'

'Will it be open on Sunday?' asked Janet.

'I don't know but it can't harm to find out,' I replied.

We followed the sign and strolled up a lane towards the castle walls. The museum was housed in a whitewashed building sitting in the shadow of the medieval ramparts. I walked up to the entrance and pushed the door.

'It's open,' I whispered.

The others followed as I stepped inside.

'*Hola.*'

The greeting had come from a young man at reception.

'*Hola*, is the museum open?' I asked.

The young curator's eyes lit up.

'Yes of course.'

One by one the others joined me.

'The entrance fee is one euro,' he added.

'Is that each?' I quipped.

The young man smiled.

I handed over the money and we followed the clearly marked route. This small and intimate museum consists of objects and machines from the pre-cinema era as well as original canvas posters, photos, and documents relating to the Portuguese cinema industry. An industry that, up until then, I didn't know existed. The majority of the exhibits were donated by French film critic Jean-Loup Passek who once owned a property in the town. For aficionados of the cinema, I'm sure it would be fascinating. For the rest of us, it's nothing if not value for money.

'What did you think?' I asked, as we stepped outside.

'It was alright,' replied Bob.

'If you like that sort of thing,' added Melanie.

Janet laughed.

'I know where we can go next,' said Melanie.

'Where?'

'The wine museum.'

'Now you're taking. Lead the way,' I replied.

Amongst other things, Melgaço is famous for its annual wine fiesta which attracts tens of thousands of visitors from both sides of the border. It's held over a long weekend at the beginning of May. The region is best known for its Alvarinho wines. For me, the Alvarinho grape or Albariño, as it's known in Galicia, is similar to a Vino Verde, but for adults. The area around Melgaço and the neighbouring town of Monção is the epicentre of Alvarinho wine production in northern Portugal.

Melanie marched off down the street and the rest of us followed.

At the end of the street Melanie stopped. It was clear she hadn't a clue which way to go.

'It's this way,' I said.

'Are you sure?' she asked.

'Tsk! Come on.'

Left, right, and left again and we were standing outside the entrance to the Solar do Alvarinho. Melanie and I had been once before and despite us calling it a museum, it's actually an exhibition centre dedicated to promoting the region and its products. It's housed in a renovated manor house and distributed over two floors. The first floor houses the tasting room.

'Come on then,' I said, eager to sample some wine.

Melanie and I led the way. The assistant in the tasting room was keen to practise his English, and even keener to let us taste the wine. We took on the role of pseudo experts, swirling, sniffing, and sipping. Our true credentials were exposed when we swallowed rather than spat. In between tastings we feigned interest in production methods and cultivation techniques, but all we really wanted to do was sample more wine. In the end our embarrassment got the better of us. We thanked our host for his generosity and wandered downstairs to the exhibition room, shop, and bar. After the hospitality we'd experienced in the tasting room it seemed only fair to treat ourselves to a bottle of Melgaço's finest.

'Would you mind if we called at the supermarket before we head home?' I asked, as we strolled back to the car.

'Are they open on Sunday?' asked Bob.

'All day.'

Bob was happy to oblige. I was hoping to stock up on Castelinho, a beautifully smooth red wine from the Douro region.

'Over there,' said Melanie.

Three euros nine cents. What a bargain. I placed a dozen bottles in the shopping trolley and headed for the checkout.

The drive back was a quiet affair. A hearty lunch and a few glasses of wine has that effect. I think Janet nodded off at one point. Within the hour we were back. Jazz had been waiting patiently on the front porch for our return.

'Aw, look at her,' said Janet.

'Are you coming in for a drink?' I asked.

Janet looked at Bob who stared back at Janet.

'Just a quick one,' she replied.

'Do you like roasted chestnuts?' I asked, as we made our way through the kitchen and out onto the back porch.

'I'm not sure,' confessed Janet.

'I didn't use to like them, but I love them now,' admitted Melanie.

'Right then, let's have some,' I said.

Galicia and chestnuts share a long history. In years gone by, chestnuts formed an integral part of the region's diet. Only with the introduction of the humble potato did their popularity wane, but their legacy remains in woodlands throughout the area.

I've always loved roasted chestnuts and after several explosive attempts to bake them in the oven, we bought a specially designed chestnut roasting pan. It's similar in size and shape to a frying pan except deeper. The biggest difference is the holes, one centimetre in diameter and equally spaced over the base of the pan. These allow flames from the burner to lap the sides of the nuts. The secret is to keep turning them. Leave them too long and they'll catch alight, and nobody likes burnt nuts.

When we first moved to Galicia, we would forage for them in the surrounding countryside. Since we bought

Campo Verde, that's changed. Despite not owning a single tree, overhanging branches from our neighbour's chestnut trees provide us with hundreds of nuts. I might moan about raking up the leaves, but harvesting chestnuts is fair compensation.

After collecting them, they need to be spread out across a hard, dry surface. This helps them dry out and prevents the larvae of weevils from feasting on them before we get the chance. A telltale sign of infestation is a perfectly round hole in the husk and a small mound of dust next to it. Before roasting we check each one carefully. Nothing puts you off your nuts like the sight of a barbecued maggot. I doubt it would kill us, but it's not very pleasant.

Janet watched with interest as I chose the plumpest nuts from our stockpile and plonked them in the pan. I lit the burner and placed it onto the flames. There's nothing quite as intoxicating as the smell of smouldering husks. Twenty minutes later they were ready to eat. Try as I might, I can't resist the temptation to taste them before they're cool enough to handle.

'Ow, ow,' I said, juggling a hot nut between my fingers.

'Just wait,' cautioned Melanie, who then proceeded to shell one herself.

'There you go,' I said, offering the first one to Janet.

Nervously, she nibbled the edge. I could see from her expression that she wasn't impressed. Melanie and I tucked in with gusto, and even Bob had a few.

'It's about time we were making a move,' said Bob.

The curtain was falling on another fabulous day. We bid them goodbye and went back into the garden to enjoy the final rays of the setting sun. Our impromptu Sunday lunch had turned into a day of culture. A grand tour through stunning scenery. Food for the mind as well as the body, and glorious weather to boot. What more could you wish for from a quiet autumn Sunday?

16

A Fitting Finale

The holiday season was drawing to a close. On Wednesday, *Campo Verde* would welcome its final guests of the season. The question was, would the weather hold? I checked the forecast. The answer was a resounding no.

'I think we ought to clean the house this morning,' I suggested.

'I thought the next guests weren't arriving until Wednesday.'

'They're not, but the weather forecast is terrible.'

'Oh dear.'

'We can nip into town on the way there.'

'What for?'

'To take the wine to be tested.'

Melanie's eyes widened.

'How much will that cost?' she asked.

'I don't know. If it's too much I won't bother.'

At least she didn't ask how much was too much.

I wandered over to the shed with two empty bottles I'd set aside for collecting the samples. The two wines couldn't have been more different. The first vat contained a mix of white Palomino grapes and Mencía (red grapes with white flesh). The resultant mix was reminiscent of rosé, whereas the wine in the second vat was a deep inky red. I filled each bottle, squeezed a cork into the neck, and went back inside.

'Right then, I'm ready when you are.'

Fifteen minutes later we were parking outside Otecoa.

'That'll be fifteen euros each,' said the shopkeeper.

Crikey! I hadn't expected it to be that much. Melanie's silence spoke louder than words.

'You can collect the results on Thursday and pay then,' he added.

I handed over the samples and we left.

'Perhaps we should accidentally forget to pick them up,' said Melanie, as we strolled back to the car.

The thought had crossed my mind, but I knew she was joking. At least I hoped she was.

A damp misty start had developed into a bright sunny morning. It seemed inconceivable that the weather would change overnight. On route to Vilatán, a golden ticker tape of autumn leaf fall hinted at what lay in store for us on arrival. I wasn't wrong; there were leaves everywhere.

'Before you make a start, can you help me collect the chestnuts?' I asked.

Melanie was only too happy to oblige. Three hours later, the house was ready for the next guests and our stockpile of chestnuts had doubled.

The rain arrived on cue. I rechecked the forecast in the hope of giving the new arrivals some good news, but alas, there wasn't any. Today's guests were Allan and his wife Margaret who had previously stayed at *Casa Bon Vista.* On that occasion, his expertise saved us from making a life-changing mistake. During their Meet and Greet I'd mentioned I was about to try my hand at distilling *aguardiente* (the local firewater). It's a harsh spirit distilled from the remnants of the winemaking process. Allan had listened with interest.

'Do you know the difference between ethanol and methanol?' he'd asked.

Unbeknown to me, Allan was a retired industrial chemist. After admitting my ignorance, he'd alerted us to the dangers of drinking pure methanol. He'd explained that distillation produces two liquids, ethanol, the spirit that gets you blind drunk, and methanol, the one that causes blindness. Under his guidance, we'd managed to avoid the latter and in so doing were able to see the wood for the trees, so to speak. Coincidentally, we were planning to distil this year's *aguardiente* immediately after the Meet and Greet.

'What's the forecast like?' asked Melanie, as I walked into the lounge.

'Not good. If they're lucky they might have a few days of sunshine before they head home.'

'Are we still going to invite them for a meal?'

'Why not? If it's raining, we'll just have to eat inside.'

'Let's invite them for Sunday lunch then.'

'Sunday?'

'Yes. The clocks go back an hour so I'll have more time to prepare.'

Melanie does most of the work on these occasions so I wasn't going to argue.

Allan and Margaret were delighted to accept our invitation and seemed fairly laid-back about the weather.

'Does twelve thirty for one suit?' asked Melanie.

'Perfect,' said Margaret.

We chatted for a couple of hours and then left them to it.

'Let's call in to Monforte on the way home and see if the test results are back,' I suggested.

Melanie agreed.

'*Hola*, do you have the results of the wine analysis?' I asked.

The shopkeeper thumbed through a pile of unsealed envelopes and plucked one out.

'Bricks?'

'That right, Craig Briggs.'

He lifted the flap and pulled out the two analyses. Each one was headed *Asesoramiento Vitivinícola* (Viticulture Advice). He read through the details and scribbled 30–40 next to the words *Sulfuroso libre mg/l* (free sulphates in milligrams per litre).

'You need to add sulphur to them both,' he said, pointing at the relevant information.

I'm sure this was very good advice for anyone in the know, but it meant nothing to me. He handed me the sheets, I gave him thirty euros, and we left.

'Well?' asked Melanie, as we walked back to the car.

'Well what?'

'Well, what did that tell you?'

'It told me I haven't got a clue what I'm doing.'

Melanie wasn't impressed with my flippant remark and stomped off. She had a point, but it's only by discovering our shortcomings we can ever hope to improve. The test results had exposed a cavernous gap in my knowledge, but had left me more determined than ever to fill it. As I chased after her, I set myself a goal: one day I would produce wine I'd be happy to pay for.

As soon as we got home Melanie started preparing lunch and I began setting up the still.

Distilling *aguardiente* is a classic man-in-a-shed activity. It's a time-consuming process requiring a small amount of skill and a large amount of patience. The quicker I made a start, the sooner I'd get to bed.

The chemical process is as straightforward as boiling a kettle. I began by shovelling the remnants of the winemaking process, skins, pips, stalks, and spent yeast into the still. Mine is a hand-beaten potbellied still fashioned from copper. To that I added a few litres of water.

I'd hardly got started when Melanie called me in for lunch.

'Slow down,' she said, as I wolfed down my sandwiches.

'Would you like a coffee?' she asked.

'Will you bring it out to me?'

'OK.'

Back in the shed, I fitted the conical cap to the top of the still and attached a pipe from that to the condenser. Once all the joints were sealed, I lit the gas burner. All I could do now was wait, and wait, and wait some more. The burner heats the contents of the still, causing steam to rise into the cone. From there it drifts along the pipe and into the condenser where it's converted back into liquid, only this time it's alcohol.

By midnight the first drops of methanol had started to drip from the spout of the condenser. I waited until I had four hundred millilitres and then tipped it out in the garden. Two hundred is the recommended amount but I wasn't taking any chances. After that it produces a bottle of *aguardiente* every twenty minutes. I use a Gay-Lussac alcoholmeter, to test each bottle's alcohol content. The first is always the strongest. Ninety-seven percent proof was a good start. By three in the morning, that had dropped to below fifty percent. At 3:10 am, I called it a day and rolled into bed. Melanie was sound asleep, and had been for hours.

On Sunday morning, wind and rain scuppered any hope of serving Paella à la Briggs. Allan and Margaret would have to make do with chicken in pepper sauce accompanied with saffron rice, and a caramelised apple flan and custard for pudding.

'Is there anything you want me to do?' I asked.

'You can set the table if you like.'

Clang, clang, clang, clang!

'Who's that?' asked Melanie.

I stared out of the French doors. To my horror, Allan and Margaret were standing at the gates.

'I don't believe it.'

'What?'

'They're here.'

'Who?'

'Allan and Margaret.'

'You're joking.'

'No.'

'What time is it?'

I glanced at my watch.

'Eleven forty.'

'Eleven forty! Well don't just stand there. Let them in.'

Melanie's command transformed my astonishment into action. I opened the door and went to greet them.

'Are we early?' asked Margaret, seemingly unaware of the time.

'Just a bit,' I replied, leading them up the drive.

'We did agree half past twelve, didn't we?' she asked.

'That's right but it's only eleven forty.'

Allan and Margaret stopped in their tracks and stared at one another.

'Did you forget to turn your clock back?' I added.

'It had completely slipped my mind,' said Allan.

'Me too,' added Margaret.

'Oh well, never mind. You'll just have to take us as you find us.'

'We can go away and come back in an hour if you'd prefer,' said Allan.

'No, come in out of the rain.'

Melanie and I took it in turns to entertain our guests while the other showered. Despite a shaky start, lunch was a great success. We even managed to take coffee and liqueurs outside on the terrace.

Sunday afternoon marked a break in the weather that lasted for the remainder of their stay. Their Visitors book comment was a fitting end to a fabulous season.

Allan and Margaret – Bury St. Edmunds

Our second holiday in this truly special region. We feel sure we shall return for a third time. Wonderful lunches in many places, beautiful countryside, ultra-friendly people and great empathy from Craig and Melanie.

See you again (soon we hope). Thank you.

'I'm going to mow the lawns before we leave,' I said.

'OK.'

I'd not long started when I noticed Melanie standing at the bedroom window trying to catch my attention. I stopped the mower and it shuddered to a halt.

'What is it?' I called.

'I think you'd better take a look at this,' she replied.

That sounded ominous. I left what I was doing and went inside.

'What's the matter?'

'Look,' she replied, pointing at the radiator in the master bedroom.

'What?'

Everything looked alright to me.

'There, I think it's leaking.' Melanie was pointing at an oily residue on the tiles.

I knelt down to take a closer look and noticed a droplet forming on the underside of the radiator.

'You're right, it's leaking oil. Have you checked the others?'

'I've only just noticed it.'

This wasn't good. I rushed around the house checking the others; thankfully, all was well.

'It's just this one.'

'Are they still under guarantee?'

'They are …'

My pause led to another question.

'But?' she asked.

'But we cut the plugs off when we installed them.'

The radiators were designed to plug into a wall socket. For safety reasons we'd asked Félix the electrician to cut the plugs off and connect them directly into the wiring loom.

'Oh, that's not good.'

'No.'

'We'll have to ring the supplier and see what they say.'

'Right then, I'll carry on mowing.'

Ten minutes later Melanie appeared at the front door with a bag of dirty laundry and hauled it into the back of the car.

'What do you want me to do?' she shouted, over the noise of the mower.

'Can you start removing the gazebo cover? We also need to put the garden furniture in the *bodega*,' I replied.

It felt quite sad packing everything away. We had one outstanding reservation, over Christmas and New Year, but there was a certain finality to storing the garden furniture. Throughout the year we'd worked tirelessly to ensure all our guests enjoyed their stay in Galicia. That hard work had been rewarded with some unforgettable memories and lots of wonderful comments. We could rightly feel proud of our efforts. By the time I'd finished mowing, Melanie had untied the cover from the frame of the gazebo. I gave her a hand to drag it off and fold it up.

'This calls for a celebration,' I suggested, as we met in the middle of a fold.

'Watch what you're doing,' she said, as I almost dropped my end. 'What kind of celebration?'

'Let's go to Carlos's for dinner.'

'That would be nice.'

Adega do Carlos is a tiny bar tucked away down an alleyway off Rúa Cardenal Rodrigo de Castro in the centre of Monforte de Lemos. The owner, Carlos, is a larger-than-life character, literally. They serve a wonderful range of tapas and an extensive selection of *raciones*. It's said that size doesn't matter, but when it comes to *raciones* it does. A tapa is a nibble that accompanies a drink. A *racione* is a portion to be shared amongst friends.

'Let's see if Bob and Janet would like to join us. It's much better when there's a wider selection,' suggested Melanie.

'OK.'

As soon as we got home, Melanie rang Climacity, the supplier of the radiators, and I went to check the emails. An audible *ping* signalled a new message.

From: Susan Xxxx
Sent: Friday, October 30, 15:47 PM
To: Craig Briggs
Subject: Re: Holiday-Rentals enquiry – "Luxury farmhouse in a central location."

Hello Craig

Can I go ahead and make a reservation please for one week, Saturday 16 Jan until Saturday 23 Jan.

Please advise me how much and how to pay the deposit.

We have stayed in Galicia before and are interested in seeing the difference between summer and winter. I am sure your farmhouse will be ideal.

Regards from Susan and Howard Field

One year was drawing to a close as another was getting off to a flying start. It hadn't quite sunk in when Melanie burst into the office.

'What size is it?' she asked, holding her hand over the microphone.

Her question caught me off guard.

'What size is what?' I asked.

'The radiator.'

'About this size,' I said, holding my hands apart.

'Not the length, the *potencia* (power).'

'Erm it's …'

My mind went blank. The original order was for three different sized radiators: small, medium, and large. I knew it wasn't a small one; those were in the downstairs lobby and the twin bedroom. That left medium or large. Was it a large one? No, that was in the hallway. It had to be a medium-sized one. Now, let me think. The small ones were 750 kilowatts … I think. Yes, 750 kW. In that case the middle ones are 1000 kW … I think. Yes, 1000.

'It's 1000 kW … I think.'

'Are you sure?'

'It must be … Yes, 1000 kW.'

Melanie passed on the information and the conversation continued. Eventually, she ended the call.

'What did they say?' I asked.

'No problem. They'll send a new one on a carrier. When it arrives, we have to unpack it and use the same box to send ours back. The driver will wait while we swap them over.'

'And the plug?'

'She said it didn't matter.'

Result, but I wasn't surprised. During the order process they'd been very professional.

'By the way, I've got some news.'

'News?'

'Yes, and you're not going to believe it.'

'What?'

'We've got another booking.'

'For next year?'

'Yes …'

My hesitation aroused Melanie's curiosity.

'But?'

'It's for January.'

'Well that's good isn't …'

Before she could finish her sentence, the penny had dropped.

'That's right. We're not here.'

The implications of my admission took a few seconds to sink in.

'What are we going to do? That's the second booking we've taken when we won't be here.'

'I'm not sure. Do you think Veronica might look after the place for us?'

'She might do. We can ask for nothing.'

'I was going to ask Peter if he'd keep an eye on the pool for us while we're off, so we can kill two birds with one stone.'

Peter and Veronica were a British couple we'd met a few years ago.

'Right then, I'd better find out if Bob and Janet want to come with us to Carlos's,' said Melanie.

They like the quirky little bar as much as we do so I wasn't surprised when they said yes.

'Janet said they'd pick us up at eight,' said Melanie.

That was unexpected, but very much appreciated.

'In that case let's have a Teatime Taster before we get ready.'

'OK.'

'Martini?' I asked.

'That would be lovely.'

'Take a seat and I'll be with you shortly.'

Martini, or *vermut* (vermouth) as it's referred to locally, is a very popular aperitif in Galicia, but beware. A Galician martini and lemonade is a very different drink to one you might order in a British pub. If anything, the measures are reversed: a glassful of martini and a splash of lemonade.

Melanie strolled to the end of the patio and slumped into the garden swing. I'd bought her the swing as a surprise birthday gift back in May. At the time, I wasn't keen. They're a bit geriatric, but I have to admit, I've become quite fond of it. Swaying back and forth is very relaxing.

'Here you are,' I said, handing Melanie her drink.

Minutes later I'd drifted into a world of my own, rocking gently in the warm sunshine.

Bob and Janet arrived at eight and we headed into town. We parked in the town's central carpark and strolled the two hundred metres to Adega do Carlos. The streets were quiet and the air felt quite cool. Carlos greeted our arrival with a beaming smile.

'*Buenas tardes*,' he said.

We acknowledged his greeting and took a seat at one of the six tables. Carlos took our drinks order and asked if we'd like a *tapa*.

'We're going to order *raciones*,' said Melanie.

While Carlos prepared the drinks, we read the chalkboard menu.

'I'll pick *tortilla*,' I said.

Carlos's *tortilla* is delicious, thick and firm with a squidgy centre, exactly how I like it.

'What about stuffed mushrooms?' suggested Janet.

'Craig doesn't like mushrooms,' replied Bob.

'I don't mind, you order what you want,' I said.

Missing out on mushrooms usually meant an extra slice of *tortilla*.

'I'll choose *chorichillos*,' said Melanie.

'Ooh yes, we must have *chorichillos*,' said Janet.

Chorichillos are small, plump sausages similar to *chorizo*. Carlos poaches them in cider which adds to their already incredible flavour.

'And *freba*, shall we have *freba*?' suggested Bob.

Freba are thin slices of succulent pork loin fried with garlic and olive oil.

'Definitely.'

Carlos returned with our drinks and took our order.

'And French fries,' said Melanie, as he turned to leave.

'It wouldn't be complete without French fries,' said Janet.

Carlos smiled. A few minutes later he returned with a basket of bread, plates, and cutlery wrapped in blue serviettes. The *tortilla* was first to arrive: half a dozen chunks of thick potato omelette.

'Ladies first,' I said, gesturing to Janet and Melanie.

They each took a piece and then Bob and I dived in. The *tortilla* was cooked to perfection and absolutely delicious. It might not be as exciting as some Spanish dishes but it remains one of my favourites. Next up came a plate of *chorichillos*, sitting in a rusty puddle of sweet paprika and cider.

'Careful,' cautioned Bob, when Janet went to stab one with her fork.

Freshly poached *chorichillos* have a tendency to fight back. Stab them with a fork and they often squirt a jet of fatty paprika over their attacker or an innocent bystander. These plump little sausages literally melted in the mouth, leaving our taste buds crying out for more.

'*Freba*,' announced Carlos as he shuffled the plates around to make room on the table.

The garlic-infused pork loins are flash fried to capture the tenderness. As we feasted, Carlos returned, firstly with the mushrooms, stuffed with a garlic and parsley butter and then with a bowl of French fries, piled high and accompanied with a side dip of rich, spicy *salsa brava*.

'*Que aproveche* (Bon appétit),' said Carlos, as he left.

The four of us tucked in as if we hadn't eaten for a month. Talk about finger licking good. Carlos's *raciones* are excellent.

By the time we'd finished, there wasn't a morsel left. We'd even polished off the basket of bread. We settled the bill and wrapped up warm. Tonight was a night for winter coats and gloves. As we strolled past the municipal park on our way back to the car, reflections of a near full moon shimmered in the dark waters of its ornamental pond. Our autumn feast was a fitting end to a successful first season of holiday lettings, and confidence was high that we'd have many more bookings to come.

17

Size Matters

The following morning, I woke with a start. A thousand kilowatts of power had lit up my cerebral cortex like a paparazzi flashbulb.

'Are you awake?' I whispered.

'No,' moaned Melanie.

'I've just had a terrible thought.'

Melanie grunted.

'That radiator isn't 1000 kW, it's 1300.'

'Go back to sleep.'

'I can't.'

Melanie rolled over and pulled the duvet over her ears. That told me. I lay on my back and stared at the ceiling. Periodic sighing eventually grabbed her attention.

'What's matter?'

'They're bringing the wrong radiator.'

'Who are?'

'Climacity. They're bringing the wrong size.'

'What are you going on about?'

'The small ones aren't 750 kW, they're 1000.'

'So?'

'So, the one in the master bedroom is a middle-sized radiator not a small one. You've told them to send a 1000 kW radiator but it should be 1300. You're going to have to ring them back.'

'Can't it wait?'

'They could be loading it while we speak.'

Melanie rolled over and looked at the clock.

'It's only ten past eight.'

'Not everybody gets to lie in, you know.'

'Alright, if it will shut you up, I'll ring them.'

Melanie dragged herself out of bed and wandered through into the lounge, closing the door behind her. I strained my ears but couldn't hear a thing. A few minutes later she returned carrying our morning coffees.

'Well?' I asked.

'Well what?'

'What did they say?'

'It was a voice message. They don't open until nine.'

'Oh.'

Jazz had wobbled in behind her. I picked her up and lowered her onto the bed.

'Here you go,' I said, giving her a morning treat.

At least someone was happy.

When kept under observation, time likes nothing more than dragging its heels.

'Ahem,' I cleared my throat and tipped my head towards the alarm clock.

'What?'

'It's nine o'clock.'

'Why can't you ring them,' she muttered, as she wandered through into the lounge.

This time, I could hear her talking but couldn't make out a word. A few minutes later she returned. I stared at her, wide eyed.

'Emi is going to speak to the warehouse and ring me back,' she said.

'Emi?'

'The young lady at Climacity.'

I couldn't believe it. She'd only spoken to her twice and she was already on first name terms.

Ring, ring ... Ring, ring!

'That was quick,' I said, as Melanie raced into the lounge.

Moments later she returned.

'Emi said that's fine, they haven't loaded it yet.'

'That's good. We'd better nip up to *Campo Verde* later and pick up the faulty one.'

'We can call to see Peter and Veronica on the way back and ask if they'll look after the house for us,' suggested Melanie.

The drive to *Campo Verde* changes with the seasons, but pouring rain is hardly its best look. Most of the deciduous trees had lost their leaves; only the oaks seemed reluctant to let them fall. Pastures and pine forests provided the colour, but even they lacked their natural vibrancy set against a grey and overcast backdrop.

The radiators are attached to wall brackets, and secured with two screws.

'Hang on a minute,' I said.

'What?'

'This isn't a medium-sized radiator. It's a big one.'

'You're joking.'

I couldn't believe it. I'd made another mistake. I pushed past Melanie to compare it with the one in the lounge.

'This is the medium-sized one,' I called.

'Don't tell me Climacity are bringing the wrong one?'

I walked back into the bedroom.

'I could have sworn this was a middle-sized one. You'll have to ring them when we get home.'

'I will, will I?'

'If you wouldn't mind.'

'So what size is this?'

'One thousand five hundred kilowatts.'

'Are you sure?'

'Certain.'

'What time is it now?'

I glanced at my watch.

'A quarter past five.'

'The office closes at five thirty.'

Murphy's law sprang to mind: "Anything that can go wrong will go wrong".

'You'll have to leave a message,' I replied.

At least disconnecting it from the electricity supply and removing it off the wall mounts was straightforward. I slid it into the back of the car and off we went.

'Where are you going?' asked Melanie.

I'd turned off the main road.

'To Peter and Veronica's.'

I pulled up outside their house and knocked on the door. Veronica answered.

'Come in,' she said.

Peter wasn't at home. We explained why we'd called and Veronica was more than happy to look after the house in our absence.

'I was also going to ask Peter if he'd keep an eye on the swimming pool for us,' I said.

'I'm sure he will,' said Veronica.

'That's great. We'll sort out the details later and run through everything you need to know,' I confirmed.

'No problem, just let us know when.'

As soon as we got home Melanie rang Climacity and left a message. The following morning Emi returned her call.

'What did she say?' I asked.

'The replacement is already en route. If she recalls it, we'll have to pay for the delivery.'

'How much?'

'She'll ring back as soon as she knows.'

We couldn't complain. This fiasco was of our own making. Twenty minutes later the phone rang again and Melanie answered it. After a short conversation she replaced the receiver.

'Well?' I asked.

'They're going to swap it over for free, but we won't get it until Monday.'

Now that's what I call a result.

Meteorologists would have described the weekend weather as changeable. On Saturday it rained on and off all day, but Sunday was dry and bright. Melanie managed to get the laundry washed and dried and we were able to sit out in the garden for a Teatime Taster: red wine, roast chestnuts, and a flaming sunset. What more could we ask. The fine weather continued into Monday.

Ring, ring … Ring, ring!

Melanie answered the phone. I checked the time: 12:10 pm.

'That was the delivery driver for Climacity. He's in Monforte.'

Fifteen minutes later the phone rang again.

'Stay where you are and I'll be with you in two minutes,' she said.

Without a word, Melanie picked up the car key and dashed outside.

'Who was that?' I called.

'The driver. He's parked outside the church. Will you open the gates for me?' she said.

I did as requested and Melanie sped off into the village. It's often easier to meet delivery drivers and show them the way than it is to give them directions over the phone. Shortly after leaving, Melanie returned followed closely by a seven-tonne, high-sided lorry. The driver jumped down from the cab and opened the back. After rummaging around, he emerged with our radiator.

'Is there one to go back?' he asked.

'Yes, but we've been told to use this box. We won't be long,' I said, taking the package from him and carrying it into the house. Carefully, I sliced down the tape.

'You grab that end.'

We lifted it out and picked up the old one.

'What are you doing?' I asked.

'What do you mean, what am I doing?'

'It needs to go your way.'

'My end is in,' she replied.

'It can't be. Pull it your way.'

'It won't go any further.'

'Well it doesn't fit.'

My momentary confusion quickly cleared.

'They've sent the wrong one,' I said.

'You're joking.'

'No, look,' I said, pointing at the label, 'one thousand three hundred kilowatts.'

'You've got to be kidding me. What now?'

'You'd better ring Emi and I'll speak to the driver.'

While Melanie dialled Climacity, I checked that the driver had given us the right one. He had. I went to tell Melanie.

'That's the only one he's got. What did Emi say?'

'She's not working today. The bloke I spoke to told me to send it back.'

'And what about the leaking one?'

'He said we'd have to speak with Emi tomorrow.'

What should have been a straightforward exchange had turned into a nightmare. We repacked the new radiator and sent the delivery driver on his way.

The silence was deafening. I could feel my heart pounding. I placed the ball on the penalty spot and took four steps backwards. One kick stood between me and World Cup immortality. I filled my lungs. The referee blew his whistle.

I ran towards the ball, planted my left foot in the turf and swung my right, *clunk!* My dream of World Cup glory had been shattered by a chuffing radiator.

'Are you awake?' I whispered.

'Did you just kick me?'

'No.'

I thought it best to keep quiet and let Melanie come around in her own time. Twenty minutes passed before she stepped out of bed and wandered off into the kitchen. We drank our morning coffee in silence and prepared for another day in the leaking radiator saga.

'Are you going to give Emi a call?' I asked.

'What time is it?'

'It's just gone nine.'

She couldn't put it off any longer. A conversation followed.

'Pen,' she whispered.

I grabbed a biro and a piece of paper and handed it to her.

'Can you repeat that?' she asked.

Melanie wrote down a phone number, thanked her, and put the phone down.

'What did she say?'

'They're not going to swap it now.'

'Why not?'

'Her boss said we'd messed them around too much.'

'It wasn't us who delivered the wrong radiator. What are we supposed to do now?'

'She's given me the phone number of a place in Ourense that'll fix it.'

'And who's going to pay for that?'

'It's covered under the guarantee.'

Melanie rang the number. The conversation was short.

'A lot of use that was,' she said, putting the phone down.

'Why, what did they say?'

'He said they don't repair Climacity radiators.'

Talk about the right hand not knowing what the left was doing. Melanie rang Emi and explained what had happened.

'What did she say?' I asked.

'She going to speak to him and call us back.'

The saga continued. I felt like an unused extra in a Hollywood B-movie.

Ring, ring … Ring, ring!

Melanie answered it. Once again, the conversation was short.

'What now?'

'Emi said he didn't understand me and I've got to ring him back.'

She dialled again. This time he knew exactly why she was phoning.

'Do we want directions?' she whispered to me.

'Get the address. I'll look it up on the computer.'

Speaking on the phone is difficult enough without transcribing driving directions.

Google Maps made short work of showing us the way. With less than five weeks to go before we headed south for our winter getaway, time was of the essence. In theory there was ample time to get the radiator repaired, but given the events to date, I was feeling a little apprehensive. I slid it into the back of the car, and away we went.

The drive to Ourense took half an hour and I found the shop without a problem. Unfortunately, the man Melanie had spoken to had since left on a callout. All we could do was leave it with the shop assistant.

'When will it be ready to collect?' I asked.

'Give him a ring at the end of next week,' she said.

Her reply sounded like a well-rehearsed statement that committed neither her nor the repairman to a timescale. It also reduced our window of opportunity from almost five weeks to less than three. We wandered back to the car feeling somewhat despondent.

'Let's go to Chaves for lunch,' I suggested.

After the uncertainty of the last few days we could do with a pick-me-up.

'Why not?'

Lunch at the Jing Huà Chinese restaurant is always a treat and as usual, we weren't disappointed.

November's weather had so far provided us with more lows than highs. We'd had a few dry days, but when the heavens opened, there were no gaps. At times, the rain had been so heavy I'd had to pump water out of the pool to prevent it from overflowing. In between showers, I'd spent most of my time raking up leaves and when I couldn't get outside, I'd been searching online for a rotavator.

'Can you call the repair shop today and see if the radiator is ready to collect?' I asked Melanie after breakfast.

The two-week wait had felt like two months.

'I'll do it now.'

Lengthy periods of silence didn't bode well.

'What did he say?' I asked.

'It's not ready.'

'Not ready?'

'No. They've sent off for a part and it hasn't arrived yet.'

'When will it be ready?'

'He didn't know. I've got to ring again towards the end of next week.'

'Next week?'

'That's what he said.'

Our wiggle room had shrunk from five weeks to three and now down to two. Time was running out. All we could do was cross our fingers and hope for the best.

My search for a rotavator had thrown up more questions than answers. Models ranged from small electric powered ones to petrol driven mechanised monsters with prices to match. Looking at online photos was all well and good, but I prefer the hands-on approach. The only problem was convincing Melanie that a 250-kilometre round trip to our nearest DIY superstore in Santiago de Compostela was a worthwhile exercise. What I really needed was a distraction, a metaphorical sleight of hand. Another online search presented me with the solution.

'How would you like a run out to the monastery at Carboeiro?' I asked on Saturday morning.

'Where?'

'Carboeiro.'

'Where's that?'

'It's about halfway between here and Santiago.'

'I've never heard of it.'

'I came across it on the internet and thought it looked interesting.'

'It's not a very nice day.'

My floundering idea required some reverse psychology.

'It was just a thought.'

'I didn't say I didn't want to go, just that it's not a very nice day.'

'So, what do you think?'

'OK, why not?'

The first part of my plan had worked a treat. All I had to do now was close the deal.

'We'll set off after lunch,' I said.

'OK.'

I retired to the office to prepare for the clincher. At some point during the morning, Melanie would inevitably bring me a coffee; that's when I'd strike.

Sure enough, within the hour Melanie came into the office carrying a steaming mug.

'Thanks.'

She turned to leave. My quarry was making an escape.

'What do you think to this?' I asked.

I clicked on a webpage I'd been looking at earlier.

'What is it?'

'A rotavator.'

'It's alright, if you like that sort of thing.'

'I know what you mean. It's so difficult to know which one to get from an online photo.'

'Well don't ask me. I don't know anything about them.'

'It might be better if we took a look at a few and see which was best suited for the vineyard.'

'Well you can do.'

'That's a good idea. What about today?'

'I thought we were going to that monastery.'

'We are, but by the time we've driven there we'll be halfway to Santiago.'

'Santiago?'

'Yes, I was thinking we could call at that big Leroy Merlin superstore. They're bound to have a huge selection to look at.'

Melanie smiled. I think I'd been rumbled.

'They will, will they? In that case, I suppose we'd better take a look then,' she said.

The drive to Carboeiro took just over an hour along the AP-53 toll road. We exited at junction 33 and after a few improvised manoeuvres we joined the PO-6502. The monastery is hidden deep in the Galician countryside and sits on a large meander of the river Deza. From a distance it looked like a ruin, but on closer inspection there was a little more to it. With an entry fee of one euro, I can only imagine the doorman was a volunteer.

The one-thousand-year-old building had clearly seen better days. All the furnishings and adornments had long since disappeared, revealing the bare bones of this magnificent structure and the craftsmanship of those responsible for building it. What remained was a temple to the ingenuity and skill of man rather the pomp and ceremony of a religious faith.

'Well, I think we've had our euro's worth,' I said, as we climbed down the stone spiral staircase of one of the church's two towers.

'I think we have.'

'Right then, let's go and take a look at some rotavators.'

The monastery had provided a fascinating distraction from the true purpose of our trip. The visit to Leroy Merlin proved useful, if not fruitful. Having seen a range of machines I now knew exactly what size I needed. All I had to do now was find one within budget.

That evening we received an unexpected phone call from Bob and Janet. Since returning to the UK their weather had been terrible.

'Does that offer to spend a week with you on the Costa del Sol still stand?' asked Bob.

'Of course, come whenever you like.'

'What about the 31st of January?'

'That's fine. What day is that?'

'It's a Sunday.'

'No problem. Just let us know when you've sorted a flight out.'

'Will do, and thank you.'

We could only hope the apartment was as nice as it looked in the photos. They say you don't really know someone until you've lived with them. We were about to find out if that was true or not.

18

Places of Interest

Seeing is believing. Like many who had gone before us, our pilgrimage to Santiago had given me a clear vision of how to move forwards. Not small, not big, but straight down the middle. I resumed my internet search for a garden rotavator with a renewed sense of confidence. Ebay.es became the focus of my search. A tidy little number in fire-engine red with contrasting black trim caught my eye. Unsurprisingly, the model in question was manufactured in China and distributed through a Spanish company, Agroverd, based in Barcelona. At a cost of 154 euros, it represented excellent value for money. The equivalent-sized machine at Leroy Merlin was over double that price.

'Come and look at this,' I said.

Melanie was sitting in the lounge with her nose in a book.

'What is it?'

'A rotavator.'

'They all look the same to me.'

'Just tell me what you think.'

My limited knowledge of rotavators extended to a week-long loan of Roy's, a trip to Leroy Merlin, and a few days browsing the internet. Melanie knew even less, but it was her blessing I was seeking, not her expertise.

She followed me into the office and sat down in front of the screen.

'Well?' I asked.

'It looks very nice.'

'And look at the price.'

'That seems cheap. Is it alright?'

I hadn't a clue, but it had to be worth the risk.

'It's guaranteed for two years,' I replied.

'Hmm.'

'So?'

'So what?'

'Do you think I should order one?'

'If it's going to make weeding the vineyard easier then I don't see why not.'

That was all I wanted to hear. Twenty minutes later, I'd placed the order and paid the price.

'It should be here by the end of the week. With a bit of luck, I might get to test it out before we go away.'

Melanie gave an exaggerated look out of the window. It was pouring down.

'You'll be lucky.'

The following week began as the previous one had ended: wet and miserable. This November was shaping up to be one of the wettest since we'd moved here.

'What are we going to get Jeremy for Christmas?' asked Melanie, over lunch.

Since moving to Spain, Christmas shopping has taken on a whole new dimension. Nowadays, delivery options and weight take priority. From humble beginnings, brother-in-law Jeremy gained a place at Cambridge University and went on to have a successful career as an architect. It's fair to say he's not the easiest person to buy for.

'I don't know. What do we usually get him?'

'Handkerchiefs or socks.'

'Does anyone still use handkerchiefs?'

'Julie says he likes them.'

'Can you imagine blowing your nose into a square of cotton and then putting it into your pocket?'

'Ugh, don't. That's awful.'

Melanie feigned retching. At least I think she was feigning.

'I know what we can get him,' I said.

'What?'

'A dog lead.'

'A dog lead?'

'Yes, a leather dog lead.'

'Julie's not exactly a head-turner, but she doesn't deserve that.'

The two of us giggled. The thought hadn't crossed my mind.

'I was thinking more about hiding in plain sight.'

Melanie looked bemused.

'When he goes out walking,' I added.

All of a sudden, the penny dropped. When Julie and Jeremy came out for her fiftieth birthday, Jeremy had been telling us about the strange looks he gets when he's out walking.

'Nobody goes walking on their own any more,' he'd said. 'People look at me as if I'm planning to abduct their kids.'

Anyone who knows Jeremey will understand how ridiculous that is, but he was convinced he was being watched. Melanie had suggested getting a dog. Again, those who know him will appreciate how unlikely that is. I suggested dispensing with the dog and getting a lead instead. No one looks twice at someone carrying a dog lead, I'd argued.

'That's a brilliant idea,' agreed Melanie.

I'm not in the habit of wishing my life away, but I couldn't wait for Wednesday. At nine o'clock Melanie rang the repair shop in Ourense.

'It's not ready,' she said quietly.

'What!'

I couldn't believe it.

'Why not?' I asked.

'Apparently, they sent them the wrong part.'

'You're joking. So when will it be ready?'

'They should get the new part this Friday.'

'Well that's something.'

'Or Monday at the latest,' she added.

I'd gone from feeling like an unused film extra to a hamster in a treadwheel.

'She asked me to ring back on Tuesday.'

By then, there'd only be eight working days until we headed south for the winter. The margin for error was shortening with every phone call. Fortunately, each radiator worked independently of each other. At least we could programme the others. As a last resort, there was always the fire.

During the renovation we'd gone to a great deal of trouble to install an open fireplace. Not only did it provided a stunning focal point and give the house a homely feel, it also added a touch of romance. During the installation, our neighbour Pablo couldn't quite get to grips with that concept.

'But the heat will escape up the chimney,' he'd said.

'It's not really that kind of fire,' I'd explained.

His facial expression had demanded an explanation.

'It's for romance,' I'd added.

'Romance?'

'That's right. You're meant to generate your own heat, body heat.'

His expression had become even more furrowed.

'Like in the movies. When the leading actors make sweet music in front of an open fire.'

'That's stupid. What if an ember jumps out? What then?' he'd argued.

No wonder people say romance is dead.

What we hadn't counted on was it becoming an essential heat source. With time running out, it seemed prudent to prepare for all eventualities.

'I'm going to nip up to *Campo Verde* this morning and chop some wood, just in case,' I said.

'Will you need me?'

'If you don't mind.'

'No problem.'

By mid-morning we were ready for off. A veil of thick fog cloaked the Val de Lemos. As we climbed into the hills it cleared to reveal a gloriously sunny day. It wasn't exactly warm, but the conditions were ideal for manual labour. The logs I was intending to split had been reclaimed from the old floors. We'd decided to replace the wooden floors with concrete. Tiled surfaces are far more practical in a holiday rental property. The old floorboards were recycled and went into creating the new roof. Reinforced concrete joists replaced the old chestnut beams which were sawn into foot-long rounds and stacked in the *bodega*. It was these that needed splitting for firewood. Purists only burn oak, but slow burning chestnut is ideal for romantics.

'What do you want me to do?' asked Melanie.

I'd carried one of the biggest rounds outside to use as a chopping block.

'Can you bring the logs out and take the split ones back? Stack them in that corner,' I said, pointing at the spot.

Melanie was much quicker at fetching and carrying than I was at splitting. Within the hour quite a backlog was piling up.

'Just hold your horses,' I said, catching my breath.

'There's loads more,' she replied.

'By the time I've split this lot, I'll have had enough for one day.'

Spending two hours splitting logs is a good morning's work, as anyone who's ever done it will testify. Romance might not be dead, but I wasn't far off.

That weekend we caught our first sight of snow on the mountains to the north. Providing it stayed there, both me and the skiers would be happy. On Tuesday morning, Melanie phoned about the radiator.

'Do you want the good news or the bad news?' she asked.

The fact there was bad news was in itself bad news.

'Bad,' I replied.

'It's not ready.'

'I knew it, and the good?'

'The good news is that the right part has arrived and it will be ready to collect on Thursday.'

'This Thursday?'

I'd learnt from experience to ask.

'Yes, this Thursday.'

True to their word, the radiator was ready and waiting when we arrived at the shop. Eager to find out if it worked, we drove straight to *Campo Verde*. Before mounting it on the wall I wired it into the mains.

'Keep your fingers crossed,' I said, as I switched it on.

The digital display illuminated. So far, so good. I turned up the thermostat. All we could do now was keep our fingers crossed and wait.

'What do you think?' I asked, gesturing Melanie to touch it.

'I'm not sure.'

The bedroom fell silent. I tightened my grip on the casing. Was it starting to warm up, or was I imagining it?

'What about now?' I asked.

'It's difficult to tell. Hang on, yes, yes.'

Who would have thought a warming radiator could bring such excitement to a bedroom?

'You're right. It's definitely warming up.'

What a relief. I dropped to the floor and stared at the casing; not a hint of a leak. I switched it off, waited for it to cool, and mounted it on the wall. From discovery to resolution it had taken an agonising five and a half weeks and involved the manufacturer, the distributor, several carrier companies, and the repair shop. Innumerable phone calls had put Melanie on first name terms with both the distributor and the repair shop, and I'd driven over 150 kilometres fetching and carrying. For the uninitiated, welcome to life in Spain.

Bodies and souls were now free to concentrate on readying the house for the Christmas and New Year guests, and getting ourselves prepared for the trip south.

Veronica joined us at *Campo Verde* for the final clean, to see first-hand how we presented the place. The new arrivals were a young family of three so we decided to go that extra mile and dress the house for the festive season. I had very little to do outside, so concentrated my efforts on decorating the Christmas tree and hanging the Yuletide decorations. We'd even bought presents for them all, gift-wrapped them and left them under the tree.

'What do you think?' I asked.

'It looks lovely,' said Melanie.

We spent the following day packing. Not for the first time, we seemed to be taking far too much.

'What's in here?' I asked, struggling to lift one of the holdalls off the dining room floor.

'Kitchen equipment.'

'Are you sure we need all this?'

'Certain.'

Who was I to disagree?

Eventually, I managed to squeeze everything into the car with just enough space for Jazz to curl up on the seat behind Melanie.

'Have you got something I can cover the windscreen with?'

'Like what?'

'I don't know. An old bath towel or something.'

'What for?'

'So I don't have to scrape the ice off it in the morning.'

Last year's journey south had begun with me freezing my bits off while clearing the windscreen. I distinctly remember the needle-like shards of ice stinging my wrists; once bitten … Melanie unearthed an old towel and gave me a hand laying it across the windscreen. That evening we turned in early and set the alarm clock for 6:30 am. Tomorrow would be an early start.

Beep, beep, beep, beep!

Melanie hit the snooze button and let out a heavy sigh. I felt like I'd been awake for ages. Excitement, anxiety, the fear of having forgotten something, I don't know what it is, but the night before a journey I never get a good night's sleep.

'Are you awake?' asked Melanie.

'I'm not sure I've been asleep,' I replied.

'Coffee?'

'Yes please.'

Before Melanie had returned the snooze pause ended.

Beep, beep, beep, beep!

'How do you switch this chuffing thing off?' I shouted.

Beep, beep, beep, beep!

Melanie burst into the bedroom.

'Give it here,' she snapped.

Beep, beep and silence.

'Where's Jazz?'

'She took one look at me and went back to sleep.'

'I don't blame her.'

Within the hour I'd squeezed the last few items of luggage into the car, removed the towel from the windscreen, lifted Jazz into the back seat, and taken up my position behind the wheel.

'Are you sure we've got everything?' I asked.

'If we haven't, it's too late now.'

On that note, we were off.

The temperature gauge read -5°C as we drove through the village. Everywhere was deathly quiet. We joined the N-120 heading east and sped past Monforte de Lemos. Its iconic *torre* was silhouetted against the dawn twilight. During daylight hours, the scenery along the N-120 from Monforte de Lemos to Ponferrada is stunning. At 7:30 in the morning, the unlit road provided a challenging 100-kilometre drive of undulating twists and turns. On reaching Ponferrada we joined the A-6. From there the road climbs steeply into the León mountains. Two-metre-tall, black and yellow striped snow poles were a welcome sight at the side of the carriageway. The alternative was unthinkable. A service station outside the village of Manzanal del Puerto marked the summit of our ascent. As we began the descent, a tiger's eye rose above the distant horizon. A glorious sunrise guided us past the historic city of Astorga.

The next twenty-five kilometres, from Astorga to La Bañeza, is as straight as an arrow and as flat as a pancake. Running parallel to the highway is the abandoned railway track that once ferried passengers from the capital to La Coruña via Monforte de Lemos. Having skirted around La Bañeza we continued on towards Benavente. At the intersection with the A-52, the volume of traffic was noticeably heavier. We now had to contend with two cars every five kilometres as opposed to one. The next major landmark is the town of Tordesillas on the banks of the river Douro.

'We must visit Tordesillas one day,' I said, as we bypassed the outskirts.

'What is there to see?'

'I don't know but I'd like to find out.'

Less than ten kilometres along from Tordesillas are the vineyards of the Rueda wine growing region. It's an area famous for its young white wines. Row upon row of orderly vineyards lined the highway. Eventually, they gave way to a landscape of rolling hills, rounded smooth through centuries of cultivation.

'Look at that,' I said, pointing to the right.

Minutes earlier we'd passed a signpost for the town of Medina del Campo. It's a small place with an urban skyline punctuated with church towers and spires, but its most outstanding landmark is the fairy-tale castle of Castillo de la Mota. We didn't have long to wait for the next place of interest. Less than thirty kilometres from Medina del Campo is the equally fascinating town of Arévalo. I've never been to Rome or Florence, but I can't imagine another place with more church towers per square kilometre than Arévalo. I made a mental note to add it to our growing list of must-see places.

One hundred and ten kilometres from Madrid, the road merges into the AP-6, a free-flowing toll road that shortens an otherwise arduous trek through the mountains north of the capital. At its highest point the road cuts the top off the Sierra de Guadarrama mountain range. At a length of over three kilometres, the Guadarrama tunnel is a masterpiece of civil engineering. Exiting it reveals the nation's capital, Madrid. We continued on, following signs for the M-50.

Some people refer to the M-50 as the Madrid ring road, but in truth it's a U-shaped bypass around the southern edge of the city. Joining it brought us to the 500-kilometre point of our journey, and for the first time since leaving home, we were surrounded by other road users.

It took an hour to negotiate that part of the journey. By the time we joined the A-4 heading south, we'd been on the road for five and a half hours, and despite being a little over halfway, it felt as if we were on the home straight.

'Sandwich?' asked Melanie.

'Why not?'

We're not ones for stopping, well, I'm not. Instead I prefer food on the go. We've tried pulling over and relaxing, but all I want to do is go to sleep, which is not ideal on a road trip. A sandwich at the wheel is a much better idea. The volume of traffic fell with each passing kilometre. At the village of Dosbarrios we pulled in for our one and only pit stop, to refuel and take a rest break. The term "splash and dash" seemed most appropriate.

'I'll take Jazz for a walk,' said Melanie, as I refuelled the car.

Within ten minutes we were back on the road. Further south the terrain changed to a semi-arid landscape of flat dusty plains. We drove past the exit for Manzanares and continued along the A-4 towards Valdepeñas, another famous wine growing region. Their fruity reds are not to everyone's taste, but I much prefer a good Valdepeñas wine to the more famous wines of La Rioja. Both use the Tempranillo grape, but they taste completely different. The highway passes a number of famous names including Señorío de los Llanos, a huge winery on an industrial scale with enormous stainless steel holding tanks bordering the highway.

Two hundred and forty-four kilometres south of Madrid, we crossed the border from Castile and La Mancha into Andalucía. Without warning, the fast-flowing highway is replaced with a steep, winding, and very challenging stretch of road. We'd entered the Parque Natural de Despeñaperros. To give you an idea of the terrain, the word *despeñaperro* translates to "the cliff where dogs plunge". The road twists and turns, dips and climbs through a stunning river gorge. If we hadn't been on the road for almost eight hours we would have been tempted to stop for a closer look, but with 270 kilometres still to drive we were keen to continue on. Arriving at our destination in daylight was far more important than stopping to take in the sights. It took almost half an hour to travel the fifteen kilometres through the gorge.

Back up to normal cruising speed, it took less than half an hour to reach the town of Bailén where we exited the A-4 and joined the A-44 heading towards Jaén and Granada. From now until we reached Granada the landscape was filled with olive groves for as far as the eye could see. It's hardly surprising that Spain is the world's largest olive oil producer. An hour later we reached the outskirts of Granada, the final stronghold of the Moors.

We continued along the A-44, skirting past the Parque Natural de Sierra Nevada, home to Europe's most southerly ski resort. This section of road had been finished the previous year. It provided a fast-flowing carpet of silky-smooth tarmac as we sped towards the coast.

'Not long now,' I said, as the azure blue waters of the Mediterranean Sea filled the horizon.

One day this excellent stretch of road will merge seamlessly with the A7 coast road; until then, we'd have to put up with a time-consuming detour along the old N-340. We were now on familiar territory. From the coastal town of Motril we drove to Salobreña with its impressive hilltop castle and whitewashed village houses. From there the road hugs the coastline, weaving in and out of small bays before finally joining the A-7 and on towards Nerja. At junction 295 we exited the main road and followed the sign for Maro. We'd rejoined the N-340 heading back along the coast. Leaving Maro behind we continued on, following the coastal contours.

'It should be around here somewhere,' I said.

The exit to Playa del Río de la Miel is nothing more than a dirt track.

'Is this it coming up?' I asked.

'I'm not sure.'

This would be our third visit, but the last was almost twelve months ago. I pulled off the road.

'Yes, this is it. It's down there.'

The track doubled back on itself. After fifty metres a shallow descent took us along the top of the cliff.

'It looks like Francisco is here,' I said, as I pulled up alongside a car parked in the shade of a jacaranda tree.

The clock had ticked around to 5:10 pm. We'd travelled the length of Spain, from Galicia in the northwest corner to Nerja on the southeast coast. It had taken the best part of ten hours and I'd loved every minute of it. It's a fascinating drive of over a thousand kilometres that's filled with ancient history, architectural treasures, and an ever-changing landscape. We'd driven through stunning scenery from snow-capped mountains to dusty plains, and natural forest to spectacular coastline.

'Right then, let's see if he's here,' said Melanie, pushing open the car door.

19

Time and Tide

The name plate on the wall read "*Casa Maria*". It had been made using individually lettered ceramic tiles so typical of Andalucía. The gate was open so we walked through into the small enclosed courtyard and knocked on the front door. Francisco answered and invited us in. After ten hours on the road, the last thing we wanted was a thread to the needle explanation of every element of our temporary home, but Francisco was nothing if not thorough.

'Do you have any questions?' he eventually asked.

'No, that's been very informative, thank you,' I replied, shaking my head.

'If you do think of anything, you have my number.'

'Yes, we do, and thank you once again.'

I shuffled forwards, encouraging him to leave.

'OK then, I'll leave you to it.'

We walked with him to the door and waved goodbye as he closed the courtyard gate. Finally, we were able to relax.

'Look at that view,' I said, staring out of the French doors.

The cottage was perched on the clifftop with uninterrupted views over the Mediterranean Sea. A vast panorama stretching out to the edge of the world.

'Teatime Taster?' I asked.

'That would be lovely.'

Melanie opened the French doors and stepped outside. The balcony was tiny, a metre wide by two and a half metres long with just enough room for two plastic garden chairs and a small round table. I opened a bottle of wine, picked up two glasses and joined her. I'd dreamt of this moment since we first clapped eyes on the place. Sitting on the shores of the Mediterranean and staring out to sea. Watching the sun setting over the distant horizon and listening to the sound of waves breaking gently onto the pebbled beach below. Perfect.

Bright sunshine welcomed us into a new day. There's no better tonic for an aching body. Our first priority was to stock the larder. Apart from coffee and milk, the cupboards were bare.

'Right then, let's go shopping,' said Melanie.

I would happily have spent the morning staring out to sea, but needs must.

'OK.'

Playa del Río de la Miel feels remote, but the bustling coastal town of Nerja is less than seven kilometres along the coast. Within ten minutes we were pulling into the carpark of the Supersol supermarket.

'Look at these,' I said.

I'd spotted some freshly baked teacakes, and when I say teacakes, I mean Yorkshire teacakes or more specifically, West Yorkshire teacakes. For the uninitiated, they're a large bread bun, approximately nine inches in diameter and made from a light, yeast-based dough.

They're sold in either white or brown and shouldn't be confused with currant teacakes which contain currants, sultanas, and/or fruit peel.

'Proper teacakes. I didn't expect to see them,' replied Melanie.

'Let's get a couple and have a sausage sandwich for breakfast.'

I picked two out of the wicker display basket, dropped them into a paper bag, and we marched off to the frozen food section.

'There,' said Melanie, pointing at two different brands of English pork sausages. 'Which one?'

'The most expensive. After all, we are on holiday.'

That wasn't strictly true, but English sausages contain very little meat at the best of times so it seemed prudent to get the most expensive. After completing our shopping, we headed back to *Casa Maria.* Given the hour, breakfast morphed into brunch.

'It doesn't get much better than this,' I commented.

Unlike our mood, today's landscape was overwhelmingly blue. A rippling carpet of aquamarine merged into arctic blue at the boundary of heaven and earth. Closer to home, gentle undulations lapped the shoreline before whispering back into the sea. A golden sun kept us toasty warm, and in the distance, the whitewashed houses of Nerja punctuated a coastline of lilac and green. Complementing this jaw-dropping panorama were the delicious flavours of perfectly cooked, fatty pork sausages, smothered in HP brown sauce and sandwiched between two light, fluffy halves of a freshly baked teacake. What more could we ask for?

Da, d, da, d, da, da, da!

Melanie's mobile phone was the last thing we wanted to hear. My heart began to race. Had the guests arrived at *Campo Verde*, and if so, was there a problem? She hurried inside. I listened with bated breath. She sounded upbeat. Perhaps my fears were ill-founded.

'That was Lyanne,' she said, stepping back outside.

'That's a relief. For one awful moment I thought it might be the guests.'

'So did I, but they don't arrive until next week.'

'Oh, anyway, how are they both?'

'They're fine. I've arranged to meet them in Frigiliana this Wednesday at lunchtime.'

We spent the next few days unwinding, familiarising ourselves with our immediate surroundings, and generally taking things easy. The cosy little balcony became our favourite retreat. There's something quite spellbinding about the motion of the sea and the rhythm of breaking waves. Combine this with an ever-changing collage of colours and it's difficult to pull yourself away. Thoughts drifted from one subject to another, merging together without focus or reason.

'Hello.'

A voice from the clifftop nudged my daydream into reality. I turned to see who it was. Two men were standing on the cliff adjacent to the house. One was much taller than the other.

'Hello,' I replied.

'It's a great view,' he said, tipping his head out to sea.

His accent had a Scandinavian twang. His companion said nothing. I couldn't put my finger on it, but something didn't feel right.

'Yes,' I replied.

I diverted my gaze out to sea and hoped my short reply would end this unwanted interruption.

'Are you on holiday?' he asked.

His question made me feel a little uneasy. *Casa Maria* is nothing if not isolated. Why was he asking? What were his intentions?

'Yes,' I replied.

I didn't want to sound rude, but surely even the thickest of skins would get the message that I didn't want to engage.

'It's a beautiful spot. How long are you here for?'

I turned sharply to face my inquisitor. This really was going too far. Seeing my reaction, he qualified his question.

'I only ask because I'd like to rent the place for Christmas or New Year.'

His admission sounded implausible, but I felt compelled to answer.

'We're here until the 8th of January.'

'Oh, OK. I know Maria. I'll call her.'

I didn't believe him for one minute. All the contact information we'd ever seen was in Francisco's name, not his wife's. I turned to face the sea, conscious that the two of them were still there. An uneasy silence passed.

'OK, see you. Have a nice holiday.'

I turned to face him, smiled and tipped my head. They turned and walked away.

Melanie had been out walking Jazz during this unusual encounter. On their return, I thought it best not to mention it. I didn't want to alarm her. They'd gone, and for all I knew, they were just being friendly.

Before we knew it, we were readying ourselves to meet Hugh and Lyanne for lunch.

'Do you know how to get there?' asked Melanie, as we headed towards Nerja.

'I know how to get to Frigiliana, but you'll have to guide me once we get there.'

'She said there's a roundabout at the foot of the main street and we need to take the third exit.'

On the outskirts of Nerja we picked up the A-7. After eight kilometres we exited at junction 292. From there we followed the MA-5102 up into the mountains.

'I think this is the roundabout coming up,' said Melanie.

Frigiliana is everything a tourist would expect of a popular Andalucían hilltop village. Narrow streets, quaint pathways, whitewashed houses, and brightly painted, wall-mounted flower pots. Even at this time of year, a few late flowering geraniums were in bloom.

'There,' said Melanie.

Lyanne was standing at the side of the road waving her arms.

'You can park over there,' she said.

I parked the car and we went to say hello. It was lovely to see them again and catch up on all their news. We found a restaurant with distant views of the Med, and dined outside in the sunshine. Lyanne was as animated as we'd remembered and Hugh as quiet, but something had changed. Interacting with them as paying guests was very different to meeting up as friends, and despite having an enjoyable afternoon, when it came to saying goodbye, I sensed we might never see them again.

Sunset at *Casa Maria* had quickly become our favourite time of the day. Every evening presented a different canvas. Cloudy or clear, each day had its own uniqueness. That evening was overcast. Shades of blue and grey created a luminous ring around the setting sun and blinding shards of sunlight skipped across the sea, radiating out towards us like the open arms of an amorous admirer. On other occasions, wispy cushions floated slowly across the sky like glowing airships of rusty red and golden peach, and as the sun sank slowly below the horizon, it filled the heavens with a crescendo of bright orange and deep purple.

A few days of changeable weather gave us the opportunity to explore the immediate coastline. From the cottage, we walked up the shallow gradient to the main road and headed away from Nerja. The next bay along the coast is

Playa de las Alberquillas. A well-trodden footpath led from the clifftop down to the beach. Jazz walked out in front, lured by the smell of the sea and the breaking waves.

'Just you slow down,' I called.

She stopped briefly, gave me one of those "hurry up" stares and continued on. The beach was much sandier than Playa del Río de la Miel. Jazz paddled in the sea and barked at the breaking waves. Before long she turned to me.

'What do you want?' I asked, as if I didn't know.

Her eyes were calling "throw some pebbles". How could I resist?

I picked up a few and tossed them into the breaking waves, close enough to tempt her in, but far enough away that she wouldn't chase in after them. Jazz is a paddler not a swimmer. She was in her element and if I hadn't called her away, she would have had me throwing them all day.

Melanie had walked on ahead. In the distance were the remnants of the Torre de la Miel, partially destroyed during stormy seas. *Torres* are a typical feature along this part of the coast. They served two main purposes, to provide a lookout for would-be invaders, and as a defensive fortress should anyone land. As we neared the ruin, the beach narrowed and an earlier rockslide had also blocked the way.

'Do you think we should turn back?' asked Melanie.

Her slow progress had given Jazz and me the opportunity to catch up. Turning back now would mean quite a hike. I felt confident we could make it through the rockslide, around the headland, and back to the house that way.

'No, let's go on.'

Melanie looked unsure. Undeterred, I went out in front to find the easiest route.

'Come on lass,' I called to Jazz.

Jazz's size allowed her to squeeze through gaps Melanie and I had to clamber over.

'Are you alright?' I asked, turning to see how Melanie was getting along.

'I don't think we should be doing this,' she replied.

We'd come to the main blockage which was a pile of very large boulders. I climbed on top of the first one to get a better view.

'Do be careful,' cautioned Melanie.

From my lofty vantage point I could see we were nearing the midpoint of the obstruction.

'This is the worst bit. It gets easier after this,' I said.

'I can't climb up there.'

I looked around for an alternative route. Not only was the surrounding area littered with shed-sized boulders, but the beach was getting narrower as we neared the headland. To make matters worse, I was convinced the tide was coming in.

'If you're quick you can probably walk around,' I said.

This section of the rockslide had spilled into the sea. Waves were breaking against the front of the slip but retreating sufficiently to leave a narrow sandy bypass. If Melanie timed her run just right, she could probably skip around the obstacles without getting her feet wet.

'You are joking.'

'There's plenty of time between breaking waves,' I replied.

Melanie looked horrified.

'You've only got ten metres to cover,' I added.

'Ten metres! I'm not Usain Bolt, you know.'

We watched as a wave crashed into the rocks. One thousand and one, one thousand and two, one thousand and three … one thousand and six and splash, another wave pounded against them.

'You've got at least six seconds. That's plenty of time,' I said.

'Are you sure?'

I hadn't a clue, but there was one way to find out.

'Stop worrying. What's the worst that can happen?'

'I could get smashed into the rocks, dragged out to sea, and eaten by a shark.'

'There aren't any man-eating sharks in the Med … are there?'

'Oh, I see. It's alright if I get smashed into the rocks and dragged out to sea just as long as I don't get eaten by a shark.'

'Don't be daft. The worst that can happen is you'll get your feet wet. If that's all that's bothering you, take off your trainers and socks.'

Jazz had wandered through the fallen boulders and was lying on the beach watching proceedings. Melanie decided that discretion was the better part of valour and removed her footwear. That was the easy part; building up enough courage to take the plunge took a bit longer, and with each passing minute the sea kept creeping further up the beach.

'Go on then,' I urged.

'Just wait,' she replied, swaying back and forth to the rhythm of the waves.

Without warning, she set off, or rather stumbled off. All that swaying had resulted in her sinking into the wet sand. She lurched forwards and by the time she'd steadied herself, a few precious seconds had slipped by. The next wave was on its way. From where I was standing, the outcome was inevitable. Two metres short of rounding the obstacle the wave broke, stopping Melanie in her tracks. The shock of the cold water brought a sharp intake of breath followed by a shrill scream. Jazz sat up to see what was going on and I did my utmost not to laugh. As the wave receded it dragged her trailing leg from under her. Miraculously, she managed to maintain her balance, regain her composure, and make it to safety before the next wave broke.

'There you go. I told you it'd be plain sailing,' I said, as I climbed down.

'That's easy for you to say.'

In the time it had taken Melanie to commit to her course, the advancing tide had crept even further up the beach. If we didn't get a move on, we were in danger of getting cut off. It was vital to reach the headland before the tide blocked our passage. If not, it might be too late to turn back.

'Right then, we'd better get a move on,' I said. 'Come on Jazz.'

Jazz picked herself up and led the way. Twenty metres further along even she was having second thoughts. She stopped to stare at the narrowing beach.

'Come on lass. Not far now.'

I led the way, Jazz followed, and Melanie brought up the rear. By the time we reached the headland, waves were lapping at the foot of the cliff. There was no time to waste. I waited for a wave to run back into the Med and made a dash for it. Wet boots were inevitable, but I managed to avoid an extended soaking. Jazz followed and seemed none the worse for her experience.

'Come on,' I called, encouraging Melanie to follow.

This time she wasted no time and paddled around the headland.

We'd avoided the immediate danger, but there was no time to rest on our laurels. Time and tide wait for no one and we had some way still to go.

Walking on pebbles was hard work. Talk about two steps forwards and one back. Eventually, we made it to the relative safety of Playa del Río de la Miel. I'd been quite anxious at one point but managed to hide it from Melanie. Unfortunately, the elements hadn't finished with us yet. The beach was divided in two by the Miel river. We'd emerged from our brush with danger on the eastern side of the river, which at first glance was ideal as *Casa Maria* was also on that side. Unfortunately, the cottage was at the top of the cliff and the only access road was on the western side of the river. One way or another, we had to find a crossing point.

'It's not very deep,' said Melanie, as we reached the point where the river cut through the beach to the sea.

'It might not be very deep but it is a river.'

Bespoke orthopaedic boots, handcrafted in leather, are not designed for wading.

'You and Jazz cross here and I'll see if I can find somewhere easier upstream.'

'OK.'

Melanie and Jazz paddled across, and I set off inland in search of a footwear-friendly crossing. Covering the riverbank were thickets of sugar cane which made searching nigh on impossible.

'There's something here,' called Melanie.

She'd started searching on the opposite bank.

'Where are you?'

The sugar cane was so dense I couldn't see a thing. The plant shares more than a passing resemblance to bamboo, and seems equally intrusive.

'I'm over here.'

'Bugger!'

'What's the matter?'

In my search for Melanie, I'd tripped over a root and gone headfirst into a clump of canes.

'Nothing, just keep calling.'

'Calling what?'

'I don't know … sing a song.'

'Very funny.'

When it comes to singing, Melanie has the vocal cords of a cat being strangled.

'Recite a nursery rhyme, then.'

Through the thicket echoed Melanie's melodic bard.

'Mary had a little lamb she also had a bear, I've often seen her little lamb, but never seen her …'

'There you are.'

Jazz wagged her tail as I appeared through the undergrowth.

'Just be careful,' she cautioned.

'Is that it?'

'It looks safe enough.'

This section of the river was much narrower than downstream, but the action of erosion had cut a metre-deep channel into the sand. Someone had been here before and laid a single rotten floorboard across the two-metre gap. The fact that it was still here indicated its successful use, but one false step and I'd end up in the drink. Had I been thirty years younger, I might have tried leaping across, but I wasn't.

'If you're that sure it's safe, why don't you give it a go?' I said.

'Because I'm on the right side of the river.'

I couldn't argue with that, but this looked far too risky.

'Let's see if we can find somewhere else,' I said.

'OK.'

Melanie turned around and disappeared into the undergrowth. I gave the plank one final look and then did the same. Further upstream the thickets became impassable.

'Anything your side?' I called.

I waited for a response but nothing. I cupped my hands around my mouth and hollered.

'Is there anybody there?'

'There's nothing this side,' echoed back. 'You're going to have to use that bridge.'

Bridge? I'd seen thicker tightropes.

'OK, I'll meet you back there.'

By the time I'd fought my way to the plank, Melanie and Jazz were already there. I had a decision to make: full tilt, or steady as you go?

'Arc you ready?' I asked.

'Ready for what?'

'In case something goes wrong.'

'If it does, don't count on me to save you.'

'I thought you said it was safe.'

'It is … I'm just saying, if it does break, I'm not going to be able to pull you out.'

How very reassuring.

I decided the best course of action was to step on the bit supported by the ground and shuffle forwards. As soon it started to bounce, I'd make a dash for it.

Slowly I stepped onto the wood and nudged my way forwards. Melanie took a step back.

'Come on Jazz, get out of the way.'

There was no turning back. One small step to midway, one giant stride to safety.

As I reached the halfway point the plank let out a crack of disapproval. I shifted my body weight and leaned forwards. One more step and my momentum would carry me across. In the blink of an eye I'd made it, and even the dog breathed a sigh of relief.

We were still some way from home, but the dangers were now behind us. A manmade road swept around the bay. It was all uphill but finally we reached the front gate. I unlocked it and we stepped into the courtyard.

'Well, that was an adventure,' I said, as we plonked our frames into the garden chairs on the balcony.

'Yes, I think we ought to try something a little easier next time.'

'I think you're right.'

20

The Name's Bond

Our exertions along the shoreline resulted in a great night's sleep. When we eventually woke, the view from the bedroom was more reminiscent of the North Sea than the Mediterranean: every shade of grey imaginable smudged by heavy rainfall.

'How are you feeling this morning?' asked Melanie, as she walked into the bedroom carrying our morning cuppas.

'Fine, which is more than can be said for the weather.'

'No aches or pains?'

'No, all shipshape and ready to go.'

Da, d, da, d, da, da, da!

The sound of Melanie's mobile phone fractured the silence of a new day. She leapt out of bed and rushed into the living room.

'Hello … Oh hello.'

She seemed to know the caller. I waited impatiently to find out who. The conversation continued, but I was none the wiser.

'OK, leave it with me and I'll get back to you shortly,' she said, before ending the call.

'Who was that?' I asked.

'Pedro.'

'Pedro?'

'Celeste's husband.'

For a split second my heart stopped. Celeste and her family were this year's final guests at *Campo Verde.*

'What did he want?'

My sheepish tone reflected my nervousness.

'They've got a problem.'

My heart sank. That was the last thing I wanted to hear.

'What's matter?'

'There's no hot water.'

Of all the things that could go wrong, this had to be one of the worst. No hot water in the middle of a Galician winter is no laughing matter. As if that wasn't bad enough, the immersion heater was downstairs in the *bodega*, an area out of bounds to guests. I racked my brain for a reason.

'I wonder if they've overloaded the system and the power has tripped out.'

'He said he'd checked the circuit breakers and they were all in the on position. What else could it be?'

'I don't know.'

Veronica and Peter had agreed to look after the place in our absence, but all they were supposed to do was ready the house for the January guests.

'I'll have to ring Veronica and ask her to go up,' I said.

I told her what we knew and asked if she and Peter would take a look. Hours passed without a word. The only thing worse than having a problem is not being able to fix it.

Da, d, da, d, da, da, da!

I held my breath. Melanie sprinted inside and picked up the phone. Her tone seemed upbeat. I could only hope for the best.

'All sorted,' she said.

The sense of relief was overwhelming. I'd spent most of the morning trying to figure out the quickest way to get back to Galicia at the lowest cost.

'She said they absolutely love the place and thanked us for the Christmas presents,' she added.

'That's good, but what exactly was the problem?'

'Veronica said she'd only switched the immersion heater on this morning.'

'Switched it on? She can't have done. We did that before we left.'

'Well I don't know. Anyway, it's all sorted and everyone seems happy.'

Everyone except me. I could only think that rather than switch the water heater on, she'd inadvertently turned it off. Although why she'd been there in the first place was a mystery to me. We'd only asked her to ready the house for the guests arriving later in the month.

Throughout the morning the weather had improved. By lunchtime, the rain had stopped and a stiff breeze was doing its best to clear the sky.

'I thought we might go a bit further up the coast this afternoon,' I said, over lunch.

'In the car?'

Given yesterday's brush with danger, the answer was a resounding yes.

'OK.'

After we'd eaten, I lifted Jazz into the back of the car and we set off along the N-340 heading east. We'd covered less than two kilometres when I caught sight of a *torre* perched on the end of a rocky outcrop. I pulled off the main road and drove down a track to take a closer look.

'Wow! Look at that,' remarked Melanie.

It wasn't visible from the main road, but the *torre* was standing in the grounds of a private residence, and between it and the edge of the cliff was a spectacular infinity pool.

'There's an information board over there,' said Melanie.

I parked the car, lifted Jazz out, and we strolled over to take a look. Jazz wandered off; unfamiliar scents were far more interesting. The 16th century tower was called Torre del Pino and was built to overcome a coastal blind spot between Caleta and Torre del Río de la Miel. As for the villa, that was called *Casa dei Italiano*.

'What do you reckon?' I said, tipping my head towards the villa. 'Mafia?'

'Mafia!'

'Who else could afford a place like that?'

'I don't know, but can you imagine staying there for a month?'

Melanie's comment got me thinking. I didn't say anything, but I made a mental note to take a look on the internet when we got back. Who knows, perhaps the owners did let it out. If I didn't look, I'd never know.

'Come on then, let's go a bit further. Jazz, come on lass.'

She waddled back to the car and I lifted her in. We rejoined the N-340 and continued east. A few kilometres further along we crossed the border from Malaga province into Granada and the Costa Tropical. We'd entered an area known as Acantilados de Maro-Cero Gordo where a vast pine forest stretches across two valleys and runs all the way down to the sea. As we navigated a sweeping bend, the valley opened out and we caught sight of the Med.

'What was that?'

I'd driven past an opening where a track descended into the forest.

'What?' asked Melanie.

'That track.'

I slowed and pulled over.

'Let's take a look,' I added.

I checked my mirror and made a sweeping U-turn. A few hundred metres further along, I turned into the entrance and we began our descent into the enchanted forest.

'Are you sure we're allowed to go down here?' asked Melanie.

The entrance was guarded by a barrier but as it was open, I didn't see why not. The track was narrow and had been surfaced with concrete. The top section was steep with tight bends that twisted through the pines. Further down it levelled out and the bends became less severe. On and on we drove for what seemed like ages but was less than two kilometres. Without warning the track opened out into a huge gravelled parking area.

'I bet this is packed during the summer,' remarked Melanie.

I had no doubt, but today only five vehicles had made the trip. At the far end of this vast open space was a single-storey building. I drove towards it. That's when we noticed a second building on the left. The sign outside it read "Restaurante la Barraca".

'Let's take a look,' I suggested.

I lifted Jazz to the ground and we ambled over to the entrance. The sound of breaking waves hinted at our proximity to the sea. When we cleared the end of the first building, the view took our breath away. We were standing on the edge of a sandy beach enclosed within a narrow horseshoe-shaped bay. Undulating waves of azure blue rolled gently onto the beach. In the middle of summer, when the carpark is rammed and the beach is crammed, it might lose some of its charm, but on a day like today, with bright sunshine and not a soul in sight, it was absolutely idyllic. If I hadn't known better, I would have said we'd strolled onto the set of a Bond movie. I half expected a bikini-clad Ursula Andress to emerge from the sea.

A short footpath, through a tropical garden, led to the entrance of the restaurant. I pushed open the glass-panelled door and we entered a large dining room. Standing behind the bar was a smartly dressed waiter.

'Are you open?' I asked.

'Of course,' he replied.

'Can we take a drink on the terrace outside?'

'No problem. Find a seat and I'll be with you shortly.'

We walked through the dining room into a small courtyard and took a seat in the warm sunshine. The waiter came and took our order.

'This is beautiful,' remarked Melanie, as she stared out to sea.

'We must come for lunch one day,' I replied.

We sipped our beers without uttering another word, choosing instead to let Mother Nature make the conversation. Physically we hadn't travelled far, but spiritually we were on another planet.

As soon as we got home, I booted up the computer and searched for *Casa dei Italiano,* but without success. Perhaps it really did belong to the mafia.

Over the next few days the weather closed in, bringing with it grey clouds, high winds and rain, not that the surfers were complaining. The rolling waves made Playa del Río de la Miel a favourite with the locals whose exploits kept us entertained. By Christmas Eve I was beginning to think our traditional Christmas Day barbecue might have to be cancelled.

'What are we going to do if it's like this tomorrow?' I asked.

'I've got a joint of pork we can have.'

Roast pork didn't have the same appeal. All we could do was keep our fingers crossed and hope for the best.

The following morning, the weather gods hinted at a reprieve. Grey sky had been replaced with shades of blue. The ritual opening of presents gets shorter every year.

We'd spent our customary twenty euros on each other and had a laugh at the results. Gifts from others required more serious unveiling.

We spent breakfast on the balcony, staring out to sea and reflecting on how quickly another year had passed. Sausage sandwiches followed by mince pies and coffee helped lighten our introspective mood.

'What do you think?' I asked, tipping my head out to sea.

'I'm not sure.'

A band of cloud had nudged its way over the horizon. It was too early to say if it was heading our way or not.

Da, d, da, d, da, da, da!

Melanie rushed inside and picked up the phone.

'It's a message from your sister,' she called.

'Oh yes, what does she have to say?'

'She's wishing us a Merry Christmas and …'

'And what?'

'I think she's hankering after coming to see us.'

'What makes you say that?'

'She is asking how far we are from the airport and what the weather is like.'

'Tell her we're miles away and it's pouring down.'

Melanie knew I was joking. She sent a reply and came back outside to enjoy the rest of the morning.

By lunchtime the first spots of rain dappled the balcony which meant our Christmas barbecue was off the menu.

'You'd better put that pork in the oven,' I suggested.

We made the most of a damp day with an early dinner of roast pork, sage and onion stuffing, roast potatoes, roast carrots, mashed potatoes, cabbage, and lashings of gravy. We ended the meal with Christmas pudding and my preferred accompaniment, homemade custard. Not a bad substitute, but given the choice I would have preferred a chargrilled feast. After dinner I lit the open fire and we snuggled up in front of the telly to watch a rerun of *Billy Elliot.*

'Cheese and biscuits?' asked Melanie during an ad break.

'Yes please.'

Melanie brought out the cheeseboard and I pulled the cork on a rather fine red wine from the Ribera del Duero region.

Throughout the evening the phone serenaded us with messages of seasonal goodwill from family and friends. Christmas Day on the Costa del Sol hadn't quite lived up to expectations, but tomorrow was another day.

A crack of thunder shook the house and a flash of lightning illuminated the bedroom. All I wanted to do was pull the covers over my ears and block out the sound of raindrops bouncing off the roof tiles.

'It feels cold,' moaned Melanie, as she headed for the loo.

As the morning wore on, the storm drifted inland leaving behind much calmer, fresher air. The storm's disappearance marked a change in the weather and by the following day, normal service had been resumed. Having been starved of sunshine for a few days, we took the opportunity to lounge around the house and enjoy a long overdue barbecue.

We decided to spend New Year's Eve at home. Nowadays we tend to avoid such congregational days, preferring instead to choose when and how we spend our leisure time.

As the clock chimed midnight, we pulled on our fleeces and stepped out onto the balcony. A full moon bathed the beach with light and skipped across the undulating ocean. White horses galloped onto the pebbles before retreating back into the dark water. On the adjacent headland, breaking waves smashed onto the rocks, sending foaming sea spray into the air. In the distance, streetlighting created an ethereal glow over the town of Nerja.

'There,' said Melanie, pointing into the night sky.

The tracer from a celebratory rocket had launched into the darkness. Moments later it exploded in the night sky creating a circular fountain of phosphorescent light radiating outwards from the point of detonation. As one disappeared into the blackness another climbed into the sky. For a brief moment each one stole the limelight before disappearing forever. All along the coast, from Nerja to Torrox and beyond, festive fireworks welcomed in the new year.

New Year's resolutions aren't really my thing. Self-discipline and determination are not date sensitive. If anything, the opposite is true. My character has many flaws, but few would say I lack willpower. Quite the contrary; the term single-minded springs to mind. I do, however, use this time of year to take stock of the previous twelve months, and my ambitions for the year ahead. Gone are the days of financial projections and business plans. Nowadays, I have a less formal canvas and employ much broader brushstrokes.

The weather continued to delight. Only during spring can we expect such days in Galicia. We continued to enjoy our modest surroundings and dined alfresco on barbecued sausages and marinated chicken.

'What time will we need to leave in the morning?' asked Melanie.

We were three days into the new year and we'd arranged to drive up the coast to Mojacar and spend the day with June and Malcolm.

'What time did you say we'd get there?'

'About lunchtime.'

'I'm not sure how long it'll take, but if we set off about nine, that should give us plenty of time.'

That night we set the alarm clock to ensure we didn't sleep in.

Beep, beep, beep, beep!

Melanie hit the snooze button and I rolled over. Five minutes later, the piercing electronic tone battered my dream into reality. Since the beginning of the year, our mornings had developed into a peaceful interlude between sleep and lunch. It seemed a shame to break the habit, but we were looking forward to spending the day with friends and seeing a little more of Spain.

Unsurprisingly, we missed our 9:00 am deadline, but by twenty past we were heading towards Nerja where we joined the eastbound carriageway of the A-7 highway. All too soon our speedy progress was brought to a shuddering halt. Within minutes of crossing the border between the Costa del Sol and the Costa Tropical, the promised highway, connecting the provinces of Malaga, Granada, and Almeria, runs out of the political will, and necessary finances, to complete it. East of the coastal town of Almuñecar, the traffic is diverted onto the old N-340 coast road.

On any other occasion, this meander along the coast would be a pleasure, but when the clock is ticking and progress is slow, frustration takes the edge off the stunning scenery. As we neared the village of Caleta-La Guardia, we caught our first glimpse of the castle of Salobreña sitting regally above the town's whitewashed houses. From there we skirted past Motril and on to the instantly forgettable Torrenueva Costa. We'd driven into Spain's vegetable garden. Mile after mile of steel framed, plastic covered agricultural warehouses occupy every inch of the flat fertile plains from the edge of the Mediterranean to the mountains inland.

The town of Calahonda marked a change. From here the road rose steeply, climbing to the top of the cliffs. Open countryside allowed me to pick up the pace. The road twists and turns as it follows the contours of the coast and offers outstanding views of the coastline and the sea. From the clifftop we dropped down into the town of

Castell de Ferro after which the next Bedouin-style encampment of plastic covered fields blanketed the landscape. Once again, the route teased us with another completed section of the A-7. An unblemished carpet of tarmac sliced its way along the coast but our joy was short-lived. The section came to an end and we were diverted back onto the old coast road at the village of Castillo de Baños.

'Isn't this where we stopped for Sunday lunch last year?' asked Melanie.

'Yes. It's coming up on the right.'

'There it is, Restaurante el Paraiso.'

'That's the one.'

'It was lovely there, right next to the sea.'

We continued on until we reached the town of La Rábita where we rejoined the A-7. Finally, I could put my foot down. We covered the next seventy kilometres in a little over half an hour and reached the port of Almeria. This sprawling city occupies a sweeping bay. The angle of the sun, and remnants of a sea mist, made it difficult to distinguish the city's landmarks, except for one: the Alcazabar de Almeria, a fortified Moorish complex second only in size to the Alhambra Palace in Granada. The time ticked past 11:00 am as we sped around the outskirts of the city.

Beyond Almeria the landscape changed to mile after mile of semi-desert scrubland, devoid of trees. The scenery was unappealing, but the road was fabulous and the traffic light. We made good progress and forty minutes later exited the highway following signs to Mojacar. The old town is perched on a hilltop almost two kilometres from the sea, but we were heading for the coast and Mojacar Playa.

June and Malcolm lived in an apartment complex metres from the beach, but due to its design we could have been anywhere, which seemed a real shame. As for Mojacar Playa, underwhelming would be an appropriate description. The resort runs along an unwavering stretch of coastline for over four kilometres with very little of interest except the support services of summer tourism. At this time of year, it feels abandoned, even neglected. Malcolm didn't mind the peace and quiet, but June disliked the dull winters almost as much as the stiflingly hot summers.

'We'll take a drive up to the old town,' said June, after whisking us along the front.

The old town had a little more character, but we'd visited far prettier whitewashed Spanish villages.

'It's much livelier during the holiday season when the beachside *chiringuitos* (bars) are open,' admitted Malcolm.

June had made a lovely lunch and it's always interesting to visit new places, but we wouldn't be rushing back to Mojacar. We spent five hours with them before hitting the road and heading home. By the time we reached *Casa Maria* it was 8:00 pm, just enough time to enjoy a Teatime Taster on the balcony before dinner in front of the telly.

Our four-week stay at *Casa Maria* was drawing to a close. The weather hadn't been the best, but even that couldn't dampen our enjoyment of this very special place. We spent most of Thursday packing in readiness for our move.

'I'm going to miss this place,' said Melanie.

'Me too, but look on the bright side, the apartment in Elviria has a dishwasher.'

'I can't wait,' she joked.

'Let's take the dog for a walk along the beach before our Teatime Taster,' I suggested.

At times it felt as if we'd had the entire bay to ourselves, probably because we did. With the exception of a few New Year's Day walkers, and the odd surfer, we'd hardly seen a soul.

'What do you say, Jazz?' I added.

On hearing her name, she hauled herself up from her bed and wagged her tail. The mind was willing, but the body less so.

'Come on then.'

Jazz waddled towards the front door and Melanie and I followed.

The walk to the beach was all downhill. We followed the horseshoe-shaped descent around the bay and down past the abandoned paper mill. At the bottom of the hill, a narrow footpath ran between the sugar canes and onto the beach. Jazz walked ahead, keen to paddle in the breaking waves. Melanie and I followed, hand in hand. Suddenly and unexpectedly, a figure emerged from the canes, giving us quite a scare. Melanie jumped and giggled nervously.

'*Hola*,' I said.

The mysterious stranger said nothing but tipped his head to acknowledge my greeting. We walked on, but not before I caught sight of a scooter hidden in the undergrowth.

'I wonder what he's doing?' asked Melanie.

I had no idea, but I didn't like it. He looked out of place and up to no good. I didn't want to alarm her so said he might be fishing. Melanie seemed satisfied and we walked on.

Having strolled the length of the bay we turned around and walked back. I sensed we were being watched, but couldn't see anyone. Perhaps I was imagining it.

'Come on Jazz,' I called.

She'd had a great time paddling in the sea and barking at the breaking waves. When we reached the path, there was no sign of the mysterious loiterer. That evening, I made doubly sure all the doors were locked and the security bars on the balcony bolted. If anyone was up to no good, they wouldn't be breaking in here without a fight.

21

On the Pull

Without an alarm clock, the transition from dreamland to reality is usually smooth. The mind drifts seamlessly from unconsciousness into consciousness. Friday morning was one of those occasions. Pink Floyd's *The Wall* was playing in the background. After a while, I noticed the needle had stuck. The helicopter intro to the song "The Happiest Days Of Our Lives" kept repeating. That's when reality kicked in. There wasn't a record player in the house, and I don't own a copy of *The Wall.*

Slowly, I opened my eyes. I was awake but I could still hear the helicopter fading in and out as if circling overhead.

'Are you awake?' I asked.

'I've been awake for ages.'

'Is that a helicopter?'

Melanie glared at me.

'Of course it's a helicopter.'

'I wonder what they're doing.'

'Besides keeping me awake, I've no idea. Coffee?'

'Yes please.'

Melanie pulled on her dressing gown and wandered into the living room. I heard her fill the kettle and take Jazz outside for her morning constitutional. Moments later, Jazz waddled into the bedroom and I lifted her onto the bed.

'It's the police,' said Melanie.

'The police?'

'Yes. It's a police helicopter and there are two officers on the beach.'

'On the beach?'

'Yes, there's a boat.'

Melanie wasn't making any sense.

'A boat?'

'Yes. It's beached on the beach.'

She smiled. It was a bit too early for bad jokes.

'There's a boat on the beach and it's beached?' I repeated.

'Yes. A speedboat.'

Was I still dreaming?

A gulp of coffee ended that theory. Melanie had aroused my curiosity. I couldn't wait to see what was going on. We finished our coffees, pulled on some clothes, and headed out onto the balcony. The scene was as Melanie had described it except the speedboat looked more like an offshore powerboat to me, but instead of bright paintwork and sponsors' logos this one had been camouflaged in military green. In the parking area leading to the beach was a four-wheel drive vehicle. Its Guardia Civil livery was unmistakable and next to that was another, unmarked car. The powerboat was being pored over by four men, presumably detectives or CSI. The two officers of the Guardia Civil were in close attendance.

'It looks like the helicopter has gone,' I remarked.

'What do you think happened?' asked Melanie.

'I bet it's drug smugglers from Morocco, or people traffickers.'

'But why did they leave the boat?'

'I don't suppose they had a choice.'

'Why didn't they push it back into the sea?'

'Are you joking? Look at the size of it. I bet it weighs a ton.'

'That's a shame, it looks really nice. Apart from the colour. I'm not keen on green.'

'Hark at you. It's not an international boat show, you know.'

'I wonder what they'll do with it?'

'I don't know. Don't the police auction these things off every once in a while?'

'Perhaps we can put in a bid.'

'It wouldn't surprise me if the same people who parked it there buy it back,' I joked.

The disappearance of the helicopter was followed an hour or so later by the arrival of two motorboats. The weather was quite overcast and windy and the sea looked grey and foreboding.

'Anything happening?' asked Melanie, who'd started packing the kitchen items in readiness for tomorrow's departure.

'Those two boats have turned up,' I said, pointing out to sea.

'What for?'

'I'm not sure. They might be going to tow the other one away.'

My statement got me thinking.

'I bet that's what he was doing,' I said.

'Who?'

'That bloke last night on the beach.'

'What was he doing?'

'Acting as a lookout or signalman.'

'Are you sure?'

'How on earth did they manage to beach that boat directly opposite the entrance? Don't forget, there was no moon last night and look how choppy the sea is. I bet he guided them in with a torch or something.'

'Crikey! If he was a baddie he might have had a gun.'

The colour drained from Melanie's face.

'Don't worry, it's done now.'

'But if they knew we were here they might have broken in and tied us up or something.'

'Well they didn't.'

That's when a second thought occurred to me.

'I wonder if that's why that Scandinavian chap was asking all those questions.'

'What Scandinavian chap?'

My slip required an explanation.

'Why didn't you tell me?'

'I didn't want to worry you. Anyway, it's over now and they're not likely to come back.'

While I'd been conjuring up my conspiracy theory, the forensic guys and detectives had gathered their evidence and left. The two Guardia Civil officers remained to guard their prize. Even from our lofty position I could see they were immaculately dressed, but they always are.

By lunchtime the weather had improved. The sea remained choppy, but the clouds had rolled inland leaving behind blue sky and warm sunshine. For the last hour, the two motorboats had been tethered together. The three occupants were deep in conversation. After much deliberation it seemed they'd agreed on a strategy to refloat the stricken vessel. The boat with two people aboard manoeuvred closer to the beach.

'What are they doing now?' asked Melanie.

'I think he's trying to offload his passenger.'

'In these conditions. They must be crazy.'

The swell wasn't ideal for surfing but it wasn't far off. The captain of the launch faced a delicate balancing act.

He needed to position his craft close enough to shore to offload his colleague yet far enough away that the breaking waves didn't beach it.

'What is he playing at?'

Just as it appeared he'd miscalculated, the captain hit the throttle and powered the boat out of harm's way. Time and time again he tried to manoeuvre his vessel within striking distance of the beach, and time and time again the swell got the better of him.

'He's going to jump!' I said.

The crewman had moved to the side of the boat.

'Surely not.'

'He is.'

In one seamless motion he flung his legs over the side and, clutching on for dear life, lowered himself into the water.

'I bet that's cold,' I remarked.

In the time it had taken him to build up enough courage to jump, the vessel had drifted perilously close to the point where the waves were breaking.

'He's going to have to let go,' I said.

Just as it seemed the craft would be washed ashore the crewman released his grip and the captain powered his vessel out to sea, leaving his colleague at the mercy of the waves. Even with a life jacket on, the man was dragged under as a breaker crashed over him. We held our breath, and seconds later he bobbed to the surface. The strong current had hurled him towards the shore, but as it retreated it sucked his legs from under him. He stumbled to his feet before falling to his knees and scrabbling up the beach on all fours. A second wave smashed into him sending him tumbling up the pebbles. I think we were as relieved as he was when he made it to safety. While all this was going on, the two officers of the Guardia Civil looked on. It would take more than that for them to risk ruining the mirror-like shine on their standard issue military style boots.

The crewman got to his feet and looked out to sea. His companion moved closer to shore. They shouted instructions at each other which floated away on the breeze. The captain picked up a rope and hurled one end at his crewmate. His effort fell short and the sodden sailor stumbled back into the sea to retrieve it.

'I can't believe it's taken them all morning to come up with this foolhardy plan,' commented Melanie.

I had to admit, it did seem rather bizarre that after all their effort the crewman had ended up on the wrong side of the beach. He now faced the challenge of hauling the heavy tow rope across the river Miel and along the beach to the stranded powerboat, a task made all the more difficult by a rocky outcrop ten metres offshore. Inevitably, the rope snagged and once again the poor sailor had to wade into the surf to free it.

'Ouch!'

'I can't watch,' said Melanie, holding her hand over her eyes.

During his attempt to free the rope, a large wave had battered him against the rocks. The poor guy was taking a pounding, and all the while the officers of the Guardia Civil looked on. Eventually, he freed the rope, dragged it along the beach, and secured it to the bow of the powerboat.

When it comes to dragging powerboats off a beach in high seas, I'm no expert, but securing the rope to the bow did strike me as odd. I had no doubt that once the vessel was in the water, towing it with the pointy end at the front was the right thing to do, but it wasn't in the water and the pointy end was currently pointing inland. While I mulled over the mechanics of turning a powerboat 180 degrees before dragging it off the beach and into the sea, the captain of the second boat had anchored his craft offshore and hopped into the other. Whatever they were planning, it didn't involve the combined efforts of both motorboats.

The scene was set. There were two men in a boat which in turn was attached to the beached powerboat by a weighty tow rope. There was a second craft anchored offshore, a half-drowned crewmate drying out on the beach, and two pristine looking officers of the Guardia Civil watching proceedings.

The two men in the boat pointed their craft towards the open sea, tensioned the tow rope and hit the gas. Somewhat unsurprisingly, the beached powerboat acted like an anchor. The bow of the smaller craft lifted skywards and the stern buried itself in the Med. Water spilled in, flooding the inside and drowning the motor which spluttered to a halt. The bow crashed back into the sea, sending a tidal wave of water splashing into the two occupants who stared at each other dumbfounded. Without power it drifted towards the rocky outcrop, helped on its way by the action of the waves. The terrifying consequences soon sank in. The crewman on the beach ran into the breaking waves and grabbed the tow rope in a desperate attempt to pull it away from the rocks. At the same time, the men in the boat worked frantically, one bailing water out of the hull and the other trying to restart the motor.

'What's he doing?' asked Melanie, pointing to the hapless soul knee-deep in the Med.

'I've absolutely no idea.'

It seemed implausible that he alone could overcome the power of the waves and pull the boat to safety.

'I'll tell you one thing though, if they don't get the motor started soon, they're going to run aground,' I added.

'Do you think we should call someone?'

'I think we're looking at them, love,' I said, tipping my head out to sea.

'Why don't those officers lend a hand?'

No sooner had the words left her lips than one of them made a move and grabbed the rope. Together they managed to prevent the boat from drifting onto the rocks, but in so doing, it had floated perilously close to the breaking waves.

'He's not going to get it started,' I said.

To make matters worse, the craft was now parallel to the shore. The boat had reached the point of no return. The swell caught the side of it and pushed it landwards. The next wave would surely sink her. It was now or never. The captain mustered all the strength he could and tugged on the outboard's starter cord, but alas nothing. There would be no last-minute reprieve or happy ending today. Their fate was sealed. The next wave rolled in and like a toy boat in a bathtub flipped the motorboat upside down. We held our breath, waiting for the two occupants to surface. Another wave broke on top of the stricken vessel. Suddenly, the first seaman bobbed to the surface followed closely by the second. What a relief.

In all the chaos, the second Guardia Civil officer had belatedly come to help out. Too little too late. The two seamen scrambled ashore. One had had the foresight to grab a dock line and was hanging onto it for dear life; the other four came to help. The fibreglass hull bobbed up and down in the breaking waves. The action of the tide moved it closer to shore before dragging it back out to sea. The five men holding the dock line followed suit like a tug-of-war team. Back and forth they went, time after time. Talk about being at the mercy of the sea; if the danger to life and limb hadn't been so real, the whole episode would have been hilarious.

Ding dong, ding dong!

I glanced at my watch: 5:56 pm.

Throughout the day we'd been expecting a knock at the door from the local constabulary. They might not have been interested in my conspiracy theories, but surely someone would want to ask if we'd seen or heard anything.

'I bet that's the police,' I said.

'They've taken their time.'

We answered the door together. To our surprise, the caller was dressed in a blue boilersuit and parked in the lane was an ageing excavator.

'*Hola*, can you tell me how to get to the beach?' he asked.

'Just follow this road, it leads straight there,' I replied.

He thanked us, climbed back into his cab, and the contraption lurched off down the hill.

'I wonder what he's going to do?' asked Melanie.

Given what had happened so far, I hadn't got a clue.

'Let's find out,' I said.

Minutes later the excavator appeared on the far side of the bay and bounced down the track to the beach. One of the officers of the Guardia Civil went to meet him. The driver jumped down and the two men had a lengthy conversation. Any sense of urgency had long since gone. Eventually, the driver clambered back into his cab and drove onto the beach, flattening everything in his way. The four men on the beach must have been over the moon to see him. They'd been fighting the sea for well over an hour in an attempt to save their upturned craft. Another lengthy discussion followed.

Everyone seemed to have an opinion, but in the end there was only one that counted: the digger driver's. He climbed back into his cab, drove headlong into the waves, snared his catch with the steel bucket, and unceremoniously hauled it out. As he did, the sound of cracking fibreglass echoed around the bay.

'I think the next phone call will be to the insurance broker,' I joked.

Before heading home the excavator hauled the powerboat even higher up the beach, presumably to prevent a professional salvager from having it away.

The knock on the door never came and we retired to bed, having packed the car in readiness for our drive to Marbella. Never in a million years did we expect our final day at *Casa Maria* to be so eventful. Thankfully, no one was hurt, although given the state of their footwear, I think the two officers of the Guardia Civil would have some explaining to do.

22

First Impressions

We were sad to be leaving *Casa Maria*, but excited to be moving along the coast rather than heading home. My only regret was not being there to watch episode two of the powerboat salvage saga. Talking of which, our morning flit felt a bit like fleeing the scene of a crime. Mind you, if the authorities wanted a word with us, I was sure Francisco would be happy to pass on our contact details.

'Have you got everything?' I asked, as we readied to leave.

'I think so.'

Melanie's reply didn't exactly fill me with confidence. One final sweep was in order. I checked all the drawers and cupboards, and every nook and cranny.

'Right then, let's go.'

We'd arranged to meet Katherine, the manager of the apartment, at 12:00 pm. I figured an hour and a half would give us ample time to drive the 116 kilometres. We made good progress and arrived with five minutes to spare.

'Do we know what car she'll be driving?' asked Melanie.

'No. We don't even know what she looks like.'

'I presume you told her what we were driving.'

'Of course.'

'What time is it now?'

I glanced at my watch but before I'd had chance to reply, a car pulled up alongside.

'Are you Mr Briggs?' asked a young woman.

'Yes.'

'I'm Katherine. If you'd like to follow me, we'll go straight to the apartment.'

Katherine drove on ahead and I followed. The road network through Elviria was chaotic and Katherine wasn't hanging around. We sped up hills and down dales, twisting and turning, around crazy bends and up precipitous climbs. We drove past a lush golf course surrounded by apartments. Opposite that was a row of luxury villas snaking up a hillside, each one vying for a glimpse of the sea. We climbed higher into the hills before cascading down a steep valley. The consequences of the global financial crisis were all around us. Ambitious new developments had been reduced to abandoned streets, empty building plots, and roadside lampposts. Six minutes after setting off, we came to a halt outside a gated entrance. The sign outside read "Santa Maria Village".

This inappropriately named development was a modern *urbanización* of luxury apartments. As if by magic, the gates opened, although I suspect a remote control performed the trick. Katherine drove through and we followed. I couldn't imagine a greater contrast between here and Playa del Río de la Miel, which was probably a good thing. From the comfort of the car the complex looked brand new. We pulled into a roadside parking space and stepped out.

'It's this way. You can leave your luggage, it'll be safe here,' said Katherine.

I was pleased; if she'd seen how much we had, she might have thought we were moving in for good. I lifted Jazz out of the back and we followed her to block two. Despite it sounding like a prisoner of war camp, it wasn't. The apartment blocks looked clean and modern and the landscaped gardens were perfectly manicured. Most noticeable was the silence. The only sounds were our footsteps echoing off hard surfaces. Blocks one, two, and three ran along the front of the *urbanización*. Katherine led us to a ground floor or garden apartment, as estate agents like to call them. She unlocked the door and we entered.

If *Casa Maria* was homely, this place was straight out of the glossy pages of a lifestyle magazine. Katherine flicked on a switch and light bounced off the polished marble floors. On the left was a guest bedroom, furnished to a showroom standard as were all the rooms. The main living space occupied the length of the apartment: dining area, lounge, and an American style kitchen, complete with Melanie's favourite appliance, a dishwasher. Large sliding doors opened out onto a covered terrace which overlooked the surrounding countryside. We'd been spoilt for views over the last four weeks, but this was very pleasant and gave the feeling of being out in the countryside and away from it all. Doors from the master bedroom also led onto the terrace. Given what we'd paid, we were delighted with our new home.

'There's underground parking, just follow the road around to the left. This remote is for the garage door and this one is for the main gate,' said Katherine, handing me the keys to the apartment and the two controllers.

She pointed out the guest information book and checked that we were happy, which we were.

'If there's anything you need, you have my number,' she said, before leaving.

'What do you think?' I asked.

'It's gorgeous.'

We unpacked the car, had something to eat, and then headed out to the supermarket. It wasn't until we reached the first road junction that I realised we hadn't a clue where we were.

'Is it up here?' I asked.

'I think so.'

Hardly the endorsement I was hoping for. I paused for thought. Turning left seemed counterintuitive. We couldn't see the sea but I knew where it was and this road wasn't heading that way. Nevertheless, we followed our instincts and began the steep ascent. Halfway up we caught sight of the Med and, as expected, we weren't driving towards it.

'Are you sure it's up here?' I asked.

'We definitely came down this road, don't you remember?'

When following another vehicle, you spend more time watching that than taking in the scenery. Turning around wasn't an option so we continued upwards. A T-junction greeted our arrival at the summit. We had two choices, turn towards the sea or away from it.

'Now where?' I asked.

'I'm not sure.'

Thankfully, the roads were deserted.

'It can't be up there, can it?'

We hadn't yet driven a kilometre and we were already lost. Once again, I followed my instincts and turned towards the sea. The road followed the contours of the hill and eventually led us in completely the wrong direction.

'I don't think this is right,' said Melanie.

Without warning the road had ended and we were staring at a pair of imposing gates.

'You don't say.'

My sarcasm wasn't helping.

We were facing in the wrong direction and there wasn't even a turning circle. To make matters worse, the road was so narrow I had to nudge back and forth a dozen or more times to turn around. And to think, all we wanted was a few groceries. I drove back to the junction and took the other option. This led us to another T-junction. The place was like a maze.

'Now where?' I asked in frustration.

'I don't know. Everywhere looks the same.'

She wasn't kidding.

'It must be right.'

'Are you sure?'

'No.'

This time I decided to ignore my instincts and turn inland. The road came to the brow of a hill and then tumbled down a valley before climbing once again. By now, all signs of civilisation had disappeared. Gone were the luxury villas and manicured gardens; the only greenery here was weeds sprouting from cracks in the pavements.

'It can't be up here,' I said.

'I think you're right.'

At least this road was wide enough to complete a textbook three-point turn. We drove back to the junction and then continued straight on.

'This looks familiar,' said Melanie.

'I don't remember this,' I said.

Sleeping policemen are something I never forget, and do my utmost to avoid. The one in front of us ran the width of the road and was definitely overweight. I slowed to a crawl. The front wheels hit the hump and the car rolled backwards. I squeezed the accelerator and we climbed over the hillock. Half a dozen more littered the street. Some were so high I thought we might need oxygen to scale them. Eventually, we reached the foot of the hill.

'This is not where we met Katherine,' I said.

Somewhere along the line we'd taken another wrong turning. By accident rather than design, we stumbled across the main coast road. We headed east and one junction further along found the supermarket we'd been searching for. The drive back proved less taxing. We made a mental note of each turn and hoped for more success the next time we ventured out.

We hadn't been home long when Melanie received a text message.

'It's your sister,' she said.

'Oh yes, what does she want?'

'She's booked a flight and will be with us on Saturday the 23rd. She wants to know if we can pick her up from the airport?'

'Do we have a choice?'

'No.'

Melanie's Christmas prediction had come true.

'You'd better tell her yes then.'

We spent the following week familiarising ourselves with our new surroundings and after several failed escape attempts, we finally figured out how to negotiate the maze of streets to and from the main road. The world was now our oyster, or at least the Costa del Sol was.

'I thought we might take a trip to Ronda today,' I suggested over morning coffee.

We hadn't been to the town of Ronda for over two years. The drive into the mountains is quite challenging but fun, and the scenery en route is stunning.

'OK. What time?'

'There's no rush. We'll have breakfast and then set off.'

Despite being overcast we enjoyed breakfast on the terrace. At 11:30 am we grabbed our coats and headed out.

In the centre of Elviria we picked up the A7 heading west along the coast. We skirted past the exclusive resort of Marbella and on to Nueva Andalucía and the upmarket marina of Puerto Banús. Two kilometres after that we turned inland onto the A-397. This fabulous stretch of tarmac climbs steadily for almost fifty kilometres, twisting and turning as it scales the mountain. Eventually, we reached the high plateaux and continued on into the historic town of Ronda.

On an overcast day in January, the old town is a pleasure to stroll around. I can't imagine what it's like on a blazing hot day in the middle of summer when coachloads of tourists descend on the place. The town's most outstanding landmark is undoubtedly the Puente Nuevo (New Bridge). Construction began in 1751 and took forty-two years to complete. The structure towers 120 metres (390 feet) above the floor of the gorge it spans and is a masterpiece of engineering. We strolled around the town and took in the sights before heading back to the car.

'Let's take a different route home,' I suggested.

We don't really go in for planning. Most of our exploration is done on the hoof.

At the roundabout on the outskirts of town we had two choices, Sevilla or Algeciras. The former would have taken us miles out of our way so we turned right onto the A-369. The scenery was vast, an overlapping collage of mountain ranges, each a different shade of blue, fading as they stretched into infinity. The first village we came to was Atajate, a cluster of whitewashed cottages and red terracotta roofs nestled in the middle of nowhere. We continued on.

'Look at that,' said Melanie.

Perched on a hilltop, directly ahead, was the Castle of Benadalid. Below its ramparts slept another hillside village. Through accident and design, each house had unobstructed views over the surrounding countryside. The scenery was outstanding: deep valleys and distant mountains for as far as the eye could see. Beyond Benadalid the road began a long and steady descent, but the outlook remained unchanged. Four kilometres further along we came to the village of Algatocín.

At first sight the village church appeared to be perched on the edge of a precipice. As we neared it, I clapped eyes on the first signpost we'd seen since leaving Ronda. It read "Estepona 45". I had a quick decision to make. Without asking, I indicated left and turned onto the MA-8305. The road doubled back on itself and a steep descent took us through the centre of the village. It wasn't long before I began to question my decision. The road narrowed into a single track and was leading us back into the Andalucían wilderness. Mountain scenery gave way to scrubland and stunted pines. Further along it climbed steadily to the village of Jubrique. I couldn't help thinking we'd made a terrible mistake.

'Is this a dead end?' asked Melanie.

Up ahead the road appeared to come to an end. If it did, we were in for quite a trek back to the main road.

'What about down there?' I replied.

A narrow lane looked to continue on between two houses.

'It looks tight. Are you sure it's not someone's driveway?'

I hadn't a clue, but it was either that, or turn around.

'Breathe in.'

I slowed to a crawl and peered in front. The lane ran between two rows of houses and then dipped, making it impossible to see what lay ahead. My reluctance to turn back spurred me on. One hundred metres further along the lane turned sharply left, widened slightly, and continued on through the village. I breathed a sigh of relief.

'Told you,' I said triumphantly.

Two minutes later we'd cleared the outskirts of the village and merged onto the MA-8301. For the next eighteen kilometres the going was slow, but the scenery was very pleasant. Somewhat unexpectedly, we exited a tight bend and the Mediterranean came into view. I stopped at the side of the road to get a better look and let Jazz stretch her legs. A sign read "Aparcamiento los Reales". Unbeknown to us, we'd stumbled upon the Paraje Natural los Reales de Sierra Bermeja, a vast Andalucían wilderness, over four hundred metres above sea level. The views along the coast, both east and west, were breathtaking. A coastal panorama that stretched to the ends of the earth. This alone made our detour worthwhile. From this altitude the coastal resorts looked like tiny white dots on a watercolour canvas.

'Right then, are you ready to move on?' I asked.

'Ready when you are.'

We zigzagged down the mountain and picked up the A-7 coast road heading east. By the time we got back to the apartment we'd been away for almost five hours.

'Teatime Taster?' I asked.

'Yes please.'

I pulled the cork on a fine red from the Valdepeñas region. We relaxed on the terrace and watched the sun dip behind the eucalyptus trees. A fine way to end an interesting day.

Having whetted our appetite for exploration, we couldn't wait to set out again. This time we chose somewhere a bit closer to home. Marbella is one of those destinations that conjures up images of exclusivity and opulence, but doesn't always deliver. On our first visit, back in 1994, we were decidedly unimpressed. On that occasion we'd entered the town along the golden mile, a wide avenue of palatial villas owned by the rich and famous. From there we drove through the new shopping area and along the seafront. Unbeknown to us, we'd completely missed the historic centre.

Many Spanish towns and cities have an old town that's very distinct from the modern urban sprawl. The coastal resorts along the Costa del Sol are no different.

'I thought we might take a look at Marbella old town this afternoon,' I suggested over lunch.

Melanie did her best to seem enthusiastic but first impressions count and Marbs, as it's become known, had failed to float her boat.

We left the apartment at 2:00 pm. Fifteen minutes and eight kilometres later we turned off the A-7 and followed signs for the Centro Historico.

'Keep an eye out for signposts,' I said.

'Don't you know where you're going?'

'I've got a general idea.'

'It's up there,' said Melanie, as I drove past a narrow lane leading off the main high street.

'Where?'

'Back there.'

'Bugger! I'll have to turn around.'

Filtering left is rarely an option in Spain. More often than not, it involves taking an anticlockwise loop to cross the main carriageway. I drove for another two and a half kilometres before I could double back.

'It's coming up on the right,' said Melanie.

I indicated and turned into a very narrow one-way street.

Eventually, we found a carpark and made our way back towards the historic centre. The sight of orange trees laden with fruit in the middle of winter is truly amazing. To see them in an urban setting is even more astonishing. Avenues bordered with oranges are as common in Andalucía as oaks and sycamores are in the UK, and the streets of Marbella were no different.

'Let's go this way,' I suggested.

The route I'd chosen was a pedestrian alleyway with a line of orange trees running down the centre. From the moment we left the main thoroughfare I felt a heightened sense of anticipation. The architecture had changed and the alleyway led us into a bygone era. Moorish style arches adorned windows and doors, their flowing lines accentuated by red brick lintels and guarded by intricately created iron railings and security grills. We stepped out into a narrow street lined with ornamental trees, and spikey leaved plants spilled out from terracotta pots. I was struck by the harmony between urban development and nature.

'This is beautiful,' remarked Melanie.

The focal point of the old town is the Plaza de los Naranjos (Orange Square). It's a garden oasis surrounded with bars and cafés selling, amongst other things, freshly squeezed orange juice served with not one, but two sachets of sugar. We took a seat and waited to be served. Tiny finches swooped in and out of the foliage and pecked at crumbs from the tables. A bust of Don Juan Carlos I, the first Spanish monarch after the death of the dictator Franco, watched over proceedings. A waiter wandered over to take our order. The choice was obvious.

There's something very special about sitting in Plaza de los Naranjos, surrounded by orange trees, and sipping freshly squeezed orange juice.

'That was a good idea you had,' said Melanie, as she took another sip.

Even Melanie had fallen under the spell of Marbella's old town.

23

Wheel Meet Again

We added the old town in Marbella to our growing list of interesting places to visit. Julie would be arriving at the weekend and she likes to be doing. Bob and Janet were due at the end of the month, but they're much easier to please. As well as Marbella, our list included Puerto Banús, playground to the rich and tasteless, Mijas Pueblo, a typically untypical Andalucían hilltop village, Puebla Aida, a stunningly beautiful development and one of my personal favourites; and if they weren't enough, we could always take a drive along the coast to Nerja.

We spent the next few days in and around the apartment. Lighting the barbecue at this time of year was a real bonus. We enjoyed lazy lunches in the warm winter sunshine and as the sun began to set, we would jump in the car and drive to the beach. While Melanie and I enjoyed a cold beer at a beachside *chiringuito*, Jazz paddled in the sea. Only when the sun disappeared below the horizon would we head home for dinner in front of the telly.

The week passed quickly and all too soon the conversation turned to Julie and our trip to Malaga Airport.

'What time does her plane land?' I asked, over morning coffee.

'A quarter past six. What time will we have to set off?'

'An hour beforehand should give us plenty of time.'

It seemed strange that our first visit to Malaga Airport would be by car rather than aeroplane.

'What are we going to do if it rains?'

Melanie's question was a reflection on the morning's weather: grey and overcast.

'Don't even go there.'

One of the downsides of renting in an area that boasts 320 days of sunshine a year is the lack of activities when it doesn't.

The weather deteriorated throughout the day and on the stroke of four the rain began to fall. By the time we set off to the airport, it was absolutely tipping it down and gusty winds made it a thoroughly unpleasant evening.

On the whole Spain's road network is excellent, but with one notable exception: drainage. When the heavens open, roads quickly become rivers and water collects in the shallows. Driving in these conditions is difficult and dangerous. Even with the wipers on full speed they were struggling to clear the windscreen, and pond-sized puddles caused the car to aquaplane. I raised my foot off the accelerator and slowed to a safe speed. On the outskirts of Malaga, we followed signs to the airport. The exit ramp curved through 360 degrees.

'Are you sure this is the right road?' asked Melanie.

Within the space of a few hundred metres we'd gone from the smooth surface of the AP-7 to a stretch of unmade road.

'That's what the sign said.'

I continued on. If anything, the rain was getting worse. The car in front stopped at a chaotic intersection where the only road manners were bad. I fought my way through the traffic, hampered by the dazzle of oncoming headlights.

'Can you see any signs?' I asked.

'Signs? I can't see a chuffing thing.'

Having successfully negotiated the intersection, I followed the taillights of the car in front and kept my fingers crossed.

'There,' said Melanie. 'Take the next right.'

A slip road led onto a dual carriageway. The volume of traffic was terrifying. I muscled my way onto the carriageway and glanced at the time. Julie's plane was scheduled to land in thirteen minutes. I moved into the outside lane where the traffic was freer flowing. No sooner had I made the manoeuvre than a bright yellow sign cut through the torrential rain.

'You need to be in the other lane,' said Melanie.

Wouldn't you know it.

There was no time to dither. If I wasn't quick, I was going to miss the exit. I checked my mirrors. Droplets of rainwater made visibility impossible. I had no choice but to indicate and hope for the best. I held my breath and slowly edged into the nearside lane. The next challenge was taking the correct exit.

'Is it this one coming up?'

'Yes.'

'Are you sure?'

'Yes.'

I wasn't convinced but turned off anyway. Thankfully, we'd made the right decision.

'Keep an eye out for the short stay carpark,' I said.

'Slow down then.'

In my haste to make up time, I'd hit the accelerator pedal and we were zipping along quite smartly. I slowed down. A big blue P indicated the entrance. I took a ticket, the barrier rose, and we found a parking space.

By the time we'd dashed into the arrivals hall, the information board confirmed that Julie's plane had landed. A few minutes later, passengers started walking through and Julie was one of them.

'Chuff me! What's this weather like?' she said.

Not quite the hello, how are you greeting one might expect, but typical of Julie. I offered to pull her carry-on and we marched back to the car. Thankfully, the walkway was under cover as the sound of water, gushing off rooftops, was deafening. By the time we left the carpark, twilight had succumbed to the darkness of night but there was no let-up in the rain. I couldn't believe it; this was the worst weather we'd had since leaving Galicia and we had my sister to entertain for the next three days.

On the way back to the apartment, Julie brought us up to speed with gossip from England. I was concentrating so hard on the road ahead, I missed most of it. As the turn off to Elviria approached, I indicated and slowed. A pond-sized puddle covered a large section of the exit ramp. Halfway through it, the front wheel hit a submerged pothole and a loud thud reverberated through the cabin.

'What was that?' asked Melanie, who was clearly startled.

'I'm not sure but something doesn't feel right.'

The steering had gone stiff and the wheel was difficult to turn.

'What are you going to do?' asked Melanie.

What could I do? We were two and a half kilometres from the apartment.

'I'm going to carry on.'

No one said a word. We hobbled on through Elviria and into the residential suburbs. The streets were lined with private gated communities and luxury villas. Away from the centre the streetlighting was terrible. Many weren't working and those that were cast only a faint glow around the foot of the lamppost. The handling was getting worse with each passing metre. I was fighting to keep her in a straight line, and all the while the torrential rain bounced off the windscreen.

'I'm going to have to stop,' I said.

I pulled in to the side of the road.

'Wait here while I take a look.'

I pushed open the door and a showery gust blew into the cabin. I stepped onto the pavement to avoid the torrent of water flowing down the street and slammed the door shut. Raindrops dribbled down my glasses as I squinted through the darkness at the front wheel. Everything looked in order, no dents or scrapes. That's when I noticed the tyre. The water was so deep I hadn't seen it at first glance, but the tyre was as flat as a pancake. What was I going to do?

I jumped back into the car and slumped into the seat.

'What's matter?' asked Melanie.

'The tyre is flat.'

'What are you going to do?'

'I'll have to change it.'

'In this?'

'We can't sit here all night, but I can't do it here. It's pitch black out there.'

I'd come to a standstill on an unlit street. I turned the ignition on and slowly moved forwards.

'There,' said Melanie.

She'd spotted a light mounted on the wall above a garage door. I fought with the steering wheel and turned off the road.

'I think it's someone's driveway,' she added.

I knew it was, but what choice did we have?

'It'll have to do.'

The rain was lashing down, bouncing off the body panels like frozen peas.

'Do you need a hand?' asked Melanie.

'There's no point in both of us getting soaked.'

'At least let me hold the umbrella for you.'

'Would you mind?'

'Of course not.'

'Do you need me?' asked Julie.

'No, you stay here.'

I opened the door and stepped in a puddle. Things were going from bad to worse. Julie's carry-on was in the back. I hauled it out and passed it to her. She slid it onto the seat next to her.

I could hardly see a thing in the back of the car. I scrabbled around in the blackness feeling for the wheel brace and carjack.

'I can't see a chuffing thing,' I said.

Eventually, I found them both. One by one I loosened the wheel-nuts and felt around under the car for the jacking point. Wherever I stood I was working in my own shadow. Melanie did her best to shield me from the worst of the weather but swirling winds hurled raindrops at me from all angles.

Why is it that crank handles work perfectly when you don't need them, but seem determined to shred your knuckles when you do?

Slowly but surely, I raised the car high enough to remove the wheel.

'It's only flat at the bottom,' I quipped.

If I hadn't laughed, I would have cried.

I tossed the flat to one side and went to get the spare. I rolled it back through the puddles and tried desperately to line the holes up with the lugs. In my haste to remove the wheel, I'd jacked the car high enough to remove the flat, but too low to fit the inflated spare. I moved back to the jack and cranked the car higher. Eventually, the wheel lined up and I screwed on the nuts before lowering the car and tightening them fully. The flat went in the back and Melanie handed me the jack and brace. Despite her best efforts we were both soaked to the skin.

Back at the apartment we showered and changed before heading back out for dinner at the Hong Kong Chinese restaurant in Sitio de Calahonda. As usual the food was excellent. On the drive back, I gave the site of our earlier mishap a wide berth. That was one airport run we wouldn't forget in a hurry.

When we woke the following morning, the storm had passed and the weather was pleasant enough to enjoy a late breakfast on the terrace.

'Why couldn't it have been like this last night?' I said, as we sipped our coffees.

'What are we going to do for lunch?' asked Julie.

'Lunch! You haven't finished your breakfast.'

'We thought we'd go to a beachside *chiringuito*,' said Melanie.

'A what?'

'*Chiringuito*. They're privately owned restaurants right next to the beach.'

Julie liked the sound of that.

'And then what?'

'We're going to visit Marbella and have a wander around the old town.'

'Marbella?'

Her tone lacked enthusiasm.

'Yes, Marbella old town. I'm sure you'll like it, and after that we'll take a look at Puerto Banús.'

'What's that?'

'Wait and see.'

'Will I like it?'

'Put it this way, it's nothing if not interesting.'

Whether she'd like it or not was another matter. Puerto Banús divides opinion. It's one of those places that encourages wealthy individuals to display their riches. It's a prestigious marina fringed with designer shops and upmarket restaurants. Luxury cars line the quayside and tens, if not hundreds of millions of pounds' worth of superyachts sway gently in the safe haven. Some people think it's great; others are appalled. Personally, I find it fascinating and a bit sad.

While I contemplated life's inequalities, a shaft of sunlight broke through the clouds and bathed the terrace. Julie closed her eyes and leant back in her chair.

After a leisurely start we headed to the beach for lunch. As expected, Julie loved eating next to the sea, so much so that she settled the bill and, despite her misgivings, she adored Plaza de los Naranjos in Marbella's old town. As for Puerto Banús, the jury is out.

'Would you like to take a drive along the coast to Sotogrande?' I asked, as we strolled back to the car.

This was the only full day Julie had with us so I wanted to make the most of it.

'Whatever you think, you know the area,' she replied.

Sotogrande Port is part of a very exclusive private residential area twenty-five kilometres from Gibraltar. The port is designed around Venice-style canals where the rich and famous live at the water's edge and keep an eye on their motorboats moored out front. Unlike Puerto Banús, Sotogrande exudes class. Unfortunately, by the time we got there the rain had returned. All we could do was drive around the port before heading home.

That evening we stayed in. On Julie's request, Melanie made a tortilla and we spent the night chatting. Before we knew it, we'd downed a few bottles of wine and the clock had ticked around to 3:00 am.

Julie's time with us was brief but busy. The following day we took her back to the airport and said goodbye.

As soon as she'd gone, I turned my attention to the flat tyre. It seemed wise to get it repaired before our next visitors arrived. Since dumping it in the back of the car, I hadn't even looked at it. We dropped it off at the repair shop and called back later to pick it up. The puncture turned out to be an irreparable six-inch gash. Little wonder

I could hardly steer the car. The tyre had to be replaced and to make matters worse, we hadn't long had the other. I don't know about the tyre being deflated, but I was.

Less than a week later we were back at the airport to collect Bob and Janet. A longer stay and improved weather gave us the chance to utilise our list of places to visit. We had a non-stop week which everyone seemed to enjoy. Their departure brought us ever closer to ours. The last few weeks flew by and before we knew it, we were getting ready to head home.

'Where has the time gone?' I asked.

'I know what you mean, it doesn't seem two minutes since were packing up to leave *Casa Maria* and now we're getting ready to go home.'

'Have you enjoyed it?'

'It's been wonderful.'

'Do you think we should do it again next winter?'

'That would be lovely.'

Taking an extended break had worked out well. The weather could have been a little kinder, but it was definitely better than enduring a Galician winter. The accommodation had been the perfect balance of coastal retreat and urban luxury, and all at an affordable price.

'OK. When Katherine comes tomorrow, I'll ask her.'

The following morning, we were rudely woken by the alarm clock at 6:45 am. An hour later Katherine arrived to check we hadn't wrecked the place and return our security deposit.

'Would it be possible to book for next year?' I asked.

Katherine was more than happy to reserve the place for us.

By 8:00 am we were on the road and homeward bound. The drive back went smoothly; the weather was kind and the car didn't miss a beat. It wasn't until we started climbing into the León mountain range that the cloud cover thickened and the wind strengthened.

'Welcome home,' I quipped.

'Did you feel that?' asked Melanie.

A gust of wind had momentarily swept the car off course.

'It's certainly windy out there.'

We exited the A-6 at junction 400 and joined the N-120. After eleven kilometres we reached the border between the regions of Castile and León, and Galicia. It's marked by a spectacular gorge and a series of tunnels through the Serra Enciña da Lastra mountains. The gorge is so deep that from the car it's impossible to see the river Sil snaking through the bottom. From here the road flows down to the town of O Barco before continuing on to A Rúa, Montefurado, Quiroga, and finally, Monforte de Lemos. The sight of Monforte's iconic *torre* signalled an end to our 1000-kilometre journey, well almost.

'What's happened?' asked Melanie.

We were less than five kilometres from home. The driver in front had switched on his hazard warning lights. I took my foot off the accelerator and slowed. Lying across the road was a large pine tree, uprooted by the high winds. Fortunately, there was just enough room to drive around it.

'That can only just have happened,' remarked Melanie.

Five minutes earlier and who knows what the consequences might have been.

After three months away, the house looked a bit sorry for itself. A long, wet winter had left tear-like stains running down the boundary walls from the iron railings above. The lawns were overgrown and untidy. Melanie opened the gates and I pulled the car onto the driveway. The back garden looked even worse. The high winds had ripped a large section of bamboo screen off the chain-link fencing. One end was still attached, allowing it to flap around in the wind like a Japanese dragon in a street festival.

'What's that?' asked Melanie.

I turned to face the house. Two terracotta ridge tiles had been torn from the roof during the storm and smashed on the terrace. Our winter getaway had come at a price, but we wouldn't have missed it for the world.

24

Spring is in the Air

If broken ridge tiles and flailing bamboo weren't bad enough, we'd yet to suffer the indignity of a post-getaway weigh-in. Melanie was first to step onto the bathroom scales.

'Oh, my word!' she said, before quickly stepping off.

'How much?' I asked.

'Too much. That's it, I'm going on a diet.'

I was next up. Gingerly I stepped on, arms clasped behind my back and eyes front. I waited three seconds and then slowly lowered my gaze to read the digital display.

'Chuff me! I'm joining you.'

For the foreseeable future, meals would consist of soup, soup, and more soup. Not exactly thrilling, but needs must. My dieting mantra is lose it quick and gain it slow. What's the point in dieting if you can't then enjoy life?

'Can you make some of those fluffy white bread rolls to go with the soup?' I asked.

'I haven't got any eggs.'

My bottom lip dropped.

'We could see if Meli can spare one,' she added.

Meli keeps a small brood of chickens and can always be counted on in a crisis.

'Come on then. Let's go and ask.'

We wrapped up warm and strolled down the lane into the village. The intoxicating scent of woodsmoke filled the frosty air and the unmistakable sound of a chainsaw cut through the silence. Meli's house was the first one on the right. To our surprise, she was standing in the driveway supervising two young men. They were busy sawing up a large pine tree that had been uprooted by yesterday's strong winds. It seemed we weren't the only ones to suffer storm damage.

'*Hola* Meli,' called Melanie, over the racket of the chainsaw.

Meli turned to look at us and her face lit up. She embraced Melanie and kissed her on both cheeks before doing the same to me. Her greeting felt warm and sincere and brightened up a cold and overcast day.

'*¿Hola, qué tal las vacaciones* (Hello, how was your holiday)?' she asked.

We told her what a wonderful time we'd had and asked about the tree. The storm had been much worse than we'd realised. It had blown in from the Atlantic and left a trail of death and devastation from Galicia to Asturias and up through France. Meli was grateful the tree had fallen away from the house and not through it. During a break in the conversation, Melanie asked if we could borrow an egg.

'Of course, just wait here,' said Meli, before marching off into the house.

'Borrow?' I whispered.

'I was being polite.'

Two minutes later she returned carrying an egg box.

'Here you go. Will six be enough?'

'Six! I only need one. I'll get you half a dozen the next time we go shopping.'

'Don't be silly. What am I going to do with more eggs?'

We all smiled. Meli's chickens produced more than enough for her needs.

'I'll have the box back though,' she added.

Boxes are worth more than their contents in these parts.

'No problem, I'll bring it back later today.'

'There's no hurry. Whenever you're passing.'

We thanked her, said goodbye, and wandered back up the lane to *El Sueño*. Melanie wasted no time mixing the ingredients and kneading the dough. In the time it took to prove, we nipped up to the post office to collect our mail. Before heading south we'd asked the postlady to hang on to it for us. After eleven weeks away you could be forgiven for thinking there might be a sack full waiting for us, but there wasn't. Since moving to Spain, we receive only a fraction of the post we used to. Not that we're complaining. A world without junk mail is a wonderful place.

With the exception of a few utility bills and bank statements, the rest consisted of twenty or more Christmas cards and a parcel of seasonal gifts from Melanie's mum. All a bit surreal on the first day of March.

Melanie's bread rolls brightened up an uninspiring lunch. Meal one of our diet had gone to plan; the question was, how long could we keep it up?

'I'd like to go to *Campo Verde* this afternoon,' said Melanie, over lunch.

Great minds think alike. I was keen to check the place for storm damage.

'No problem, I just want to sort out that bamboo before we go.'

Immediately after lunch I removed the flapping bamboo from the chain-link fence and salvaged what I could. Replacing it would have to wait until the wind had calmed down. Twenty minutes later we were pulling into the entrance at *Campo Verde*. Melanie jumped out to unlock the gate.

'Something is wrong with the lock,' she called.

I got out to take a closer look.

'What's matter?'

'I can't turn the key.'

'Here, let me have a go.'

With a little gentle persuasion, I managed to unlock it. On closer inspection the handle and lock looked to be sprained.

'I bet it's slammed shut in the wind and bent something,' I said.

'Can you fix it?'

'No. We'll to have to buy a new lock.'

If that was the only damage, we'd got away lightly. We left the car in the entrance and walked down the driveway. Melanie went upstairs and I checked the *bodegas* before joining her.

'Is everything OK?' I asked, as I walked into the lounge.

'Not bad, but look at the state of the fire. They didn't even clean out the ashes before they left.'

The back of the fire was stained with sooty deposits and the hearth was full of ash. Melanie takes these things personally. I adopt a more philosophical approach.

'That is what it's for, love, and they were on holiday.'

'I suppose so, and they did leave some nice comments in the Visitors book,' she replied.

I went to take a look. The first guests were the Sellier family who'd stayed over Christmas and New Year.

Pedro, Celeste & Cristina Sellier – Malaga

Dear Melanie and Craig it has been a wonderful stay, we've enjoyed very much Galicia and especially this place beside the Miño. Some people take holidays in healthy centres, we did and enjoyed many good meals and tried every single wine!! Which as a French girl, I would recommend to everyone. Thank you for this holiday, your house is superb and very practical and so peaceful. We wish you both a very good New Year.

Kiss from Pedro, Celeste and Cristina

What a great review to end our first rental season. I moved on to the next entry, the Fields from Stoke.

Howard and Susan Field – Stoke on Trent

Campo Verde is 5-star accommodation set in rural Galician countryside. Real Spain at its best. Peace and quiet for those who want to get away from it all, but only a short drive from several towns with shops, cafés and restaurants. Visited Monforte, Lugo and Chantada and found everyone friendly and helpful. This is our second visit to this area and we will be back!

It felt reassuring to know that even in our absence, guests had enjoyed their experience and the house. If these comments were anything to go by, we were definitely doing something right.

Over the next few days, the wind ran out of steam and calm returned to Canabal. Clear sky ushered in frosty mornings and beautifully sunny days. Perfect weather for pruning the grapevines.

'I'm going to make a start on the vines this morning,' I said, as we sipped our morning coffees.

It's a critical time in the vinicultural calendar. Mother Nature provides winemakers with one opportunity to prepare the vines for the coming season. Get it right, and you're well on the way to a bumper crop; get it wrong, and you have to wait a whole year to correct your mistakes. I'd hoped it would become easier over time, but it hadn't. If anything, the opposite was true. The problem was trying to remember, from one year to the next, exactly what cuts I'd made.

At the end of the growing season, when the grapes have been harvested and the vines have shed their leaves, all that remains is a spaghetti-like tangle of long wiry canes. Deciding which to remove and which to prune is a tricky business. Some cuts speak for themselves, others less so. One by one I snipped away until all that remained was a trunk and a number of trimmed canes, each with two buds. It's these buds that dictate the success or otherwise of the harvest.

The newly planted vines in the vineyard presented a different challenge. Throughout the growing season I'd removed all but one cane which I'd trained to grow straight and true. This single cane would form the trunk of the vine. What I didn't know was how tall to leave them.

The trellising in the vineyard consisted of rows of equally spaced galvanised steel posts connected by three rows of training wires. The lowest wire was ninety centimetres from the ground. Trimming them to that height seemed the logical thing to do. With only one cut to make per vine, I was finished in no time. What remained resembled a field of upturned walking sticks.

Having completed the pruning, I was itching to fire up my new rotavator and start weeding, but before that I had a minor drainage problem to sort out. The leylandii we'd planted to enclose the vineyard had suffered a few winter casualties. Overall, we were delighted with their progress. They'd grown over half a metre in ten months and the tallest ones were now well over a metre. Those that hadn't fared so well were along the eastern boundary where the land sloped into a dip. During the winter this had become waterlogged and the young trees were drowning. I decided to dig two channels perpendicular to the boundary and fill them with rocks in the hope of draining the surrounding land. Only time would tell if the affected trees would survive.

While I excavated the channels, Melanie began pruning the lacecap hydrangeas. Every year, this fast-growing hydrangea produces an abundance of creamy white flowerheads, many the size of a football. To say they're eye-catching is an understatement. Throughout the summer we're inundated with requests for cuttings from far and wide, and we're more than happy to oblige. Our neighbours do so much for us and rarely take anything in exchange. This is our way of saying thank you.

'I'm going to take these cuttings round to the neighbours,' said Melanie.

I'd finished making the drainage channels and was about to start rotavating.

'OK, see you soon.'

Melanie wandered back up the garden and disappeared inside. I dragged the rotavator out of the shed and rolled it into the vineyard. Before starting I checked the oil level, which unsurprisingly was spot on, and then filled the fuel tank. Checks completed, I was ready to fire her up. I stowed the transport wheel, opened the choke, and grabbed the starter cord. With one almighty tug, I yanked the cord and my little red rotavator burst into life. The earth was damp yet firm. I squeezed the throttle handle and the tines spun into action; as they did, the machine lurched forwards, taking me with it. Mastering this mechanical tilling machine would take time but until then, I'd have to hang on for dear life as it dragged me around the vineyard.

Forty minutes later Melanie returned.

'How's it going?' she called, over the noise of the motor.

'It's harder than it looks.'

'I bet it is. Coffee?'

'Yes please.'

A ten-minute coffee break gave me the boost I needed to crack on until lunchtime.

'What's for lunch?' I asked, as I stepped into the kitchen.

'Guess?'

'It wouldn't be soup by any chance, would it?'

'That's right.'

Melanie's reply was decidedly downbeat.

'It'll be worth it in the end,' I replied, trying my best to sound positive.

Within the hour I was back at work. By the time I'd finished the clock had ticked around to 4:00 pm. I stood back to admire my handiwork. It had been tough going, but nowhere near as difficult and time-consuming as digging it over by hand. My work hadn't gone unnoticed. Ever since I'd planted the vineyard, Terresa's husband, Chuchi, had shown a keen interest in its progress. We often caught him snooping around when he thought we weren't at home.

'What do you think?' I asked.

'They're too tall.'

Galicians are nothing if not direct. He was referring to the height of the vines.

'How tall should they be?' I asked.

Chuchi had been making wine since before I was born. It would have been foolish not to ask his advice, and besides which, the locals like nothing more than offering their opinion.

'Two buds tall, no more.'

When it comes to pruning, Chuchi knew his stuff, but I wasn't convinced. The vines in his vineyard were self-supporting whereas mine relied on modern trestles.

'Even though I'm using trestles?' I asked.

'Of course.'

Chuchi was adamant, and who was I to disagree. I fetched my secateurs and clipped the first vine to two buds.

'That's better,' he said.

Twenty minutes later my rows of upturned walking sticks were little more than pencils. I couldn't help thinking I'd made a terrible mistake.

After eighteen days of soup, glorious soup, wonderful soup, nothing but soup, our resolve cracked. Man cannot live on soup alone.

'Would you like to take a run out to Chaves today?' I asked, over morning coffee.

Melanie's eyes lit up. A trip to Chaves meant one thing: lunch at the Jing Huà Chinese restaurant.

'For a Chinese?'

Her reply was bursting with anticipation.

'Why not?'

'But what about our diet?'

'One day off won't make any difference, but if you're that worried, you can always order a bowl of chicken and sweetcorn soup,' I joked.

'No chance.'

A damp, misty start hinted at better weather to come. By 10:30 am the sun had melted away the grey clouds. We couldn't have wished for a better day.

The owners of the restaurant were delighted to see us. We hadn't been since last November. To show their appreciation of our unwavering patronage, the portions were even more generous than usual and everything was delicious.

Before heading home, we called at the supermarket and picked up a few bottles of Castelinho. That evening we contented ourselves with a bowl of soup and a glass or two of fine wine.

Springtime in Galicia is hectic. There are fields to plough and crops to plant. Neighbours are busy in their *huertas* (vegetable gardens) preparing the ground and planting potatoes, onions, cabbage, garlic, and *grelos* (turnip tops). By the end of March, fruit trees are starting to blossom. Everything and everyone was shaking off their winter blues.

'What's that?' asked Melanie.

I'd just been to collect the post. Based on the style of envelope and the address label, I had a good idea who it was from.

'I think it's from the council.'

I slit it open and pulled out a leaflet.

'Yes, it is. There's a concert tomorrow evening at the Casa de Cultura.'

'What sort of concert?'

'A guitarist from South Korea.'

'South Korea?'

I knew exactly what she was implying; how does a guitarist from South Korea end up performing in a sleepy rural village in northern Spain?

'Do you want to go?' I asked.

'Why not. It's not as if we've got anything else planned. Shall I ring Maria and see if her and Roy want to join us?'

'That's a good idea, and ask them if they'd like to nip into town afterwards for dinner.'

'What about our diet?'

'It's the weekend.'

'You're right.'

Melanie didn't take much persuading.

'Can you give me a shout when you ring her? I'd like a word with Roy.'

'What about?'

'I want to take a look at his vineyard.'

'What for?'

'To see how he's pruned his vines.'

Roy and Maria own a small vineyard and use a similar trestling system to mine. They'd learnt their pruning skills from a neighbour who, unlike Chuchi, made wine for a living. If Chuchi was right, all well and good; but if not, I needed to know what to do next year.

'I'll ring her now and then you can have a word with him.'

I waited patiently while Melanie spoke with Maria. I could tell from the conversation that they were going to join us.

'She's gone to get Roy,' whispered Melanie, as she handed me the phone.

Moments later he picked it up and I explained what I wanted.

'Come up now if you like,' he said.

A quarter of an hour later, I arrived at Roy's and we drove down the valley to their vineyard. As soon as I saw his vines, my heart sank. Chuchi's advice, although well-intentioned, was wrong.

'Not to worry,' said Roy, in his West Country accent, 'they'll grow again.'

He was right. Grapevines are nothing if not forgiving, but still, having to wait another year to rectify my mistake was a little disappointing. I thanked him for his time and dropped him back home.

On Saturday evening we readied ourselves for our first night out since returning from Andalucía. Roy and Maria were waiting outside the Casa de Cultura when we arrived.

'Have you been waiting long?' asked Melanie.

'We've just this minute arrived,' said Maria.

We wandered through into the auditorium. For a free concert, the audience count was pitifully low. Jusuk Lee, the South Korean guitarist, was an accomplished musician. In 2006 he received the prestigious accolade of Kumho Asiana young artist of the year. That alone made his appearance in Sober all the more extraordinary. His programme included Guido Santórsola, Carlo Domeniconi as well as a few test pieces intended to highlight his skill rather than be pleasing on the ear. On a cold night in March, Jusuk Lee was far better than his audience deserved, but we weren't complaining.

Dining out in the evening in Monforte de Lemos is generally a quiet affair. At the end of March, the town was deathly quiet. Our restaurant of choice was La Maja. Not that long ago the place would have been buzzing. All that changed when the young owners sold up, putting family before profit. We shouldn't complain. Galicia could teach everyone a thing or two about work/life balance.

Four weeks after returning home, it felt like we'd never been away. The sleepy village of Canabal is an easy place to return to. The dry weather had given us the opportunity to prune the vines, till the vineyard, mow the lawns, and ready the garden for spring. We'd received gifts from the neighbours and played our part in reciprocating. Since the start of the year, reservations for *Campo Verde* had been excellent. Three months in and we already had fourteen weeks booked. Manolo had replaced the two broken ridge tiles and refused to take payment, save for a can of beer, and Melanie and I had repaired the fence. Spring was in the air and what better way to spend a sunny Sunday afternoon than to pull the cork on a fine white wine, marvel at the setting sun, and enjoy a Teatime Taster. *Salud* (Cheers)!

HASTA LA PROXIMA

How it all began

The following is an excerpt from book one in The Journey series

Journey To A Dream

A voyage of discovery from England's industrial north to Spain's rural interior

1

Inception

The afternoon sun warmed my face as I wandered around the garden of our temporary Spanish home. I paused for a moment staring into a cloudless blue sky. An airliner cruised overhead, marking its progress with a long, wispy vapour trail, one more carrier heading home with its cargo of introspective holidaymakers. All too soon lazy-day memories would be replaced by a predictable routine. For many it's a daily trudge on the treadmill of life. This year however, I wouldn't be joining them. My wife Melanie and I had chosen a different path.

Living abroad was a dream I'd nurtured for many years. It all began on the Greek island of Corfu. I was seventeen at the time. A fun-packed holiday with my best friend Mark was drawing to a close. During our last night on the island I found myself alone, sitting on the beach. Waves lapped gently onto the sandy shore as I stared out across the moonlit Mediterranean. I longed to stay and not return home, but lacked the confidence to follow my impulse. More than twenty years had passed since that fleeting, rebellious moment, but now the wait was over.

My journey from dreamland to mainland Spain had begun some months earlier. A casual remark about the future of our small printing business developed into serious negotiations over its sale. Within weeks we'd received a formal takeover offer. This modest windfall could open the door to a new life abroad. What seemed like an easy decision became a very difficult choice. After weeks of soul-searching, we decided to sell up and chase our dream.

Most of our evenings and weekends were spent on the internet, trawling through foreign property sites. We focused our search on two areas, the Costa Blanca on Spain's Mediterranean coast, and the Canary isle of Lanzarote. We'd almost decided on Lanzarote when purely by chance I discovered a website promoting properties in a place called Galicia.

The advertised listings radiated rustic charm. There were quaint little cottages, romantic ruined farmhouses, and majestic manors, all at unbelievably low prices. Night after night I scoured the internet, desperate for information on this little-known region of Spain.

Galicia is situated in the northwest corner of the Iberian Peninsula. To the east it's bordered by the regions of Asturias, and Castilla and León, and in the south by the country of Portugal. To the north and west it borders the Atlantic Ocean. Its rugged coastline is aptly named Costa del Muerte (Coast of Death). For centuries, ships and their crews have met a watery grave along this treacherous stretch of coastline. The interior is characterised by high mountains and deep river valleys. It's an unspoilt rural landscape where man and wildlife live in harmony.

Cleverly worded marketing is one thing, but to satisfy our curiosity we needed to fly out and take a look.

At the end of February that's exactly what we did. We flew with British Airways from London Gatwick to Porto in Northern Portugal for a three-night break to explore Galicia and view some properties.

After collecting the hire car we headed north. The scenery through Portugal was stunning. Wide valleys and rolling hills meander their way through forested mountain ranges. Small hamlets speckle the landscape as the main highway carves its way through lush, green valleys on tall concrete stilts. Within an hour we'd drifted over the border into Spain.

Our destination in Galicia was the village of Caldelas de Tui. Hours of internet surfing had led to the discovery of a restored manor house reincarnated as a rural hotel. Within its grounds several outbuildings had been converted into small self-catering cottages, one of which would provide a countryside retreat for the duration of our stay.

Once across the border we headed for the cathedral city of Tui. After leaving the main highway we trundled along winding local roads and into the city centre. The streets were deserted. There was no sign of activity anywhere, pavements were empty and shops closed. Unbeknown to us, we'd arrived during lunchtime siesta. Previous holidays on the Mediterranean coast hadn't prepared us for such urban abandonment.

'It must be around here somewhere,' I said, as we drove through the empty streets. 'Why is there never a signpost when you want one?'

'Where is everybody?' asked Melanie.

'I've no idea.'

Up to this point the trip had run like clockwork. It hadn't occurred to me we wouldn't be able to find the hotel. We drove aimlessly around the city looking for any signs of life. Even the petrol station was closed. After an anxious fifteen minutes Melanie spotted an old man sitting on a doorstep.

'There's someone,' she said, waving frantically to the right.

I jumped on the brakes and we ground to a halt. A narrow pavement separated the road from a row of small cottages. An old man was sitting on his doorstep basking in the wintry sunshine. Melanie lowered her window and asked for directions. Her enquiry met with silence. A curious expression spread across the old man's weathered face. Holiday Spanish had not equipped us for such native encounters. Fortunately, I'd printed off details of the hotel from the computer.

'Show him the printout,' I said.

Melanie leapt from the car, presented him with the printed sheet and repeated the question. He squinted at the paper, studying it carefully. Time drifted on and still he stared.

'*Es un hotel* (It's a hotel),' said Melanie, urging a reply.

She glanced across at me, looking for inspiration. I thought he might have dozed off and was just about to tell her to get back in the car when slowly, he lifted his head. He looked at Melanie and then at me, shrugged his shoulders and handed her back the printout. Without speaking a word, he'd made it perfectly clear he hadn't a clue where it was. We thanked him and continued on our quest.

A deserted city and a clueless local had done nothing for our confidence. I began to fear we were nowhere near our intended destination. Another ten minutes passed before we spotted our next would-be guides, two young men walking along the street. I pulled alongside and Melanie shouted out of the window. Both men approached the car and looked carefully at the printout.

'Yes, I know where it is,' said one of them.

An enormous sense of relief flooded the car. He wasn't sure of its exact location but pointed us in the right direction.

'Ask again when you get a bit closer,' he added.

We left the historic centre of Tui and sped off into the countryside. The scenery was beautiful. Narrow country lanes wound their way through picturesque villages and quaint hamlets. After ten minutes we still hadn't come across our elusive hotel.

'Do you think we've missed it?'

No sooner had I asked than we spotted the village sign, Caldelas de Tui.

'Can you see a hotel anywhere?' I asked.

'No,' said Melanie, 'but there must be a sign somewhere.'

I spotted a young man walking towards his car and pulled up alongside.

'Do you know where this hotel is?' asked Melanie, showing him the printout.

'Yes.' he replied. 'Follow me, I'm going that way.'

At last we'd found someone to help. He jumped into his car and headed off up the road. With a flash of his lights and a toot on the horn, he guided us to the main entrance.

The printed photos failed to portray the romantic beauty and charming character of this restored manor house. Entry into the grounds was through a pair of grand wooden gates, guarding an imposing stone entrance. We walked through the gateway into a flagged courtyard. A well-dressed woman stepped out of a small office. With a beaming smile she introduced herself as the housekeeper and welcomed us to the hotel. Politely, and without fuss, she led us through the courtyard and along a gravel path to a delightful stone cottage.

A roaring fire welcomed our arrival. The warm air was filled with the intoxicating aroma of wood smoke. Large pine logs crackled and hissed as they flamed in the open hearth. In the lounge, a long bay window framed a landscape of distant snow-capped mountains fringed with dark-green forests. A combination of exposed natural granite and polished plaster lined the interior of our weekend retreat. The roof space was open: exposed wooden ceiling joists lay on thick chestnut rafters. The cottage was idyllic, a quiet and peaceful location set amongst pine forests and orchards.

After a good night's sleep we set off to meet the estate agent. He'd arranged to meet us in the nearby coastal town of Baiona. We arrived in good time and waited outside the tourist information office as agreed. Waiting in the bright, warm sunshine was pleasant enough, despite a stiff sea breeze, but as time drifted on I began to feel a little uneasy.

The promenade of an out of season seaside resort hardly seemed the most appropriate meeting place for an estate agent and his clients. Surely a bona fide agent would have an office where we could meet.

About the Author

Craig began writing a weekly column for an online magazine in 2004. Over the last few years he has written a number of articles for the Trinity Mirror Group and online publications such as CNN, My Destination, and Insiders Abroad.

In 2013 he published his first travel memoir, *Journey To A Dream*. It tells the story of a turbulent first twelve months in Galicia. Since then he has added *Beyond Imagination*, *Endless Possibilities*, *Opportunities Ahead*, *Driving Ambition*, *The Discerning Traveller*, and *A Season To Remember* to The Journey series.

As well as writing, Craig is an enthusiastic winemaker and owns a small vineyard.